OPTIONS
ON
FUTURES

WILEY TRADING

OPTIONS ON FUTURES

New Trading Strategies

John F. Summa
Jonathan W. Lubow

John Wiley & Sons, Inc.

Library of Congress Cataloging-in-Publication Data:
Summa, John F., 1957–
    Options on futures : new trading strategies / John F. Summa and Jonathan W. Lubow.
        p. cm.—(Wiley trading)
    Includes index.
    ISBN 0-471-43642-9 (cloth : alk. paper)
        1. Options (Finance)   2. Futures.   I. Lubow, Jonathan W., 1967–   II. Title.
    III. Series

    HG6024.A3 S86 2001
    332.64'5—dc21   2001046566

Printed in the United States of America.
10 9 8 7 6 5 4 3 2 1

To my mother and in memory of my father.
—J.F.S.

To Jessica, Caroline Rose,
and Knick.
—J.W.L.

PREFACE

Most traders who achieve success do so only after a long period of trial and error. However, costly mistakes committed by aspiring option traders might be reduced by making a strategic shift in their trading approach. We firmly believe that it is better to be an option *writer* (seller) rather than an option *buyer*.

Option writers have a trading edge because they do not need to fight time-value decay. Time value is the portion of an option's price that decreases with each passing day in the life of an option contract. With time-value decay as an ally, furthermore, an option writer does not need to predict the direction of the market to profit. We will defer further discussion of time-value decay to subsequent chapters. For now, it is enough to say that we consider option writers to have a built-in edge over buyers.

The best teacher is the market itself—grading trading ideas with debits and credits to a trader's account. Failing grades in the form of repeated losses eventually lead most traders to weed out dead-end ideas, or get weeded out themselves. But you don't have to lose your grubstake to discover that option buyers are at a definite disadvantage. Chicago Mercantile Exchange (CME) data that we present inside this book reveal that most buyers get it *wrong*. In fact, 70 to 90 percent of CME options held until expiration end up being worthless, which means that the option writers are laughing all the way to the bank. We are, therefore, primarily option writers, and this book emphasizes option selling over option buying strategies.

What exactly do we mean by writing options? Whether we are talking about stock options or commodity futures options, by writing options we mean entering a trade by selling to open an option position. This is option writing, also known as option selling. When selling an option, the option writer is making one side of a market, one that results in receipt of options premium as a credit in the trader's account. For instance, let's assume a buyer of an out-of-the-money July $2.40 corn call option pays a premium of 10 cents when July corn is trading at $2.00. Each penny of a corn option is worth $50, therefore this option has a value of $500. Because this option is out of the money, in this case by 40 cents, this entire value represents just time value. The time-value premium goes to the option seller and is retained should the call option expire out of the money, and thus *worthless*.

A call option expires out of the money, having no intrinsic value, when the strike price of the option ($2.40) is above the price of the underlying futures contract ($2.00) at expiration. For put options to be out of the money, the futures price needs to be higher than the strike price. *Time* and *intrinsic value, strike prices,* and the concept of *in* and *out of the money* are all fully explained later in this book. For a quick definition, however, you can consult our glossary in Chapter 15.

Successful trading is not easy. However, we believe that it is easier to trade options on futures than it is to trade futures outright. Many beginning traders try their hand at futures trading, but soon discover that trading futures is quite difficult. The average trader is often undercapitalized and operating in an environment filled with better-funded traders who typically have more experience and thus more knowledge of market conditions. After all, why should an average futures trader in, let's say, cocoa, do better than Nestlé operating in the same market? We believe that our option strategies offer a more realistic trading style for new and even experienced traders who may be contemplating trading futures outright.

The temptation to trade options from the long side as a buyer remains a powerful one. This is especially true for those trading in the commodities markets, which have the potential to make explosive moves and thus produce windfall profits. Buying options may indeed appear to be even more of a no-brainer in commodities for this reason, but in reality it is quite difficult to make money as many soon painfully learn. Option buyers typically purchase an option with the intention of selling it later at a higher price, or holding the option contract until expiration hoping the option ends up deep enough in the money to be a profitable trade. This approach offers the potential for unlimited profits and tremendous leverage, but option buyers only make money if the underlying futures make a big move before the options expire. Furthermore, buyers miss out on the major advantages offered by option selling.

Option writing requires a little more work in the form of diligence and monitoring, yet carries with it higher odds that the trader will win because time is an ally, not a foe. The logic is simple for the writer: Markets tend to spend most of the time in definable ranges, making big moves in short bursts. Option sellers, deploying the appropriate writing approaches, can capitalize on this technical fact of life for most markets, thus profiting as options lose time value and eventually expire worthless.

As the reader will discover, many of our trading strategies involve selling *and* buying options as part of a *net selling strategy.* The long side of our strategies is often used to hedge our risk. This is the case with S&P 500 option credit spreads, for instance, which we discuss at length in this book.

Option writing may not be for everybody, but once a trader develops some familiarity with premium selling and options on futures markets, a new world of opportunities awaits. There are never any guarantees in life, but given a well-thought-out trading plan and appropriate money management, we believe that the option writing strategies presented here offer the potential for long-term success.

JOHN F. SUMMA
JONATHAN W. LUBOW

New Haven, Connecticut
Randolph, New Jersey
November 2001

ACKNOWLEDGMENTS

We would like to thank the following people for their help with the writing of this book: John Sarich for his generous and skillful aid with compiling statistical data, Ed Carr for his eagle-eye comments and criticism of earlier drafts, and Claudio Campuzano, Jennifer MacDonald, and Pamela van Giessen at John Wiley & Sons for their assistance with many of our questions about the editorial process. Special thanks also goes to Bertrand Desruelles, George Greco, Lisa Hardy, Frank Piccolo, and Michael Tucker for their encouragement and support.

J.F.S.
J.W.L.

CONTENTS

INTRODUCTION

Thumb through any copy of the *Wall Street Journal* or *Investor's Business Daily* and in the money-and-investing section you'll encounter, typically adjacent to the stock option pages, a special feature devoted to options on futures markets. This fertile world of trading opportunities—from soybeans, gold, sugar, and heating oil, to options on stock index futures and Treasury bonds—unfortunately remains largely untapped by many traders. Most individual option traders in today's online trading environment remain confined to trading stock options. Yet, a basic understanding of options can easily be parlayed into trading options on futures.

With a combined total of over 25 years' trading in the various markets for options on futures, we feel well positioned to share our accumulated good and bad experiences. By revealing the power of *commodity options,* a term used interchangeably with *futures options* or *options on futures* throughout this book, we hope readers can begin to add these versatile markets to their trading repertoire. With advantageous margin rules and an ample supply of liquid markets available for traders, options on futures present the aficionado and the rookie alike with many choice trading opportunities.

For anybody who has traded options, this book should open a new dimension to trading. Many traders have seen how fast their premium can disappear, and felt how frustrating this can be. Imagine how it would have felt to have profited from that premium decay? How much better off would most traders be today if all that premium decay was money going *into* their pocket, not

1

out? Imagine having the ability to profit even when your opinion on market direction is wrong, or your trade is poorly timed. Despite the substantial risk assumed by the option seller, we can't emphasize enough the huge advantage resulting from the ability to profit on trades that are unrelated to market direction. It is this trading edge that makes the key difference in the long run, and that separates our approach from those who take long positions and rely on predicting market direction for their success.

Option sellers need fewer conditions to profit and can win even if the market goes nowhere, a reality that characterizes market behavior a lot of the time. Buyers of options, however, require the correct market direction, and they also need a move by the market in sufficient *magnitude* to produce a profit. That is, in addition to the option being in the money at expiration, the move of the underlying futures must be large enough to cover the premium paid to purchase the option for the trade to be a winner.

This book is divided essentially into two sections. Chapters 1 and 2 present a closer look at the major advantages of option writing using options on futures. We then turn to S&P 500 futures, and options on S&P 500 futures, walking the reader through key characteristics and pricing fundamentals in Chapters 3 through 5. Next, Chapter 6 addresses how we trade this popular market using deep-out-of-the-money credit spreads. We then look at the dynamics of Standard Portfolio Analysis of Risk (SPAN®) margin requirements for S&P credit spreads in Chapter 7. In the final part of the first section of this book, Chapter 8 looks at the parameters of profitability of actual trades we executed using S&P 500 option credit spreads—including a review of the setups, rationale for making the trades, and discussion of any follow-up adjustments to the positions. Throughout this book, we should note that unless otherwise indicated the profit-and-loss figures and calculations do not include commissions and fees.

The book's second section broadens our discussion to include commodity options, such as grains and exotics (i.e., the so-called softs, such as coffee, cocoa, etc.). In Chapter 9, we look at the essential characteristics of commodity futures and futures options. Next, in Chapter 10, we present the selling approaches we have used in these markets—namely naked option selling, ratio spreads, and ratio writes. This is followed in Chapter 11 by a reconstruction of actual trades we established in these markets using the option writing approaches presented in Chapter 10. Among other things, we explain the conditions present in the market that led us to initiate the trades, along with the trading setups and any remedial or preemptive actions needed to either limit losses or take profits. Finally, in Chapter 12, we present a buying strategy—the *synthetic call*—which combines long futures and options, a strategy we occasionally deploy when conditions merit.

The book's remaining chapters cover trading tips, technical analysis, and option and futures terminology. The appendix sections, we should note, include lots of useful data to which we refer from time to time throughout the book. Among other useful information contained in the appendix sections, readers will find price range data for major futures markets that can be incorporated into any option trading plan.

We truly believe that our no-nonsense, hands-on approach sets this book apart from most other books covering option strategies. By presenting and reviewing in detail *actual* trades, the reader should be able to get a solid feel for these markets and the workings of our option writing strategies. Instead of overloading another book with page after page of hypothetical option models and trading scenarios, we present only what we know has worked for us. This book, therefore, doesn't offer a tour of all the option strategies available to a trader.

With so many books on trading options available to the public, yet so many losing traders, what purpose could another option book serve? Not much, unless it is offering something new. We have compiled a practical, how-to-win manual on trading futures options. After all, making money is what really matters—not learning all about options.

Chapter 1

TRADING OPTIONS THE "WRITE" WAY

As we have already pointed out, one of the central themes of this book is the argument that being a *net seller* rather than a *net buyer* of options is generally a better approach. While there are certainly long position trades that offer profitable opportunities, including synthetic calls (discussed in Chapter 12 of this book), we are convinced that selling premium offers traders a strategic advantage for two central reasons: (1) time becomes an ally, and (2) directional movement of underlying futures contract is not required to profit. For the majority of the trading public, however, this unfortunately is not how trading is conceived.

While it may sound complicated, the mechanics of selling options is simple. There is no writing, literally speaking, going on when an option is sold. Selling options, furthermore, does not mean that a trader owns them first. For example, if a trader were interested in writing some March S&P 500 options, a trader would simply tell the broker to sell five March 1250 S&P calls at market. Once the order is filled, the trader is short five calls. That is how somebody becomes an option writer. The term *writer* actually is left over from the days before standardized listed options existed, when somebody would agree with another party to actually write an option contract. Today, option markets are organized and maintained by exchanges. The clearinghouse division of the Chicago Mercantile Exchange (CME), for

5

example, monitors about $20 billion in performance bond assets (margin) each day. The performance bond system, which we discuss at length in Chapter 7, backs up and makes possible the trading of options and futures positions taken by traders. On a typical day, over $900 million moves through the CME's trade-matching and clearing system.

The Buyer's Dilemma

Why is option buying such a loser's game? Let's look at a typical buyer of options, whose name is Richard. Richard is the owner of his own successful retail business and a relatively inexperienced option speculator. He came to us one day with a question about a trade. Typical of most new option traders caught up in the buy-and-hold approach to option trading, he had purchased some call options on a technology stock, hoping for a swift vault higher and a windfall of cash. He was bullish on the stock and had purchased some calls instead of buying the stock, which provided great leverage and limited downside risk. Purchasing the stock requires much more capital and has the potential for bigger losses if the stock declines. Meanwhile, the stock had stalled and remained locked in a trading range after Richard took his position in his call options.

He wanted our opinion on the market. We told him that it is very difficult to know what direction that particular stock might take, which is why selling options is a more viable approach. Since we are not in the business of stock options, and we rarely recommend the outright purchase of options on commodities, there was not much advice we could offer regarding this particular position. We could only warn him about the difficulties associated with buying options. Eventually, Richard decided to cut his losses and get out after time-value decay had wiped out half of his option premium. Had he been an option seller, Richard could have closed the position with a nice profit—collecting one-half of the option premium that had decayed.

Unfortunately, the market made a large move shortly after Richard got out. Had he stayed in, Richard would have at least had a chance to get back to breakeven. But the ravages of time-value decay had tested his patience, and as so many traders do, he cut his losses just when he should have stayed with the trade. The windfall of profits had eluded him this time. But he was ready to try again. This time he was bullish on another stock he had received a tip about, and was thinking of buying call options in anticipation of a large move by the stock, which was expected when the company released its next earnings report.

As mentioned previously, many traders like Richard are attracted to the *potential* for profit in the purchase of an option. Approached as if playing the lottery, the typical trader repeatedly risks a little—the premium paid to purchase an option—in the hopes that a winner will pay many times more than what has been lost cumulatively. Losing many times is frustrating, but stomached by most traders looking to catch the "big kahuna." Yet, traders too often fail to see an important flaw in this logic.

Many traders like Richard don't realize something that becomes quite obvious later. Risk may be limited in any *one* trade (the price of a lottery ticket), but there is no limit to *how many times* a trader can lose. In other words, there is no rule that says a trader can't lose premium *repeatedly* until wiped out, which is what eventually happened to Richard. The odds are that most option buyers will lose. Not initially perceived is the mathematical fact that if an option expires worthless, 100 percent of the initial investment is lost. Another factor that hurts the ability of the option buyer to make money is the psychological inability to let a profit run. Had Richard stayed with his tech company options and gained from the rally that eventually occurred, like so many traders, he may have hung on for even more profit. The stock rally eventually faded even though the call options had gotten back to above breakeven. Had Richard stayed with the trade after the initial rally, the options would have gone from being profitable to becoming a 100 percent loser, since they ended up expiring worthless after all the gyrations.

On those rare occasions when an out-of-the-money option becomes profitable, skittish buyers might be inclined to sell that option at a small profit for fear that the market will indeed move the other way again, as it did in Richard's case, turning a winner into a 100 percent loser. Yet, this small profit will not cover repeated losses of the option buyer. For the option buyer to be profitable, in the long run the trader needs to hold onto the rare winner until it becomes a massively profitable trade. This is very difficult to do consistently well.

The Numbers Speak for Themselves

While it may not be obvious to many traders, a look at some facts should provide a needed dose of realism. Most buyers of options are putting themselves on the losing side. How bad is it? While data are not easy to come by, Exhibit 1.1 presents some recent statistics we obtained from the CME. In the period from January 3, 1997, through December 31, 1999, more than 75 percent of all CME options held until expiration during this three-year time period expired worthless.

Looking at just the S&P futures options provides an even more telling picture. Of the total of S&P 500 options held to expiration during the period January 3, 1997, through December 26, 1999, over 80 percent expired worthless. As Exhibit 1.1 shows, furthermore, a larger percentage of puts expired worthless. This may be due to a bullish bias of the market during this period

Year	CME Options (%)	S&P Options (%)	S&P Puts (%)	S&P Calls (%)
1997	76.3	81.7	94.1	54.8
1998	75.8	82.2	93.1	43.9
1999	77.5	84.7	94.5	66.7
1997–1999 (average)	76.6	83.3	94.0	55.3

Exhibit 1.1   Percentage of CME options expiring worthless. (CME total and S&P options (1997–1999).)
Source: CME.

despite some sharp market declines. In each of the three years surveyed, over 93 percent of S&P put options held to expiration expired worthless.

Since the trading of options is a zero-sum game, it should not come as a big surprise that all these expiring options end up benefiting the option writers. By zero-sum game, we are speaking of the fact that all open interest in options represents two parties—one a buyer and the other a seller—and therefore ultimately always a winner and a loser. To understand this concept more clearly, it may help to think about how a poker game works, but one that is played between individuals, not against the house (i.e., a casino).

The total available money to win or lose is what is available at the table of the two players. If one player wins a hand of poker, the other loses, since only one person can win each hand. The total won by the player with the winning hand will equal what the other player loses. Thus we have a zero-sum outcome, where the winning amount minus the losing amount equals zero.

Since most buyers lose the majority of trades, option writers end up the winners most of the time. Becoming an option writer, therefore, gives a trader of options on futures a statistical edge. In our view, time-value decay, which works in favor of the writer from the moment a position is opened, gives option writers the decisive edge.

The Importance of Time Value

Why is time value so important? Time-value decay, as shown in Exhibit 1.2, is not a function of movement of the underlying futures, but of the passage of time instead. While it can be affected by changing volatility levels, it nevertheless marches to its inevitable terminal end—zero. Therefore, as a seller of time value, the option writer actually needs fewer conditions to profit. Since we are essentially selling time value with most of our positions, it is possible to profit without any movement of the underlying futures.

Contract Month	Option Strike	Premium
May	1250	21.80
June	1250	35.40
July	1250	43.10
Sept	1250	57.60
Dec	1250	71.10

Exhibit 1.2 Time-value decay. Here, the structure of premium decay for a just-out-of-the-money 1250 S&P 500 call option strike is evident. The nearby May contract has the least time value. These prices existed at daily settlement on April 27, 2001.
Source: CME.

Let's assume a trader is bullish on the S&P 500 futures and wants to purchase calls with the intention of holding until expiration. For example, on February 23, 2001, the S&P June futures settled at 1260.60, and our bullish call buyer believed the market was ready to move higher. The option buyer might decide to purchase a call to try to profit from his or her belief in the market's ability to rally. Perhaps an out-of-the-money June call option at the 1300 strike is chosen. By purchasing the S&P 500 call with a strike price of 1300, the trader is betting on a move from the level of 1260.60 to above the strike price. The price of the 1300 June call on this day was 43.20. Each point of the S&P 500 is worth $250. The cost of the S&P June call was, therefore, $10,800 (43.20 × $250 = $10,800).

To illustrate why call *buying* is an uphill struggle, the S&P 500 call has to move at least 43.20 points *above* the strike price of 1300 upon expiration *just to get to breakeven*. We will be using the term *strike price* throughout this book and will explain in more detail in Chapter 5 what a strike price is. For now, by strike price we mean the price at which an option buyer can exercise an option. In other words, the index must move *first* to above the strike price to get in the money. The *second* condition is that it must move high enough to cover the cost of the call (the premium paid), which means it must expire above 1343.20 (1300 + 43.20 = 1,343.20) for the buyer to profit if the option is held until expiration (see Exhibit 1.3). Meanwhile, the option writer (seller) is betting that the option expires below 1343.20 (breakeven) or best of all, out of the money. For the option to end up out of the money, the S&P futures must expire below the strike price of 1300. The call buyer loses 100 percent in this case, and the option writer keeps the entire premium as profit.

If, on the other hand, an option *writer* is bullish on the S&P 500 futures, this trader might sell a June 1200 put option when the S&P futures are trading at, let's say, 1247.50. Here, we are using naked S&P puts as an example only to illustrate the advantage of time decay. By selling a put option, the conditions for profit are much less demanding. The June 1200 put option was selling for 39.20 points, which means that breakeven would be at 1160.80, or 39.20 points below the strike price of the put option. If an out-of-the-money June 1200 put were sold, therefore, the option writer would make money given the following scenarios:

1. A sideways market (trading range).
2. A bullish market (unlimited rise).
3. A moderately bearish market (expires above 1160.8).

The third market condition results in a profit if the S&P decline is not *too* big. As long as the put option remains out of the money on expiration, or if it is in the money but above the breakeven point of 1160.8, the trade will be a winner. If bullish, the seller, like the buyer, expects a move higher. The difference

Trade	Option	Strike	Price	Breakeven
Sell	S&P put	1200	39.20	1160.80
Buy	S&P call	1300	43.20	1343.20

Exhibit 1.3 S&P 500 short put versus long call.

is that the seller has greater probability of winning because of time-value decay.

As the reader will see with most of the S&P 500 put spreads that we present, even a 15 percent decline in the S&P 500 futures may not turn the trade into a loser. Selling in general, therefore, greatly increases a trader's chances for success provided the proper money management and risk controls are in place. In other words, an option writer will always need to have a preconceived game plan covering a number of different market scenarios. As the reader will see later, there are indeed numerous effective hedging and remedial actions available should a trade get into trouble and thus require adjustment. This does not mean that losses are not possible. They will always arise. But we can attempt to control the severity of losses.

Obviously with the passage of time, as we get closer to the expiration of an option, the value of an out-of-the-money option will tend to diminish. To profit, however, an option writer need not wait until expiration. Before expiration, the option can often be bought back at a nice profit, which means the option writer doesn't need to wait until the option actually expires. Often, when the market moves strongly in the option writer's favor, the trade can be closed early. Of course, if an option expires worthless, the seller keeps the full premium that was originally collected. Nevertheless, if the premium has diminished significantly from either a move in the underlying futures, or the passage of time (or both), the trade can often be closed early and a new position established, collecting new premium. This is often the case when markets are trending strongly.

For example, if we take our June 1200 S&P 500 put trade discussed earlier, under strong bullish market conditions the premium would drop quickly. If the S&P 500 futures were to make a 10 percent move higher during the first month, premium would fall rapidly, thus giving us a nice profit long before expiration. Often, rather than waiting for the last two months to pass, during which only marginal gains are possible given the small amount of time value left on the put option, the option trader can write another put option for additional premium, perhaps in a contract month further out in time or by selling a different strike in the same month, while closing the original trade at a profit. This would make sense if the trader is still bullish on the S&P 500. Under these ideal conditions, a much higher profit rate becomes possible from options writing.

As mentioned previously and worth reiterating, the general selling approach just outlined goes counter to the mind-set of most traders. Our own experience and the data suggest that the majority of individual traders lose from buying options. Yet, the buying approach continues to appeal to the retail-trading crowd. By taking the other side of the market as a net seller of options, on the other hand, traders can gain a statistical edge by breaking their dependency on the market's direction, while profiting from the daily erosion of time value. The rest of this book explains how to implement trading strategies designed to best exploit the selling of time value.

Chapter 2

WHY TRADE OPTIONS ON FUTURES?

Trading options on futures has three critical advantages over trading stock options and outright futures: (1) greater potential for diversification, (2) better margin leverage, and (3) a steady supply of overpriced options to sell due to high volatility.

Diversification

To win in the option game it is essential that traders acquire knowledge of all option markets. As many veteran option pros know, diversifying across numerous markets is good risk management. Yet, the average option trader is someone who is generally confined to the field of stock options. The ability to truly diversify gives a trader a statistical edge, the hallmark of any winning strategy. Options on futures should, therefore, be part of any option trader's arsenal. Offering the possibility for diversification across different and unrelated markets, options on futures provide a perfect arena for creating a viable trading plan.

The smart trader knows how important it is to take positions in markets that are not dependent on one macro event, like a Federal Reserve interest policy change or a crop report, for example. A key advantage for options on futures traders is the ability to *diversify across numerous unrelated markets*, markets that have no dependence on one another and are thus immune from just a single market event. As Exhibit 2.1 illustrates, for example, there is little correlation between corn, natural gas, and orange juice. This is true for many other futures markets, as well.

Stock option traders, meanwhile, can be demolished by one big stock market event. The high degree of correlation between stocks and the overall stock market, for example, makes it difficult for the stock option trader to establish a portfolio of diversified and unrelated positions. This is particularly true because most stock option trading volume is centered on stocks comprising the S&P 500, Nasdaq 100, and the 30 Dow Industrials. These stocks are thus highly correlated with the movement of the major stock market indexes, leaving them vulnerable to market shocks. Exhibit 2.2 presents volume data on equity options, which show

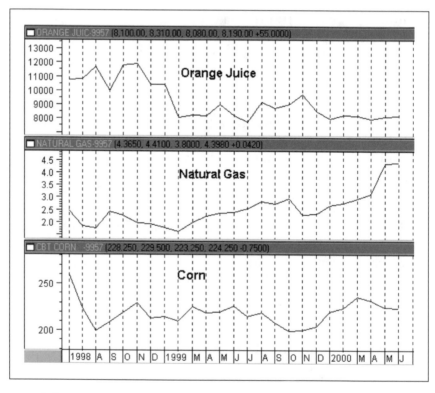

Exhibit 2.1   Uncorrelated corn, natural gas, and orange juice markets.
Created using MetaStock Professional.

AMD	4,335	MSFT	35,969
ORCL	5,076	CSCO	26,811
YHOO	5,526	GEN ELEC	18,057
JUP	6,718	WAL	14,932
I B M	6,919	GLW	11,844
MOT	7,112	C	4,128
WCOM	7,144	BRR	12,043
CIEN	7,314	STK	9,324
AOL	8,019	LU	8,103

Exhibit 2.2 Concentration of big-cap stock option volume. These 18 stocks represented 25 percent of all of the stock options volume on April 27, 2001.
Source: CBOE.

that most equity option volume takes place within a narrow universe of mostly big-cap stocks.

For example, if a trader buys IBM calls and the Dow Industrials decline (IBM is a component of the 30 Dow Industrials) due to a major market event (e.g., the Asian crisis of 1998), the call position is probably going to be losing even if the fundamental story about IBM remains unchanged. Therefore, even if a trader's opinion is correct about individual stocks, several similar equity option positions may lose due to a larger market-wide event. Options on futures, on the other hand, offer the astute option trader opportunities to take multiple uncorrelated positions. The correlation is very low or near zero between the major futures option markets, as seen in Exhibit 2.3.

Energy	Heating oil, crude oil, natural gas, unleaded gas
Grains	Wheat, corn, soybeans, oats
Exotics	Cocoa, orange juice, coffee, lumber, sugar, cotton
Meats	Feeder cattle, live cattle, lean hogs
Currencies	Swiss franc, British pound, Japanese yen
Indices	S&P 500, DJIA, Nasdaq 100
Metals	Silver, platinum, gold
Inter. rates	Eurodollars, T-bonds, T-notes (10-year)

Exhibit 2.3 Major commodity option markets.

Low Margin, High Leverage

With low margin requirements for many futures and options on futures markets, diversification becomes possible even for traders operating with little capital. The ability to diversify using options on futures, therefore, is helped by the special advantage of most individual options on futures: their especially small *initial margin requirements*.

Let's compare margin requirements for stocks versus futures so you can get a better feel for how valuable this advantage really is for traders. The low margin and high leverage of futures translates into the same for the corresponding option contracts. For stock purchases, the Federal Reserve Board's Regulation T permits a two-for-one margin. This means, for example, that if you have an account value of $50,000, you can purchase up to $100,000 in stocks (assuming the stock is marginable; not all stocks are). We can reduce this margin rule to simply stating that there is a 50 percent margin limit on positions ($1.00/$2.00 × 100 = 50 percent). A trader can buy $2 worth of stock for every $1 in account value. Many aggressive traders take full advantage of this margin rule. In practice, this represents a loan by the broker to the investor charged at the broker's loan rate.

With futures, on the other hand, margin money is typically put in treasury bills, so interest is *earned on margin money!* More important, in options on futures markets, which are regulated by the Commodity Futures Trading Commission (CFTC), an agency of the U.S. government, a much lower margin ratio is tolerated. For example, the value of the S&P 500 futures is $250 per point. If we take an example of the S&P 500 futures with a daily settlement of 1260, the value of that contract would be $315,000 ($250 × 1260 = $315,000). We know the current margin requirement to trade an S&P futures contract is $21,563. Therefore, we can determine the margin percentage required to trade that contract. With the S&P 500 futures, $21,563 allows you to control $315,000 worth of stock, representing just 6.8 percent of the value of the contract, which is more than a 14-to-1 leverage ratio, compared with 2 to 1 for stocks. There are even better ratios of margin-to-contract value available in other markets, as can be seen in Exhibit 2.4. While higher leverage means higher risk, it also means that you can get better use of your capital, provided you manage risk appropriately.

This futures margin advantage translates into tremendous leverage when using options on futures, especially if selling. Let's make a simple comparison to stock options using our example of the S&P 500 futures, but this time assuming a settlement at 1247.50. The value of the S&P 500 futures contract would be $311,875 ($250 × 1247.50 = $311,875). This amount represents $311,875 worth of underlying component stocks that make up the S&P 500 stock index. If we were to sell at-the-money *stock options* matching this market value, the margin requirement would be 20 percent of the value of the stock. To short an S&P futures option, on the other hand, an option writer would only need a fraction of what stock option traders are required to deposit as margin.

Let's return to our example. The S&P 500 futures we assume settled at 1247.50. If we were to write a call option on the S&P 500 futures that was basically at the money (having a strike of 1250), the option writer would need to deposit $18,674 in initial margin to trade a contract worth $311,875. Compare this with the equivalent of selling at-the-money call options on $311,875 worth of stock and the leverage advantage becomes quite obvious.

Futures Contract	Market Price	Contract Size	Contract Value	Initial Margin Requirement	Percentage of Contract Value	Approximate Leverage Ratio
Soybeans	$4.40/ bushel	5,000 bushels	$22,000	$945	4.3	23:1
Gold	$260/ ounce	100 ounces	$26,000	$1,350	5.2	19:1
Crude	$28 barrel	1000 barrels	$28,000	$3,375	12.0	8:1
Cocoa	$1050/ton	10 tons	$10,500	$980	9.0	11:1
S&P 500	1260	250 × index	$315,000	$21,563	6.8	14:1

Exhibit 2.4 Futures margins and leverage ratios.

We can approximate the margin that is required to sell the equivalent of $311,875 worth of stock options. Let's say XYZ is selling at $31.187 per share. If we sold 100 calls at the money, this would represent $311,875 worth of underlying stock. This allows us to make a valid comparison. We are using this example to be able to compare the leverage advantage of futures options over stock options. To write these 100 at-the-money options, a trader would need to deposit 20 percent of the value of the stock, or $62,375. If the stock is below the strike price, the trader is generally allowed to subtract the amount it is out of the money. Nevertheless, based on the 20 percent rule alone, selling call options on $311,875 worth of stock is much more costly. The same formula applies to writing naked puts.

The S&P options would require $18,674 in initial margin compared with $62,375 in margin for stocks. Compare 5.98 percent of the underlying asset value for S&P options to 20 percent for stock options and the reader should see that there is a tremendous margin advantage. The low margin requirement for this S&P 500 call option is determined by a system known as Standard Portfolio Analysis of Risk (SPAN), which is now used by most futures exchanges. We explain SPAN margin in more detail in Chapter 7. One of the advantages of this more logical margin system, for example, is its global reading of risk. Traders can establish credit spreads on both sides of a market and only be charged margin for one side, assuming equal risk for both sides. If one side is riskier than the other, only the riskier side is charged margin. Stock option traders and those trading the OEX, are hit with a double charge, which can significantly impact the profit rate on option writing strategies. This extra margin is applied even though both sides of a dual credit spread, for example, cannot expire in the money.

Volatility and Overvalued Options

The third advantage of trading options on futures is *volatility*—both historical and implied. Volatility measures fluctuation in the price of a futures contract. *Historical volatility* is the actual past price movement of futures, and *implied volatility* is what the market expects of the future in terms of likely price movements. Implied volatility that is greater than historical volatility means that an option's market price is greater than its theoretical price and thus considered overvalued. High-implied volatility relative to historical volatility (overpriced options), therefore, provides excellent net selling opportunities. Option writers search for these conditions, as well as high implied volatility compared with past implied volatility. Selling these options can provide an edge in trading, since any fall in price back toward the theoretical value of the option and average levels of volatility often means profits are made even with no movement of the underlying futures market. Option writing is thus an excellent way to capture overvalued option premium and turn it into profit.

Exhibit 2.5 contains implied and historical volatility levels for natural gas futures. The broken line represents implied volatility and the solid line indicates historical volatility. Implied volatility has risen above historical volatility, an illustration of overpriced

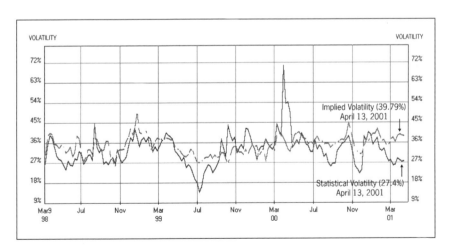

Exhibit 2.5 Implied and statistical volatility for natural gas futures. On April 13, 2001, implied volatility for natural gas futures was 39.79. With statistical volatility at 27.4 on the same day, we have overvalued option premiums.
Source: OptionVue 5 Options Analysis Software

conditions, seen at the far right side of Exhibit 2.5. The energy complex, which includes natural gas, heating oil, and crude oil, is one of the most volatile of the commodity groups. Often these markets offer great writing opportunities, as the option prices can become very overvalued. In addition to these markets, there are others (e.g., cocoa, orange juice, silver, lumber, cotton, the British pound, the Swiss franc, sugar, and coffee), which all occasionally offer high volatility and thus writing opportunities.

While there are certainly other advantages to trading options on futures as opposed to stock options (and to outright futures) that will be touched on throughout the book, we have highlighted in this chapter what we feel are the most important ones. To summarize these advantages, they are (1) the potential for diversification due to the unrelated nature of most commodity markets, (2) the low margin requirements and capital leverage resulting from SPAN margin rules, and (3) plenty of tradable volatility and potentially overpriced options to sell. Turning these advantages into profit is the subject of the rest of this book.

Chapter 3

S&P 500 FUTURES BASICS

In the two previous chapters, we outlined the major advantages of an option writing approach, and the key reasons traders should add options on futures to their trading repertoire. In this chapter, we explain the basic mechanics of S&P 500 futures, primarily looking at essential properties and characteristics. Yet there are several key relationships to options on futures we need to understand first before we begin to explain essential terms and characteristics of futures in general, and the S&P futures in particular. We begin this chapter, therefore, by highlighting two special features of futures in relation to options on futures.

Futures, Option Prices, and Exercise

There are two important concepts related to option price settlement and exercise that should be highlighted. First, day-to-day option price settlements are influenced primarily by changes in the price of the underlying futures. Stocks underlie stock options. Futures underlie options on futures. While other factors may be at work, such as time-value decay and volatility levels, the most important cause of a change in an option price is always the movement of the underlying futures contract. For example, we don't watch the level of the cash commodity or the level of a stock index. *Instead, we are concerned with the price movements of the underlying futures contract in relation to the strike price of an option we have sold.*

23

Exercise is the second key concept to understand. With few exceptions *options on futures exercise into the underlying futures, not the cash commodity or stock index.* For example, at expiration, or if assigned ahead of expiration, a put option writer receives a long futures contract, and a call option writer receives a short futures contract priced from the strike of the option. We will come back to the question of assignment in subsequent chapters covering S&P 500 and commodity options. For now, some simple examples will help illustrate this important aspect of the relationship between futures and futures options, which applies to most futures markets.

If an option writer sells one September $4.00 soybean put option and September soybean futures trade below $4.00 (i.e., in the money), the put buyer may exercise the option. If the put holder chooses to exercise the option should the underlying soybean futures move lower to $3.50, the put writer would have a *long* September futures position established in his or her account. The position would show a purchase price of $4.00 and would thus have unrealized losses of $0.50 ($4.00 − $3.50 = −0.50, or −$2,500). Just like with a stock option put seller who has stock put to him or her, the futures option put seller has a long futures position put to him or her. If this were a stock option put writer, just like the preceding case, the account would show a stock position priced from the strike price to the current market price of the stock, showing a loss.

The opposite is true for call writers. If assigned once in the money, a call writer would show in his or her account a *short* futures position, priced from the strike to the current market level, and therefore showing a loss. To provide an example using S&P options, if a trader had sold a March S&P call option with a strike of 1250 and the March S&P futures moved above 1250 to 1300, and the buyer of the March S&P call option decided to exercise the option, the call writer would be assigned a short futures position, with his or her account showing a loss of 50 points. Stated another way, the seller would be short from the 1250 strike while the March futures contract was trading at 1300, a loss of 50 points. He or she can either cover and thus offset the short position, or stay with the trade. If the price of the underlying futures at expiration is 1300, the short position would expire with a 50-point loss, resulting in $12,500 debit to the account minus the amount of premium received for initially selling the option. Meanwhile, the call buyer, who gets a long futures position priced from the strike (1250), has a gain of 50 points. Any premium paid for the call initially would have been lost with the exercise by the call holder.

Futures Properties and Characteristics

While it may at first seem somewhat daunting for anybody new to futures, *understanding* the functioning of these markets is actually rather simple. Keeping in mind the two key concepts we mentioned earlier, we now briefly explain the basic features of a futures contract required for any speculator or hedger.

A futures contract, similar to a listed option contract, has standardized terms and conditions. But unlike an option, which gives the buyer the *right* but *not the obligation* to exercise the contract, being long futures *requires* delivery of a specified quantity of a commodity, or cash if a stock index like the S&P 500, at a specific time in the future. As speculators, however, we have no interest in delivery. Long futures positions we take are always offset (closed) ahead of first-notice day, before it is possible to be assigned a delivery. There will never be 10,000 metric tons of cocoa delivered to your front yard.

At the end of each trading day, futures contracts are marked to market. This means that there is a settlement price determined at the close of trading and all accounts are adjusted based on this price. As required by the exchanges, a trader must have sufficient margin in an account to remain in open positions. Changes in the settlement price thus determine if additional margin needs to be deposited, or if excess margin remains, in the account. The alternative is to exit the trade. A gain in any position, on the other hand, results in excess margin accumulating in an account. If margin excess gets very low, a trader needs to keep a careful watch on the day-to-day changes in futures settlement prices and the impact these changes may have on margin requirements. A good broker will help with this. Unlike stockbrokers, who may interact very little with investors, options and option futures brokers play a much more interactive role, which is why finding a reliable broker is so important.

The S&P Futures

The S&P 500 futures contract is one of the oldest and most popular. Compared with the Dow Jones Industrials and the NASDAQ 100 futures contracts, the S&P futures contract is far ahead in terms of volume traded on a daily basis. It represents a composite stock index, the S&P 500, which is made up of 500 large-cap, blue-chip stocks. The index is a weighted measure based on capitalization of each of the listed companies. The index is generally considered to represent the broad market because the index comprises 80 percent industrials, 15 percent financial stocks, 3 percent utilities, and 2 percent transportation issues. For traders who want to speculate on movement of the broad market, the S&P futures contract offers an excellent tool. If a trader believes the market is headed higher, for instance, the purchase of the S&P futures (going long) will allow such a bullish trader to profit from a move higher.

To profit on a decline in the broad market, on the other hand, a trader can sell the S&P futures (go short) in anticipation of a price decline. Buying or selling the S&P futures carries with it unlimited risk as well as unlimited profit. As the reader will see later, options on the S&P futures can be used instead of the futures contract to limit risk. Later in this book, we will present our option writing strategies for profiting on either bullish, bearish, or neutral outlooks.

The S&P futures price tracks movement of the underlying cash index, with the index itself priced based on changes of each stock that make up the S&P 500 stock index. The S&P 500 futures contract acts as a surrogate for the purchase of the index stocks themselves, which is useful for speculators and stock portfolio hedgers.

As the reader can see from Exhibit 3.1, the chart of the S&P futures looks very much like the index itself. However, the

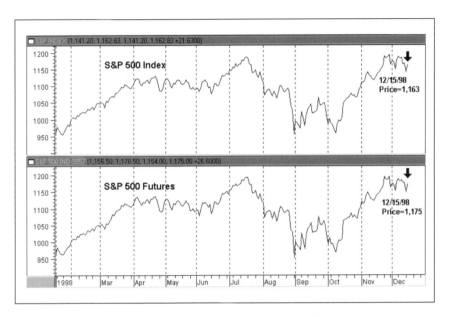

Exhibit 3.1 S&P 500 cash index and S&P 500 futures. The S&P futures generally trade at a premium to the cash index as can be seen here.
Created using MetaStock Professional.

futures price is generally higher than the index due to a premium on the futures. The premium results from the opportunity costs of money.

Futures Pricing, Margin, and Settlement

Each market for futures contract has its own unique price terms. This concept is easy to understand if we consider how this differs from stocks. For example, IBM and GM both are valued in terms of shares. If you know the price of each share, you can determine the value of 100 shares simply by multiplying by $100. Aside from a few exceptions, there isn't any uniformity of pricing terms with futures. A soybean contract represents 5,000 bushels of soybeans but a cocoa contract represents 10 metric tons of cocoa. In other words, while all stocks are denominated in shares, futures are denominated in bushels, metric tons, gallons, troy ounces, and so forth. The value of a futures contract is, therefore, based on its price multiplied by a certain quantity of the commodity in question. To take the soybean example again, each contract represents 5,000 bushels of beans. If the price of the futures contract is $4.20 per bushel, the value of the contract is $21,000 ($4.20 × 5,000 = $21,000).

As we saw with the exercise examples at the outset of this chapter, there are certain concepts about the S&P futures we need to be aware of when trading options on S&P 500 futures. In addition to these concepts, traders will need to know some of the key characteristics, namely price terms and product specifications, of the S&P futures. Exhibit 3.2 provides specifications and terms for the S&P 500 futures contract.

Let's bring to life some of these terms and specifications using the example of an S&P futures trader. We will call him Bob. Suppose Bob goes long the S&P futures at 1250.00, believing that the S&P futures will rise. For each point rise in the S&P futures, Bob will gain $250. The contract is worth $312,500 (1250 × $250 per point = $312,500) and requires $21,563 in *initial margin*. The required *maintenance margin* (i.e., the minimum level of margin allowed below which an account must be brought back to initial margin) is $18,500. The maintenance margin is thus the mini-

Contract	Size	Tick Size	Delivery Months	Last Day of Trading	Settlement Type
S&P 500 futures	$250 × level of S&P 500 index	0.10 = $25 Minimum tick size is 0.10	March, June, September, and December	Thursday prior to the third Friday of the contract month	Cash

Exhibit 3.2 S&P 500 futures contracts specs and terms. Stock index futures, such as the S&P 500, settle in cash. The minimum trading price change (tick) for the S&P futures contract is 0.10; a tick change up or down amounts to $25 each for every 0.10 change in price.

mum sum of money, smaller than the initial margin requirement amount, that needs to be on deposit in a trader's broker account to keep an option or futures position open. Any drop in the account value below this maintenance level triggers a margin call. The trader then must deposit additional funds, make adjustments to open positions, or close positions to bring the account back in line with required initial margin levels.

Let's say Bob opens an account with $25,000. He will be able to go long one contract of the S&P futures with this amount. But if the account value falls to below the maintenance margin ($18,500) while in a position, Bob will be required to bring the account value back to the initial margin level of $21,563 if he would like to stay with the position.

Having entered his long position at 1250, Bob plans to sell (offset) at 1350 if the S&P futures get there. By closing (offsetting) the position at 1350, where Bob has a good-till-canceled (GTC) limit order placed, he hopes to make a nice profit. As long as the S&P futures continue to rally, there will not be any losses, and obviously Bob will not be subject to any margin calls. Unrealized gains in the account, furthermore, expand excess margin. But what if Bob is wrong? What if the S&P futures reverse and head lower? If Bob remains with the position, he will eventually suffer a margin call if his account value falls below required maintenance margin levels. The account is debited or credited for the position's daily gains or losses. Positions are revalued or marked to the market at the end of each day.

If Bob had bought (gone long) the S&P futures contract at 1250.00 and the futures rose to 1350.00, and Bob had closed the position, he would have gained $25,000 ($250 × 100 = $25,000). If, on the other hand, the S&P futures had fallen to 1200.00, Bob would have lost $12,500. Initial margin to establish a position is $21,536. If Bob had begun with a $25,000 account, however, the decline in the S&P futures would have triggered a margin call long before reaching 1200 since the position is marked to the market daily, showing unrealized losses. Bob, for example, would have had to either exit the trade early or put up more margin money to stay with the position when his account value fell to or below $18,500, which would have occurred with a 26-point drop in the

S&P futures ($250 × 26 = $6,500) ($25,000 − $6,500 = $18,500). If Bob's account fell below the designated maintenance margin level, he would have had to meet a margin call to continue holding that position.

Let's take a closer look at the pricing of the S&P futures. Terms for the S&P futures, like terms for S&P option contracts, are standardized. The same terms apply to all S&P options and futures traded. Exhibit 3.3 provides hypothetical daily settlement prices for the June S&P 500 futures two months prior to expiration on April 27, 2001. We can see that the price of the June futures has risen 18 points (1800 basis points) to 1258.50. This price change of 18 points represents a gain of $4,500.

Let's take another example of a bullish trader, whom we'll call Lisa, who went long even earlier than bullish trader Bob, buying the S&P futures at 1210 instead of 1250, and holding until expiration.

If the June S&P futures expired at 1305, Lisa would have profited by 95 points, which becomes a cash credit to her account upon expiration. Upon expiration, the S&P futures and the S&P stock index will have the same price. The speculator, Lisa, who

Mth/		Session				Pt	Est	Prior Day		
Strike	Open	High	Low	Last	Sett	Chge	Vol	Sett	Vol	Int
JUN01	1252.00	1259.50	1244.50	1259.00	1258.50	+1800	60K	1240.50	77036	45431
SEP01	1261.50	1270.00	1256.00A	1270.00	1269.40	+1850	2030	1250.90	616	4500
DEC01	1274.00	1280.20B	1268.20A	1280.20B	1280.00	+1880	42	1261.20	83	224
MAR02	—	1290.40B	—	1290.40B	1290.40	+1900	25	1271.40	1	62
JUN02	—	1302.40B	—	1302.40B	1302.60	+1920		1283.40	6	68
SEP02	—	1314.90B	—	1314.90B	1315.60	+1970		1295.90		
DEC02	—	1327.40B	—	1327.40B	1328.60	+2020		1308.40		7
MAR03	—	1339.90B	—	1339.90B	1341.60	+2070		1320.90		
TOTAL							EST. VOL		VOL	OPEN INT
TOTAL							62918		77742	50295

Exhibit 3.3   Settlement prices for S&P 500 futures (April 27, 2001). The June S&P 500 futures settled at 1258.50 (Sett) representing a point change (Pt Chge) of 1800 basis points, or 18 points. Each point is worth $250.00, or $2.50 per basis point.
Source: CME.

bought the contract at 1210 would have realized a profit equal to $23,750 (95 × $250 = $23,750), which is the amount that would be credited to the account at expiration. This is a cash settlement. Looked at another way, if the contract had settled 95 points below the price where Lisa had gone long, and she held until expiration posting all the necessary margin, her account would have been debited the same amount.

In both of these cases, settlement at expiration results in either a final cash credit or debit to Lisa's trading account, based on how the futures contract is marked at the special opening quotation when the S&P futures expires. This occurs four times each year, the third Friday morning of each futures expiration month. The S&P 500 index quotation is calculated to the nearest 0.01, and on expiration, it is based on the official opening values of all 500 stocks making up the S&P 500 index.

S&P Contract Months, Front-Month Contracts, and Pricing Terms

As the reader will see, expiration dates differ both across markets and across contract months for most futures contracts. While stock options always expire on the third Friday of the contract month, futures contracts (e.g., corn, gold, S&Ps, etc.) have a different cycle. Different commodity contracts, such as gold, corn, and S&Ps, can have the same delivery month, but will not expire on the same day of that month, nor in the same month. While the S&P futures always expire on the open of the third Friday of the contract month, gold and corn will typically expire on their own unique days. Fortunately, there are brokers who can help with this information, and increasingly this information is available on the Internet, either from a data service or from the exchanges themselves at their web sites.

The S&P 500 futures have four trading months: March, June, September, and December. As with all futures, there is a *front-month* contract, which is where the bulk of trading activity (open interest and daily volume) will be found. The bulk of trading volume and open interest always shifts ahead of the expiration of the current front-month contract to the next-nearest month as positions are rolled into what becomes the new front-month contract. For the S&P futures there can never be two front-month contracts at the same time, for instance, because there is only one set of hand signals in the S&P pits in Chicago, and they are only used for the front-month contract. The price of the front-month contract is lower than the deferred months because it possesses smaller carrying costs in the form of interest on money. All futures contracts, therefore, will be greater than the price of the S&P 500 cash index, and the further out in the time the contract is the greater the premium over the S&P 500 index.

These basic characteristics of the S&P futures can be viewed in Exhibit 3.4. Exhibit 3.4 provides a typical CME price table of S&P 500 front-month and deferred contract months, beginning with March 2001 and running through to December 2002. As the reader will see, the price patterns and open interest of the front-month contract (March) are easy to interpret.

To determine which contract is the front month, a quick check of the open interest should give a clue if in doubt. To the far

Mth/		Session				Pt	Est	Prior Day		
Strike	Open	High	Low	Last	Sett	Chge	Vol	Sett	Vol	Int
MAR01	1303.00	1312.50	1296.50	1305.80	1305.50	−2760	65K	1333.10	68514	440620
JUN01	1318.00	1327.00B	1313.00A	1319.00B	1319.90	−2800	12K	1347.90	6381	47971
SEP01	1345.00	1345.00	1327.60A	1337.60A	1334.90	−2870	3	1363.60	48	1351
DEC01	1355.00	1359.10B	1343.10A	1352.10A	1349.90	−2920	4	1379.10	189	846
MAR02	—	—	1358.10A	1367.10A	1364.90	−2920	10	1394.10	5	401
JUN02	—	—	1374.10A	1383.10A	1379.90	−3020	10	1410.10		298
SEP02	—	—	1389.10A	1398.10A	1394.90	−3020		1425.10		4
DEC02	—	—	1404.10A	1413.10A	1409.90	−3020		1440.10		
TOTAL							EST VOL	VOL		OPEN INT
TOTAL							77995	75137		491491

Exhibit 3.4   S&P 500 futures prices, open interest, and volume. Prices are as of February 16, 2001, at 4:00 P.M. The front-month contract is the month with most of the open interest. Here, we see March as having the highest open interest (Int) levels of 440,620.
Source: CME.

right of Exhibit 3.4 is the open-interest column (Int is the heading). Each line represents total open interest for each contract month. To the far left, each line contains the S&P futures contracts available. Listed in Exhibit 3.4 are two full years of contracts (March, June, September, and December for 2001 and 2002).

In Exhibit 3.4, we see that the March 2001 contract has an open-interest figure of over 440,000 contracts. Open interest represents the number of contracts that remain open (either from a trader executing a buy-to-open or a sell-to-open order to establish a position). A position is open until it has been offset.

Let's take the March 2001 S&P futures contract as an example. Going from left to right along the top line beginning with the contract month/strike column, first we see MAR01, which tells us that we are looking at the futures contract for March delivery. Next, we have the open, high, low, and last prices for the previous trading day. The open for this particular day was 1303.00, the high 1312.50, the low 1296.50, and the last 1305.80. Next is the settlement price, which is 1305.50, and then the point change for the day, shown as −2760 (basis points). Finally, we have a volume of 65K, representing the total contracts traded that day.

The price change here is presented in basis points, where 100 basis points equal 1 index point (each basis point is valued at $2.50). Therefore, in this case, we have a decline of 2760 basis points, or 27.60 index points. The minimum size for a price change is now in dime-size ticks as opposed to nickel-size, which had been the protocol prior to October 31, 1997, when the contract was split. The minimum trading price change (tick) for the contract is $0.10 (one dime), which amounts to $25. For example, a move from 1250.10 to 1250.80 is an increase of 7 ticks, or $175 in the price of the futures contract. As we have already pointed out, each commodity and financial futures contract has its own unique set of price terms and characteristics. The trader must get familiar with individual contracts and their terms. Starting with the S&P futures makes the most sense, as this is one of the most widely traded and followed contracts.

It should be obvious at this point that for speculators, buying and selling futures is akin to buying and selling a stock—buy low and sell high, or sell high and buy low (if shorting). The key difference has to do with leverage and margin, as we have demonstrated. We realize that this chapter is a simplified discussion of S&P futures. Nevertheless, we believe that this chapter provides the necessary background for understanding S&P futures in order to trade S&P options, which is one of the primary focuses of this book. The next two chapters cover the essential characteristics of S&P options and options pricing fundamentals, and then we turn to trading strategies using S&P options.

Chapter 4

THE OPTION PRICING STORY

Now that we have covered the basic mechanics of S&P 500 futures, it is time to look at option pricing fundamentals before turning to the terms and properties of S&P options in Chapter 5. Futures options, like any options, have a number of price-determining variables. In other words, the value of any option is a function of several variables that make up standard option pricing models. In this chapter, we will present a nontechnical version of the price fundamentals story, highlighting the features of the price equation relevant to our style of trading.

The value of a futures option is the function of three key factors:

1. The amount of time remaining on the life of the option.
2. The relationship of the underlying futures to the option strike price.
3. The amount of past and future market volatility (historical and implied).

Interest rates play an insignificant role in this story, so we will not concern ourselves with this variable.

Influences on an Option Price

Exhibit 4.1 provides a list of the major factors influencing an option price. These represent *direct* influences on the price *level*

35

Options	Increase in Volatility	Decrease in Volatility	Decrease in Time to Expiration	Increase in the Underlying	Decrease in the Underlying	Increased Interest Rates	Decreased Interest Rates
Calls	+	−	−	+	−	+	−
Puts	+	−	−	−	+	−	+

Exhibit 4.1   Influences on an option price. A plus sign indicates direction of change in an option's premium given a change in the factor influencing an option's price. For example, the result of a decrease in time to expiration will lower the value of both call and put options, all other things remaining equal.

of an option's premium. After we discuss each of these, we will look at some terms that allow us to measure these influences. These are known as *delta* and *theta,* and these variables measure the *rate of change* of the price level.

Time Value

Time value is the portion of the price of the option that is not intrinsic value. It is also known as extrinsic value. As the reader can see in Exhibit 4.2, which contains the decay of time value for an out-of-the-money S&P option assuming no change in the underlying futures, time value decreases with each passing day, from 19 points of premium to 0.1 point as expiration nears. Time value decays for the following simple and intuitive reason: As the length of time remaining until expiration decreases, the probability that the underlying will make a move into the money diminishes. That is, the less time there is remaining until expiration, the less likelihood the option will make a profit for the buyer. Therefore, the price of the option will be lower, reflecting less time value. A call option is in the money when the underlying futures price is greater than the strike price. A put option is in the money when the underlying futures price is less than the strike price. When the underlying futures are near the strike price, there will always be more time value on the option than if the underlying futures were further away from the strike price.

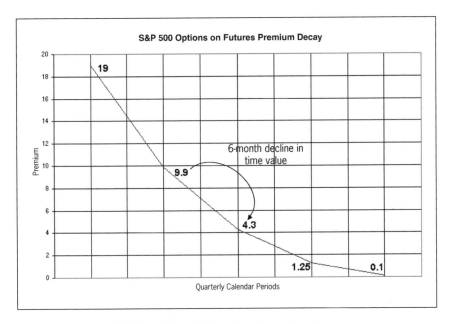

Exhibit 4.2 S&P option time-value decay.

This is because there is a much greater chance for a near-the-money option to get in the money and thus have intrinsic value.

The chance that an option contract will get in the money within a year is more likely than during a period of one month. The more time the underlying futures have to make a move, the more time value there will be in the option price. Stated another way, the level of time value is a function of the time remaining until expiration. For example, when an option buyer pays for an out-of-the-money option, the price represents time value only. The buyer is betting that the option will get in the money, and thus acquire intrinsic value, before expiration. The option seller, meanwhile, bets that the option will expire worthless, looking to keep the time premium. To better understand what we mean by an option being in or out of the money, let's now look at the second major influence on the price of an option—intrinsic value.

Intrinsic Value

Intrinsic value is the portion of an option's value arising from an option being in the money. Intrinsic value of a *call* option, for example, arises if the underlying futures are trading higher than the strike price of the option. Intrinsic value of a *put* option arises when the underlying futures are trading below the strike price. Let's take a look at an example of a call option at expiration to illustrate intrinsic value.

An S&P 500 1250 call option at expiration will have 10 points of intrinsic value if the S&P futures settle at 1260 (1260 − 1250 = 10). Now, let's take an example of an S&P put option at expiration. If the put option strike price is 1250 and the S&P futures settle at 1240, the put option has 10 points of intrinsic value (1250 − 1240 = 10). At any time before expiration, given these same prices and strikes for the call and put examples, intrinsic value will be the same, but the option premium will also include time value. For example, if the S&P 1250 call option has a premium of 15 when the futures are trading at 1260, the extra 5 points in premium represents time value. The same would apply to the put option if it had a premium value of 15. If the premium declined to 13 with no change in the underlying futures, intrinsic value would remain the same, and time value would now be 3.

To summarize, at any point in an option's life, if the futures price is greater than the strike price, a call option will have intrinsic value equal to the futures price minus the strike price. The remaining premium represents time value. For a put option, on the other hand, we calculate intrinsic value by subtracting the futures price from the strike price. The difference represents intrinsic value. The remainder of the premium, as with calls, equals pure time value.

Finally, when the underlying futures are trading at the strike of the option, which is known as being *at the money* (and thus has no intrinsic value), the time value will always be at its highest point. Deep-out-of-the-money options lose most of their time value just as deep-in-the-money options do. Think of it like this: If the option is very far out of the money, then time value, known also as extrinsic value, will be very small given that the chance for a move from deep out of the money to in the money is less likely. If the option is already deep in the money, on the other hand, the time value will be very low too. This is due to the fact that once an option gets deep in the money, the ability for the buyer to derive any additional leverage decreases and thus so does the time value. Since deep-in-the-money options offer very little leverage to a trader, there is little time value to be found in the premium.

Volatility

Historical volatility measures the degree of past fluctuation in the price of a futures contract, or how rapidly the price has been changing. Implied volatility, on the other hand, measures the expected volatility, so this is really a measure of future volatility. How does this figure into trading decisions and pricing? Generally speaking, high implied volatility results in a higher premium on the option. Lower implied volatility leads to a reduced premium on the option. If we write options that have high volatility priced in them, and volatility declines, our position will gain, assuming all other things remain the same. (See Exhibit 4.3.)

It is worth pointing out that implied volatility is not always the same for each of the option strikes. Some options may have what is known as a volatility skew, which can be exploited when constructing certain trades. For example, S&P put options tend to have more implied volatility than S&P call options. This can be seen in put premiums. Put premiums that are the same distance out of the money as calls typically have more premium. We will talk more about exploiting volatility skews in the second half of this book covering commodity options.

As option writers, we are primarily interested in selling overvalued options, essentially options with high implied volatility relative to historical volatility, and when implied volatility is at an extreme compared with past levels. By writing options with high implied volatility, we are looking for an eventual conver-

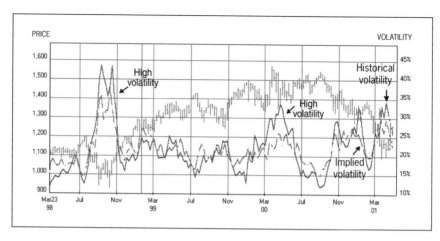

Exhibit 4.3 Implied and historical volatility chart for S&P futures.
Created using OptionVue 5 Options Analysis Software.

gence toward normal historical levels of volatility. This gives our trades as option writers an added edge.

This edge results from a greater likelihood that the implied volatility will drop toward the historical norm while we are in a trade, which will lower premiums, all other things remaining equal. Given that time value is always taking its toll on the premium value of an option, as option writers we profit *even faster with a decline in volatility.* Often, we can close positions well ahead of expiration, given favorable changes in volatility combined with the erosion of time value. Again, this profit arises not from the movement of the price of the underlying but from changes in volatility and the passage of time. However, it should be pointed out that a favorable move of the underlying would only accelerate gains in an option writer's strategy.

Delta and Theta

Previously, we have covered the major factors that influence an option's price. In the following subsections we will discuss delta and theta, which allow us to measure the effect of these influences on a particular option or position.

Delta

The delta of an option is a measure of the change in an option's premium resulting from a change in the underlying futures. For example, if the S&P 500 futures rise by 1 percent, and an option's premium increases by 0.5 percent, the delta would be 0.5, or an increase in an option's premium by exactly one-half of the percentage change in the underlying futures. Delta will depend on the distance of the futures from the strike price of the option and how much time remains on the option and is typically expressed as a number between zero and 1.0 (for calls) or between zero and –1.0 (for puts). Deep-out-of-the-money calls have deltas closer to zero, as do deep-out-of-the-money puts. Calls and puts closer to the money have deltas nearer to 0.5 and –0.5, respectively. For options that are in the money, the delta will approach 1.0 if it is a call option, and –1.0 if it is a put option. A near-zero delta would mean that a change in the underlying would have little or no impact on the option price. At the other extreme, a delta of 1.0 would mean that a change in the underlying produces a one-for-one change in the option's price.

Let's take an example using the S&P futures and futures options. If the S&P 500 futures rise by 20 points with a delta of +1.0, the call option's price should rise by 20 points. But if the S&P futures were to rise by 20 points with a delta of +0.4, then the call option's price should rise by 8 points with all other things remaining equal (0.4 × 20 = 8). Taking the same move of the underlying futures, but considering a put contract instead, with a delta of –0.4, the price of the put option should fall by 8 points (–0.4 × 20 = –8). A negative delta, in other words, means that a rise of the underlying futures results in a *fall* in the premium on a put option.

An important related variable in the option pricing equation is *gamma*, which measures the *rate of change* of the delta variable. Gamma measures the rate at which an option's delta changes as the underlying changes. Gamma is calculated by dividing the change in delta by the change in the futures price. It measures the change in delta that is caused by a change in the underlying. Typically, the option price gets a lot of gamma in it as we approach expiration and the underlying is near or just in the money.

As the reader will see, an important concept known as *position delta* is used to help determine how a move of the underlying will affect an option position. A delta neutral position should not be affected much by a small move of the underlying in either direction. Delta neutral positions will not eliminate all risk, but can be used to contain small moves throughout the life of an option writing strategy. Large moves that happen quickly can sharply and suddenly change a delta neutral position to delta short or long, with the possibility for unrealized losses on the position. Keeping a position delta neutral requires close attention to daily price changes of the underlying and adjustments to the position if the market is moving. It is best carried out with the help of a good broker. This dimension of trading comes into play primarily with the ratio spreading that we do on many of the commodity option markets.

Theta

As we explained earlier, an option price is itself always influenced by the time remaining until expiration. But there isn't a one-to-one relationship between the passage of a unit of time (i.e., one day) and a decline in time value.

Theta, which is always negative, is the *rate* of time decay. Theta increases as options approach expiration. For each day that passes in the life of an option, the amount of value the option loses in the form of time decay is not constant. Theta, therefore, increases as we get closer to expiration. On the other end of the curve, the slope is nearly flat, indicating that the passage of time results in very little decay of time value.

As the reader will see with the S&P spread trade examples presented in Chapter 8, however, the decline in the value of deep-out-of-the-money credit spreads is not just a function of theta. These spreads can shrink to a negligible amount if the options move further out of the money. This permits the option writer to close the trade at a nice profit and free up margin for a new trade. Therefore, it is not always necessary to wait until the last few weeks for the time value-decay slope to turn sharply downward (more vertical and less horizontal) to collect a nice profit.

In summary, we learned in this chapter how option prices are influenced by time, intrinsic versus extrinsic value, and volatility. We moved on to explain how delta and theta allow us to measure these influences. While there is more to the option pricing story than we have presented here, this chapter should equip the reader with the necessary essentials for understanding our trading approach presented in subsequent chapters.

Chapter 5

UNDERSTANDING S&P 500 OPTIONS

At this point, the reader should have a practical grasp of the important features and functions of the S&P 500 futures, as well as the pricing fundamentals of options on futures in general. Understanding S&P 500 options, therefore, should be a natural segue at this point. Following a short historical digression on futures options, in this chapter we will describe the major characteristics of S&P 500 options. While we do touch on commodity options and futures contracts in this chapter, as we did in the previous one, we are deferring a fuller discussion of these nonindex products to Chapter 9, where we will introduce commodity futures and options, followed in Chapter 10 by the strategies designed to work with these instruments.

Brief History of Options on Futures

Options on futures contracts were introduced formally in 1982 following the sanctioning of these instruments by the U.S. government. While options in various forms have been traded for many years, it was not until this time that option markets became standardized and exchange based. While the Chicago Board Options Exchange (CBOE) began offering stock option products in 1973, it would not be until 1982 when the Commodity

Futures Trading Commission (CFTC) approved the trading of options on domestic commodity futures contracts. These developments provided the legal and financial framework for the growth of option markets.

The Chicago Mercantile Exchange (CME), the largest futures and futures option exchange in the world, opened its index and commodity option market (IOM) in 1982, the same year the S&P 500 futures contract began trading. The S&P 500 stock index futures began trading on March 21, 1982, and options on the S&P 500 stock index futures commenced the following year on January 23, 1983.

Other options on futures contracts were introduced later. While live cattle futures were introduced on November 11, 1964, it would not be until October 30, 1984, that options on live cattle futures appeared. British pound futures options, meanwhile, started trading on February 25, 1985, and 90-day U.S. Treasury bill futures options got started on March 10, 1986. More recently, Nasdaq 100 stock index futures options were launched on March 10, 1996. Also, options and futures on the Dow Jones Industrial Average index began trading in late 1997. These are just a few of the many futures option contracts available to traders today.

The arrival of the Internet and online trading added an additional spur to the growth of stock option trading. By the late 1990s, it seemed that stock option speculating had become almost a national pastime. There is no doubt that the historic bull market of the 1990s contributed to this unprecedented enthusiasm, as well. This surge in stock option trading, however, did not spill over into options on futures markets, as the majority of the option traders are familiar only with stock and stock index options traded at the CBOE. Lack of education about options on futures, unfortunately, has kept many traders away. We hope this book helps fill that void.

Options on futures data available from the CME, presented in Exhibits 5.1 and 5.2, offer some indication of trading volume of these instruments over the past five years. In terms of overall volume, keep in mind that the CME represents only one of the options on futures exchanges. Exhibit 5.3 contains volume data

Year Change	Volume	Percent Change
	CME Total	
1996	35,270,185	—
1997	40,764,159	+15.6
1998	42,991,388	+5.5
1999	32,723,766	−23.9
2000	36,007,913	+10.0
	CME Index Options	
1996	4,700,632	—
1997	4,899,259	+4.2
1998	5,148,507	+5.1
1999	4,898,058	−4.9
2000	5,088,836	+3.9

Exhibit 5.1 CME historical options on futures volume. Annual data cover the period from January through December of each of the years listed.
Source: CME.

Options Contract	Volume	Percent of Total
Eurodollar	21,634,276	36.0
S&P 500	4,352,249	12.0
Live cattle	622,590	02.0
Japanese yen	567,896	02.0

Exhibit 5.2 CME options on futures volume leaders. Volume is concentrated in four markets: (1) live cattle, (2) Eurodollars, (3) Japanese yen, and (4) S&P 500. The data presented cover the period from January through December 2000.
Source: CME.

47

Calendar Year	Oat Options	Corn Options	Wheat Options	Soybean Options	Bonds (30-year)	Notes (10-year)	Ag. Group Total	Fin. Group Totals	CBOT Total
1990	7,334	2,116,302	482,941	2,089,382	27,315,411	936,754	5,015,477	28,444,924	33,461,799
1991	4,486	2,048,422	692,327	2,165,167	21,925,578	890,293	5,105,826	23,014,276	28,125,965
1992	15,307	1,833,816	2,165,167	1,930,334	20,258,741	2,564,191	5,145,395	23,533,861	28,701,626
1993	17,373	2,031,284	713,670	2,927,072	23,435,164	4,844,272	6,177,860	30,333,411	36,531,698
1994	20,495	2,144,461	827,930	2,710,656	28,142,549	6,437,215	6,256,931	37,534,091	43,806,394
1995	35,250	3,783,446	1,243,567	3,149,635	25,639,950	6,887,102	8,767,223	36,283,780	45,056,867
1996	45,037	6,602,010	1,886,909	5,135,124	25,930,661	7,907,650	14,563,288	36,725,763	51,304,320
1997	21,654	4,963,603	1,698,969	5,339,936	30,805,885	6,032,088	13,159,368	39,311,358	52,642,632
1998	51,852	4,267,274	1,346,272	3,845,804	39,941,672	9,296,742	11,187,734	52,609,469	64,050,508
1999	56,418	4,205,325	1,516,037	4,792,245	34,680,068	9,738,808	12,129,126	47,054,651	59,413,936
2000	52,760	5,135,111	1,563,557	3,890,510	17,267,458	10,629,021	11,823,282	31,842,462	43,866,151
Totals	327,966	39,131,054	14,137,346	37,975,865	295,343,137	66,164,136	99,331,510	386,688,046	486,961,896

Exhibit 5.3 CBOT historical options on futures volume for leading groups and contracts.

Source: CBOT.

48

for the Chicago Board of Trade (CBOT), which is the second largest options and futures exchange.

The bulk of CME-traded options on futures volume is concentrated in four markets: (1) live cattle, (2) eurodollars, (3) Japanese yen, and (4) the S&P 500. Exhibit 5.2 provides volume data for these four markets for the period from January through December 2000, giving some indication of their liquidity. Eurodollar options lead in volume, followed by the S&P 500 stock index futures options. The four largest markets in 2000 represented 52 percent of total CME volume.

Like futures contracts, options contracts have a two-fold character. They serve as an instrument for commercial traders, those typically long or short the 'basis', or cash commodity, who need to hedge against unwanted price moves. At the same time, they provide a vehicle for speculators. It is the speculator who provides much of the liquidity in these markets, and who is taking on the risk that hedgers are transferring through their trading operations. Hedgers are, meanwhile, willing to pay to reduce risk, a potential source of profit for speculators.

S&P Options Characteristics

A notable feature of S&P options is their relationship to the underlying cash index. Unlike the S&P 500 and S&P 100 stock index option products traded on the CBOE, the CME's S&P 500 options trade day to day based on the price of *S&P futures*, not the underlying S&P 500 cash index. The CBOE S&P stock index options, on the other hand, trade directly based on the S&P 500 and S&P 100 cash indexes.

Another important feature of S&P options is the existence of serial and nonserial S&P options. The S&P futures have a cash settlement at expiration in December, March, June, and September just as S&P options do for the same trading months of the S&P futures. However, serial-month S&P options exercise into the *next nearest futures contract month*. For example, January and February (both serial months) options exercise into the March futures contract, April and May options (serial months) exercise into June futures. Therefore, on the third Friday of the serial contract month, the options would settle based on the prices of the March and June futures. Daily settlements of these serial-month contracts is likewise based on daily settlement prices of these next nearest futures contracts. Serial-month options are created to provide traders with a contract that has a closer expiration date than three months, and because there is demand for them. For example, once December options expire along with the December S&P futures, the next nearest option would be March. By offering January and February options, for instance, the exchange offers shorter-term options for traders.

Exercise and Option Assignment

Most stock option traders know that the transfer of stock is involved in stock option assignments. With options on futures, however, assignments involve buying or selling of the underlying futures contract. Exhibit 5.4 illustrates the essential mechanics of assignment of S&P options. If assigned, a call writer gets a short futures position and a put writer gets a long futures position.

Let's look more closely at assignment, using an S&P put option with a strike of 1250. If the holder of the S&P put option exercises the option when the September S&P futures are trading 1225, the writer of the put option would be assigned a long futures position at the option strike price. That is, the writer would get a

Call/Put Writer	S&P Call Writer	S&P Put Writer	Cash Settlement
If assigned	Gets short futures	Acquires long futures	Pay cash

Exhibit 5.4 Assignment of S&P 500 futures options. A call writer is assigned a short futures position and a put writer is assigned a long futures position in the event of exercise by the option holder (buyer).

long futures contract priced from 1250 (the strike price). Essentially, therefore, with the futures at 1225, the long futures shows an unrealized loss of ($25 \times \$250 = \$6,250$).

By exercising, meanwhile, the option put holder or buyer gets a short futures position, as shown in Exhibit 5.5. Using the same examples as previously, this short position is priced from 1250 (the strike price), and thus the option holder's account shows an unrealized gain of 25 points ($6,250). The short futures can then be offset for a profit of $6,250. The option writer can likewise offset the long futures at a loss of $6,250. As the reader can see, assignment takes place in the form of the creation of a long or short futures position in the accounts of the option writer and buyer, respectively.

It is worth noting, finally, that if the option were exercised on the last day of trading of a nonserial month, the holder would receive an S&P 500 futures contract that expires at the open on the following day and that settles in cash. This would give the same results as previously mentioned, assuming that the same prices prevailed. For call options, the same process is at work, but the call holder gets a long futures, and the call writer gets a short futures.

To summarize, upon exercise a long call holder acquires a long futures position and a long put holder receives a short futures position. The call seller, meanwhile, acquires a short futures position and a put seller receives a long futures position. These assignments take place at the option strike prices.

Call/Put Buyer	S&P Call Buyer	S&P Put Buyer	Cash Settlement
If exercised	Acquires long futures	Gets short futures	Receives cash

Exhibit 5.5 S&P 500 options exercised. If an option buyer chooses to exercise his or her option, the buyer of a call would receive a long futures position and the buyer of a put would receive a short futures position.

Expiration Date Rules

Understanding when options on futures expire is easy. You call your broker. Information is also available on the Internet at the exchanges. Therefore, the lack of standardization between different futures and futures option contracts should not be a hindrance to getting started trading these markets. Even though there are widely differing last trading days for futures and option contracts, today's software and a good broker make this a secondary concern.

Nevertheless, we will point out some basic concepts to help understand expiration. First of all, the S&P futures and options are easier because they settle in cash. Unless a serial-month option contract, they expire together on the third Friday of the contract month. Other options on futures, however, will expire ahead of first-notice day. The S&P futures, because it is a cash settlement contract, does not have a first-notice day. First-notice day is the date for commodity futures on or after which the holder of a long futures can be assigned a delivery notice for the underlying physical commodity. All commodity option contracts expire ahead of first-notice day. Therefore, as speculators in options on commodities, we never worry about first-notice day or delivery because we have to get out of our position ahead of this date. It is worth noting, furthermore, that due to the expiration of commodity options ahead of first-notice day, many commodity options actually expire in the month *prior* to the contract month of the futures.

Unit of Trading and Price Quotations

All options on futures trade one-for-one relative to the underlying futures contract. That is, one S&P 500 futures contract is equivalent to one S&P 500 futures option contract. For example, one option contract can be exercised for one futures contract. Regarding quotation protocol, futures options are generally quoted in the same value per unit as their related futures contract (i.e., one tick's value for the S&P 500 futures is equivalent to the value of one tick of option prices). In one exception to the rule, T-bond futures options trade with a minimum tick value of $\frac{1}{64}$ ($15.625), while the futures contract is based on a minimum price change of $\frac{1}{32}$ ($31.50).

Turning again to the S&P futures, we already know that one S&P 500 call option is equivalent to one S&P long futures contract; and a one-point change in option premium represents the same dollar value of a one-point change in the futures ($250). Each tick value, furthermore, is worth $25, and there are 10 ticks per point (or per 100 basis points) for a total point value of $250. Options that are worth fewer than 2 points, however, can trade in increments of 0.05. Generally, though, tick and price quotations are consistent for a futures contract and its corresponding option contract.

Strike Prices and Serial Options

Generally, strike prices are at five-point intervals with S&P 500 options. However, each listed futures option market is different, having its own strike price intervals. Option chains with the latest prices (last and settlement), open interest, and volume exist at each of the exchanges.

With many option markets there are contract months that are not the same as the futures delivery months. As we already explained, these are known as serial months, and they cover months without futures contracts. For example, there are four futures contracts—March, June, September, and December—for the S&P 500 futures. However, as previously mentioned, serial options also exist on the S&P 500 futures, which expire in every month between the delivery months for the futures contract (i.e., April put options that expire into June futures). These serial options exist on markets such as currencies, government securities, major metals, and several other liquid commodity markets.

Transaction Costs

With any market, transaction costs must be considered when attempting to trade. This is especially true with option writing.

An option writer's profit is generally limited to the premium collected. Therefore, the premium received must be large enough to provide a reasonable profit and cover commission costs. Our rule of thumb is to simply never write options for less than $300 in premium per contract. As you will see with S&P 500 option credit spreads, which we discuss in Chapter 8, we are able to take in on average $1,000 in premium per contract with deep-out-of-the-money spreads, which is plenty of premium relative to commission costs for traders. For example, if a spread trade costs $60 per leg in commissions, then a trader pays total commissions of $120, which means that the transaction costs represent 12 percent of the premium received. This is very acceptable. However, a spread on soybean options, which carries less premium, may not always generate a reasonable premium-to-commission ratio. The determination must be made on a trade-by-trade basis.

Margin Requirements

The subject of margin, meanwhile, will be taken up in Chapter 7. For now, it is important to keep in mind that initial margin and maintenance margin are set by the exchanges, and the amounts differ by contract market. Usually, the higher the value of a contract, the more margin that is required per contract.

Some markets, such as corn and wheat, have relatively low margin requirements, even for writing naked options. Others, such as the S&P 500 stock index futures options, require a larger sum of money to write naked options.

It is worth noting that hedged positions, such as credit spreads, can substantially lower the margin demands when trading S&P 500 options and commodity options. For example, a deep-out-of-the-money credit spread can be written with as little as $1,500 initial margin for S&P 500 options. On average, these credit spreads are priced with a margin-to-premium ratio of 2 to 1. And if the spread is put on both sides—that is, a call and put credit spread done simultaneously—there is little or no additional charge for the second spread (the other wing) if the second wing has less or equal risk. Therefore, a trader can often collect premium equal to 100 percent of initial margin.

In summary, we briefly discussed the history of options on futures and the current level of trading of these instruments on the major exchanges. We then reviewed essential characteristics of S&P options related to exercise, assignment, expiration, and pricing and quotation protocol. We finished by highlighting relevant aspects pertaining to transaction costs and margin requirements. In Chapter 6, we shift our focus to trading strategies, presenting the basic building blocks of our approach to trading S&P 500 options—deep-out-of-the-money credit spreads.

Chapter 6

THE LONG AND SHORT OF AN S&P CREDIT SPREAD

The strategy emphasized in this book for trading S&P 500 options on futures is the *basic credit spread,* which is also known as a *bear credit spread* if written with call options and a *bull credit spread* if written with put options. Later in the book we will move on to commodity futures options, where we explain ratio writing, naked option positions, and other trading setups. With S&P 500 futures, meanwhile, writing credit spreads offers an excellent hedged approach to trading and one that, if done correctly, does not eat up loads of trading capital through onerous margin requirements associated with either taking outright positions in S&P futures or selling naked options on S&P 500 futures. And because we prefer deep-out-of-the-money spreads on the S&P 500, the odds of winning each trade are very high.

In the previous chapters, we have attempted to explain the mechanics of futures markets using the S&P 500 futures as an example. It makes sense for consistency to remain focused on S&P 500 futures through the first half of the book because it will help to cement an understanding through increased familiarity with this liquid and potentially profitable market. In this chapter, therefore, we will illustrate our credit spread examples using the S&P 500 futures options. We begin by discussing long and short calls and puts, and finish by building deep-out-of-the-money call and put spreads on S&P 500 futures.

To construct a credit spread, it is necessary to first cover some basics, to make sure the reader understands long and short option positions, which are the key building blocks of spread trades of this type. For readers with some knowledge of options and futures, this will serve as a review. A credit spread has two legs, meaning that there are two sides to the trade setup: a short and long option with different strikes. It is called a credit spread because a trader's account receives a credit upon entering the spread. This is because the short leg is sold for more than it costs to purchase the long leg. We don't discuss spreads that result in a debit to a trader's account, because this strategy is a net option buying approach. We are net option premium sellers, primarily. To help the reader better understand the concept of a credit spread, we will first review some basic option strategies, using these as stepping-stones toward understanding what constitutes a credit spread.

The Long Call Option

The purchase of a long call option is a simple strategy established as a directional trade when a trader has a bullish outlook on the underlying futures. A long call strategy involves the outright purchase of a call option. There is no corresponding sale of another option in this type of strategy. For example, instead of buying the underlying S&P 500 futures should a trader have a bullish view of the broad market, the trader could simply purchase an S&P 500 call option. Generally, this type of call strategy involves buying an out-of-the-money call option, which means the S&P futures will be trading below the strike price of the call option. The further out of the money the call option, the less value the call option will have. By deploying this strategy, a trader is able to make a bet on the direction of the S&P 500 without purchasing stocks that comprise the S&P 500 index (requiring more capital and effort) or incurring the huge risk and margin of trading the futures contract. Instead, a relatively small amount of capital and effort is required to purchase the call option. This type of trade thus offers tremendous leverage and simplicity, which is what lures buyers into taking a long position in a call or put option, even though most lose at this game. It is a limited-risk trade with an unlimited profit potential. The maximum risk is known beforehand. It is equal to the amount paid for the option. The premium is the maximum that the trader can lose. Finally, there is theoretically no limit to how much can be made.

The profit-and-loss profile is quite simple to visualize for a long call. In Exhibit 6.1, a hypothetical profit-and-loss picture is presented for an S&P 500 June long call position with a strike price of 1280. As can be seen in Exhibit 6.1, the loss is limited on the downside, indicated by the horizontal slope beginning at the kink (the strike price of 1280) and moving leftward (zero intrinsic value). Breakeven is at 1290.00, 10 points (which was paid for the option) above the strike price of the June 1280 call. The June S&P futures are at 1267.50, so the call option is out of the money. The potential losses are limited to the amount paid for the option $(10 \times \$250 = \$2,500)$ because no matter how low the S&P futures

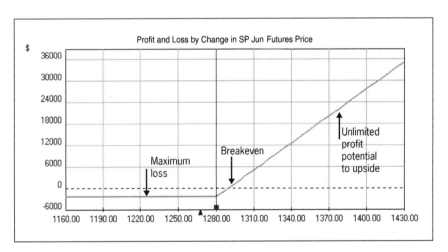

Exhibit 6.1 S&P 500 June 1280 long call profit-and-loss function. Here, the June call option trades on June S&P futures, which are indicated by the solid black triangle along the horizontal axis at 1267.50. The vertical line represents the strike price at 1280.00. The dashed horizontal line is the breakeven level. *Created using OptionVue 5 Options Analysis Software.*

trade, the buyer of the long call can only lose what was paid for the option. The northeasterly pointing line beginning at the kink represents unlimited profit potential, with profits rising once above 1290 (breakeven).

From the kink moving upward to the right, sloping northeasterly (positive and increasing intrinsic value), losses become less until they reach the zero level, or breakeven point. This is the level at which the trader has covered the cost of the call option. The price of the underlying futures has reached a level above the strike price of the option that covers the premium paid by the buyer. The horizontal axis along the bottom of the chart plots different levels of the underlying futures at expiration. Thus, as the underlying moves higher (moving to the right along the horizontal axis), we move farther to the northeast (from the kink), indicating higher profit on the position. As we noted earlier, there is theoretically an unlimited profit potential, should the underlying futures continue to rally throughout the life of the option contract. What is important here is the functional relationship between the movement of the underlying futures and the level of potential profit or loss.

Until now, we have abstracted from the role played by time decay. If we add theta (the rate of time-value decay) to the graphic display of profit and loss, however, we do not alter the basic shape of the profit-and-loss function. Instead, what happens is we get a shift downward in the profit-and-loss function as time passes. This is easy to understand if you think of the role time plays in the pricing equation, which we covered in Chapter 4 on pricing fundamentals. Time-value decay will decrease an option's premium, all other things remaining equal.

Exhibit 6.2 includes theta in a profit-and-loss function for a June S&P long call option, which can be visualized by the multiple profit-and-loss functions. We know that time value will fall to zero at expiration. But at any point before expiration, usually there will be some time value remaining and, therefore, more than just intrinsic value in the option price. As time passes, the profit-and-loss function will shift downward and to the right (a southeasterly direction), because at any level of the underlying (which is not indicated in Exhibit 6.2) there will always be less

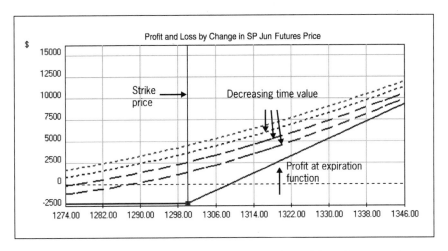

Exhibit 6.2 S&P 500 June 1300 long call profit-and-loss function showing impact of time decay. At any level of the underlying futures the passage of time will lower the profit-and-loss function. The solid profit-and-loss function reflects profit or loss at expiration.
Created using OptionVue 5 Options Analysis Software.

time value embodied in the option price, represented by a lower profit-and-loss function at any given level of the underlying.

Given any level of the underlying futures, therefore, the profit-and-loss function will have moved more in a southeasterly direction—reflecting loss of time value. We know that intrinsic value accrues once the option is in the money. Time value, however, will always take its toll on the option price. In Exhibit 6.2, we have drawn three additional profit-and-loss function lines to show exactly how time decay lowers the potential profit as time progresses. The reader will notice that it does not alter the main characteristics of the strategy of buying a long call option. That is, incorporating the time-decay dimension to a long call does not alter the ability of this strategy to theoretically make unlimited profits while having only limited risk.

The long call option strategy, while itself a popular approach to option trading, actually forms one part of a strategy called a *credit spread*, which is why we chose to illustrate it here. The second part involves selling a call option in the same contract month that is closer to the money than the purchased option. Before constructing a credit spread, we will therefore first lay out the basics of option selling. More specifically, we will show the basic mechanics of selling using an S&P 500 call option as an example.

The Short Call

When an option writer sells an option—whether a put or a call—this is considered a naked position if not covered by the purchase of an option on the same underlying futures at a different strike. The term *naked* thus refers to a situation where the potential for loss is theoretically unlimited. In other words, in theory a trader is exposed to unlimited losses when writing naked options, as if the trader were long or short the underlying futures. We will return to the subject of writing naked options later in Chapter 11, where we present actual trades involving the sale of naked commodity options. For now, we will explain the basic mechanics of naked option writing for the purpose of illuminating the call and put credit-spread strategies. A call credit spread, as the reader will see later, combines both a long call and a call that is written, or sold (the short leg), using different strikes to generate a credit to the account.

A naked call, or call that is written, is a strategy employed by a trader who is neutral to bearish on the underlying futures. This is not a directional trade, as with the long call. Instead, it has the advantage of making money under three conditions, as opposed to just one for a long option. A naked call will make money under the following three conditions: (1) the underlying futures remains in a relatively narrow range, (2) the underlying futures trades lower by whatever magnitude, or (3) the underlying futures trades moderately higher. *Money, therefore, can be made without relying on the market to move directionally.* The most favorable condition for a naked call strategy is the second. A decline of the underlying futures will cause the premium to drop faster. Day-to-day passage of time will lower the premium on the naked option as well, but not as quickly as a strong bearish move of the underlying futures.

Exhibit 6.3 presents a profit-and-loss function for a June S&P naked call option with a strike price at 1300. Profit from a naked option is limited to just the premium received when it is written, in this case 4.4 points, or $1,100. Intrinsic value begins to accrue, meanwhile, at the kink on the chart in Exhibit 6.3, and increases southeasterly along the profit-and-loss function. Breakeven on expiration is at 1304.40, at which point intrinsic value just equals premium received by the writer. This point represents exactly the amount received for writing the call option added to the strike price of 1300. The vertical line at the kink indicates the strike price. Above 1304.4, at expiration, losses will be incurred and are potentially unlimited should the trade remain open with the underlying futures rising.

On the other hand, if the call option remains out of the money, as can be seen in Exhibit 6.3 (along the horizontal axis left of the kink), the price of the option declines to zero at expiration, having a maximum profit indicated by the horizontal

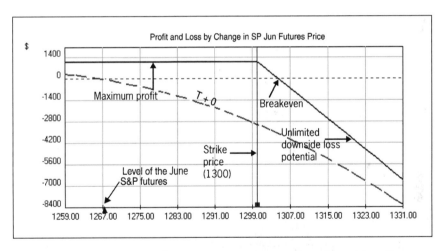

Exhibit 6.3 S&P 500 June 1300 naked call option profit-and-loss function. Here, the June call option trades on June S&P futures, which are indicated by the solid black triangle along the horizontal axis at 1267.50. The dashed line (T + 0) is the profit/loss function at the time the trade is established. Premium received for writing this option was 4.4 points. Breakeven is at 1304.4.
Created using OptionVue 5 Options Analysis Software.

chart from the kink leftward. Maximum profit would be $1,100. But as the reader can see in Exhibit 6.4, when theta is factored in, the erosion of time helps the position gain even if the underlying moves against the call option writer. Here, with the multiple profit-and-loss functions representing different points in time, the position begins to show a profit even if the underlying June futures price remains stationary at 1267.50.

Remember, the call buyer likes a quick upward move of the underlying futures. This is because the call won't lose as much time value and the option price will increase faster. To the contrary, the same mechanism works in reverse for the call seller, who prefers little upward movement of the underlying futures when there is a lot of time value on the option because this can quickly raise the value of the option price, and thus result in potential losses. As time passes, however, a call seller can tolerate moves higher by the underlying due to the depressive effect on the option's price caused by time decay.

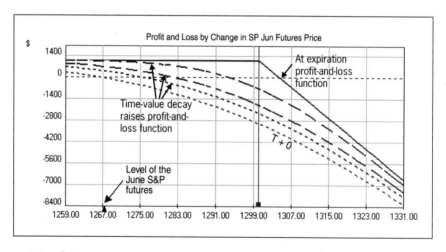

Exhibit 6.4   S&P 500 June 1300 naked call option profit-and-loss function with time decay. Here, the June call option trades on June S&P futures, which are indicated at 1267.50. Even with no movement of the underlying, with time-value decay the naked call option begins to show a profit before expiration.
Created using OptionVue 5 Options Analysis Software.

Note that the farther away (lower) from the strike price the underlying futures trade (e.g., out of the money), the less extrinsic value on the option. For an in-the-money naked call option, a sharp move of the underlying futures toward the strike price drops the premium even faster. In this case, both intrinsic and extrinsic (time) value are declining.

Summarizing the main features of a long and short (written) call, we can state the following: A naked out-of-the-money call writer profits as long as the underlying futures do not trade higher by too much and if the underlying futures trades sideways, or if the underlying futures trade lower by whatever magnitude. The long call strategist gains only if there is a large bullish move of the underlying futures by expiration. The move must be large enough to leave enough intrinsic value in the option to at least cover the cost of the option.

The Call Credit Spread

As we already mentioned, credit spreads, as opposed to debit spreads, involve writing an option at one strike and buying another option on the same underlying futures at a different strike further out of the money. Earlier we reviewed the two legs separately (the long call and the short call). Now we can assemble the spread position with these two pieces. We will continue to use the example of a call credit spread, which could also be called a *bear credit spread* because the position profits more quickly if the market is bearish. Yet, as the reader will see, the strategy profits even if conditions are neutral to slightly bullish. Generally, if a trader's outlook were neutral to bearish, a call credit spread would be an appropriate strategy to trade.

All credit spreads offer traders the advantage of limited potential losses and hence lower margin requirements, which is an essential idea behind this strategy. As the reader will see later, this becomes very important for a market like the S&P 500 futures, which has a high minimum margin requirement to write naked options. There *is* reduced potential profit with a credit spread. Nevertheless, this is compensated for by the limited loss nature of this strategy, as well as a lower margin requirement.

Let's pick up the discussion with our previous example of a naked call. We know that if the market should move sharply higher, the potential for unlimited losses exists. This is evident in Exhibit 6.3 in the shape of a June naked call option profit-and-loss function that slopes downward, or southeasterly from the kink. Yet there is a way to cap the losses on this position while still preserving a nice profit potential by turning the naked into a credit spread. (See Exhibit 6.5.)

On June 1, 2001, the September S&P futures were trading at 1267.50. Let's say we want to set up a September deep-out-of-the-money call credit spread, which expires on September 21. To construct this deep-out-of-the-money call credit spread, we will *sell* the 1450 strike and *buy* a *higher* call option at the 1500 strike. Exhibit 6.5 provides a profit-and-loss function for this

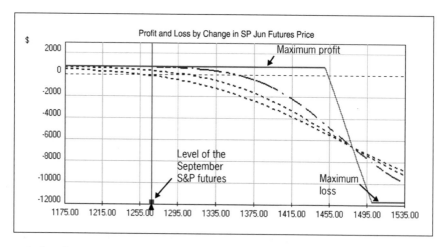

Exhibit 6.5 S&P 500 September call credit spread with 1450 × 1500 strike prices. The September S&P futures are indicated at 1267.50 by the solid black triangle along the horizontal axis. The bottom right-hand corner of the profit-and-loss function shows the function flattening out at the maximum loss level. *Created using OptionVue 5 Options Analysis Software.*

credit spread. Let's take a look at the prices so we can see how we arrive at a net credit when establishing this position.

We sold the lower strike of 1450 for 5.30 points, or $1,325 ($250 × 5.3 = $1,325) and bought the higher strike for 2.4 points, or $600 ($250 × 2.4 = $600), leaving a net credit of 2.9 points, or $725 (5.3 − 2.4 = 2.9 points × $250 = $725). This spread is approximately 15 percent out of the money. Initial margin requirement for this trade is $2,217. Typically, we establish S&P 500 credit spreads three months out in time, meaning three months before expiration, in order to capture enough time premium and still be deep out of the money.

This September S&P call spread will profit as long as the underlying September futures settle below 1452.9 (1450 + 2.9 = 1452.9; the short call strike price + the premium received). Full profit arises if the short leg of the spread stays out of the money and thus expires worthless (below 1450). Here, the writer keeps the entire premium, not just part of the initial credit. If the underlying futures settle at 1451, only 1.9 points of the initial credit of 2.9 would be retained because the short call expired 1 point in the money.

Of course, in practice we probably would not sit in a credit spread if the underlying got too close to the short side of the spread. Instead, there are a number of follow-up moves that a trader can take to limit losses and reduce margin demands on an account. The margin requirement will increase generally if the underlying futures get closer to the short strike price of the spread. Since positions are marked to market daily, it is absolutely necessary to be well capitalized to stay with the trade should the underlying futures experience a sharp gain during the life of the spread. As the reader will see in Chapter 8, it is possible to take follow-up action to avert major losses.

Just what kind of margin requirements would arise under different scenarios (taking into account the size of a move and at what point in the cycle of the option's life) will be explored in the next chapter. *Anticipating margin needs is a crucial element in achieving success with credit spread trading, which above all means establishing the proper position sizes so that a trader can handle a large move of the underlying against the position.*

The Long Put Option

We have presented the long call option position. Now let's do the same for a long put position. A long put, much like a long call, is a directional trade. A trader who is bearish on the underlying futures would buy puts to speculate on an anticipated decline. Just like with the previous long call example, this is an outright purchase of an option. There is no additional sale or hedge leg in this trade. Buying a put is an alternative to shorting the underlying itself, and has many advantages over shorting the futures but still suffers from the buyer's dilemma we spelled out in Chapter 1. If the trader expects the market to trade significantly lower, a trader could purchase an out-of-the-money S&P put option. The further out of the money the trader goes, the less the puts will cost. Exhibit 6.6 provides a profit-and-loss profile for this type of option strategy.

Exhibit 6.6 presents a profit-and-loss function for a June S&P long put option with a strike price of 1240. With the June futures contract trading at 1254, it would have to decline below the strike price (1240) by more than the amount paid for the option in order to profit.

This strategy does provide tremendous leverage even though time-value decay works against a put buyer, just like for a call buyer. The put offers limited upside risk just like the call provides limited downside risk—limited to the premium paid for the option. Meanwhile, the put buyer has the potential for unlimited profit on the downside should the market sell off sharply. Also, an increase in volatility will add more value to the put option, which can happen with a strong downward move of the underlying futures. But as we pointed out earlier regarding the advantages to selling options, most buyers lose because time value works against the buyer of an option and most stock and commodity markets tend to spend most of the time in trading ranges, which ultimately benefits the sellers. Buyers tend to

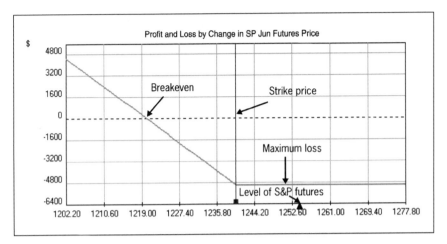

Exhibit 6.6   S&P 500 June 1240 long put profit-and-loss function. Here, the June S&P 500 futures are indicated at 1254.00 along the horizontal axis by the solid black triangle. Profits are realized at expiration if the June futures are trading below 1220, which is where the solid profit-and-loss function crosses breakeven. Premium for this option was 20 points, which makes breakeven 1220 (1240 − 20 = 1220).
Created using OptionVue 5 Options Analysis Software.

spend many a night hoping for some news event to move the market enough to profit.

The profit-and-loss profile for the long put, as with the long call, is very straightforward. This profit-and-loss picture is presented in Exhibit 6.6 for our June S&P long put. The limited-loss aspect can be seen in the horizontal slope from the kink moving rightward. From the kink moving to the left, sloping northwesterly, losses become less, until they reach zero as the underlying futures decline (movement along the horizontal axis). At the 1220 level of the underlying futures, the trader has covered the cost of purchasing the option (20 points in premium). If the underlying futures continue to trade lower from this point, at expiration a profit is registered. The solid northwesterly sloping line crossing the dashed horizontal line (breakeven) is where profits would begin to accrue.

Just like with the long call example earlier, the horizontal axis plots different levels of the underlying June S&P futures. Thus, as the underlying futures move lower, (leftward along the horizontal axis) we move farther to the northwest along the vertical axis once we pass breakeven, indicating higher profit on the put position. Theoretically, an unlimited profit is available should the underlying continue to decline. Again, this can be seen in the profit-and-loss line sloping upward in a northwesterly direction.

The functional relationship between the movement of the underlying futures and the levels of profit or loss is the important concept to understand. Now we need to insert time decay into the equation, which makes it a bit more complex. First, by projecting into the future the impact of time-value decay on any position, we do not alter the fundamental functional relationship between the underlying futures and the profit-or-loss levels. Yet, we do see that time is a drag on the ability to make a profit for long puts, just as it is with a long call option. Exhibit 6.7 provides multiple profit-and-loss functions that capture this drag effect on potential profits. For example, the more time value that remains on the option, the greater the impact on the profit level that any favorable move of the underlying futures will have. This dynamic is captured in Exhibit 6.7.

A shift downward in the profit-and-loss function reflects the passage of time. Given any level of the underlying futures ahead of expiration, the more time value remaining in the option's price, the higher the profits if a profitable trade. In other words, if the underlying futures move down to 1230 from 1254 in Exhibit 6.7, the trade becomes profitable early on. As the reader can see, at 1230 profits will appear and then disappear if the underlying futures stay at that level. The erosion of time value eventually turns a winner into a loser.

While we don't like to buy put options outright, as the reader will see shortly, the long put option can be used as one leg of the put credit spread strategy. The other leg, meanwhile, is the short put option (writing a put option at a higher strike to generate a net credit). We will now review in more detail what constitutes

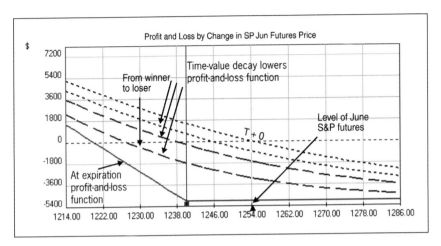

Exhibit 6.7 S&P 500 June 1240 long put option profit-and-loss function with time decay. Here, the June S&P 500 futures are indicated at 1254.00.
Created using OptionVue 5 Options Analysis Software.

a short put and how its profit-and-loss profile looks before turning to assembling both legs into a put credit spread.

The Naked Put Option

If a trader is neutral to bullish, an appropriate strategy might be selling a put option. The straight sale of a put, which is known as a *naked put*, does not require large moves of the underlying to make a profit, unlike a long put strategy. The naked put will make money under the following conditions: (1) the underlying futures remains in a relatively narrow range, (2) the underlying futures trades higher by any magnitude, and (3) the underlying futures trades lower moderately. In our example, we will sell a 1200 put option when the underlying futures is at approximately 1254 one month prior to expiration.

Exhibit 6.8 captures these conditions, with the naked S&P put strike price of 1200 (indicated by the kink). Breakeven is shown where the southwesterly sloping profit-and-loss function crosses the horizontal dashed line. The premium received for this put was 20 points, making breakeven at 1180.

Maximum profit will be limited, as with the short call, to the amount of premium received from writing the naked put ($20 \times \$250 = \$5,000$).

As the underlying moves higher, the put option gets farther away from the money. The put option will lose value and the writer will experience gains up to the maximum profit level. Exhibit 6.8 shows the level at which the profit-and-loss function becomes horizontal beginning at the kink (strike price).

Exhibit 6.9 shows this relationship with time-value decay plotted at different points in time before expiration. The process works in reverse when compared with our previous long put example. This time the passage of time adds profit. This can be seen at 1254 on the horizontal axis, the level of the S&P futures. The profit-and-loss functions move higher with a stationary underlying futures generating higher profit until the maximum level is reached.

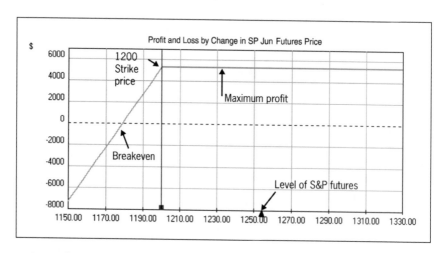

Exhibit 6.8 S&P 500 June 1200 naked put option profit-and-loss function at expiration.

Created using OptionVue 5 Options Analysis Software.

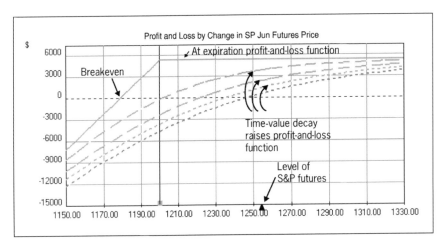

Exhibit 6.9   S&P 500 June 1200 naked put option profit-and-loss function with time decay.
Created using OptionVue 5 Options Analysis Software.

The Put Credit Spread

Just as with the call option credit spread, in order to construct an out-of-the-money put credit spread we sell one option and buy another in the same option month. This vertical structure, however, works exactly the opposite way that calls work. In the case of puts, the trader *sells the higher strike and buys the lower strike to generate a credit.* Recall that for a credit to be generated in our example of a call credit spread, it was necessary to sell the *lower* strike and buy the *higher* strike to generate a credit.

We are going to write this put spread when the September S&P futures are trading at 1267.50, just like in the case of the September call spread. Since it is a September put spread, it will expire on the third Friday of September along with the S&P September futures. Exhibit 6.10 provides the prices and strikes. We will construct this spread 17 percent out of the money using the 1050 and 950 strikes. We are selling the higher strike and buying the lower strike to generate a credit.

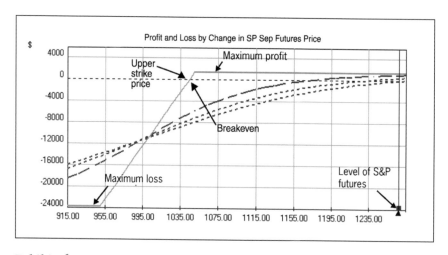

Exhibit 6.10   S&P 500 September put credit spread with 1050 × 950 strike price. The September S&P futures are indicated at 1267.50, approximately 17 percent out of the money. The first kink in the expiration profit-and-loss function (solid line) is the upper strike in the put spread (1050). Losses would be incurred if the S&P futures were to trade below 1045 (1050 minus the premium received of 5 points) and would be limited by the long put with a strike of 950 (the second kink in the lower left-hand corner of the diagram). Typically, these trades are closed before the underlying reaches the upper strike to minimize losses.
Created using OptionVue 5 Options Analysis Software.

Let's take a look at the prices so we can see how we arrive at a net credit. By selling the 1050 strike, we collect 8.6 points ($250 × 8.6 = $2,150). We then buy the lower 950 strike for a debit of 3.6 points ($250 × 3.6 = $900), leaving a net credit of 5 points, or $1,250 (5 × $250 = $1,250). Initial span margin for this spread is $2,657. If this spread expires out of the money, the profit rate based on initial margin would be 47 percent. Clearly, it is possible to write at least four of these spreads per year, which means a profit rate of up to 200 percent is possible under ideal conditions.

The first part of this chapter highlighted basic call and put options strategies: long puts and calls and short puts and calls. We then constructed one of our favorite trading strategies: the S&P credit spread, which combines both long and short options. We presented a call credit spread and a put credit spread. The basic idea is to profit from time value-decay by writing deep-out-of-the-money put and call credit spreads. By writing deep-out-of-the-money credit spreads, there is a high probability that spreads will profit, especially given that proper position sizing and money management and follow-up action is undertaken at the appropriate moments. In the following chapter, we will provide a simulation of SPAN margin requirements for credit spreads written on the S&P futures. This will give the reader a more solid feel for the functioning of credit spreads and the degree of risk associated with this strategy when deployed on the S&P futures.

Chapter 7

SIMULATING MARGIN REQUIREMENTS FOR AN S&P CREDIT SPREAD

In this chapter, we discuss some of the practical aspects of Standard Portfolio Analysis of Risk (SPAN®)* margin, and then present simulations based on different scenarios for the underlying futures and changes in time remaining on the spread. We will compare the performance of the naked put option with the put spread on the underlying S&P futures. This is purely an analytical exercise, but one that nonetheless realistically represents the behavior of margin requirements and spread and naked put values given different assumptions about the movement of the underlying futures. Essentially, by looking at a June S&P naked put and put spreads under different assumptions, we get a glimpse of how a trade might behave under actual trading conditions.

What Is SPAN®?

We have explained in a previous chapter that one of the advantages of trading options on futures pertains to the benefit that traders derive from SPAN, a sophisticated performance bond

---

*SPAN and PC-SPAN are registered trademarks of the Chicago Mercantile Exchange, Inc.

system (i.e., margin) created by Chicago Mercantile Exchange, Inc. (CME) and now used by many exchanges worldwide, including all of the major commodity exchanges in the United States.

The Standard Portfolio Analysis of Risk, or SPAN, calculates perceived overnight trade risk on all open option positions simultaneously. SPAN will calculate margin requirements for a complete portfolio of option and futures positions in a manner that is more logical and realistic than other methods. Older margin systems and those used to determine margin on stock and index options are considered inferior in design. The bottom line is that SPAN offers much lower margin requirement based on its global analysis of risk. We should point out that not all brokers enable a trader to operate at SPAN margin levels, which are the exchange minimums. To maximize the potential of option selling strategies outlined in this book, however, it is essential to find a broker who allows the trader to get SPAN margin minimums.

By performance bond of course we mean *margin*, the money that must be posted to a trader's account to open and hold any option or futures, or combination of option and futures positions. These SPAN margin requirements were designed and are maintained to ensure that daily minimum risk requirements for futures clearing firms, individual members of the exchange, and retail customers are being met.

To understand the practical aspects of SPAN for trading and, in particular, selling options, we will present here an S&P put option credit spread and naked put position given different scenarios for the underlying S&P futures. It should be understood at the outset, however, that margin requirements differ by contract market, essentially determined by historical volatility, daily futures settlement prices, and time remaining until expiration, as modeled in the SPAN algorithm. Based on a set of 16 scenarios (i.e., what if the futures are up ⅓ of range? what if volatility is down? etc.) known as *risk arrays*, SPAN predicts what maximum daily losses might be for any position, and then generates the necessary margin requirements to keep the position open. We will only be looking at S&P option positions here.

Before we turn to a simulation of margin demands for a June S&P put spread and naked put option, however, we should explain what it means to (1) post margin, (2) receive a margin call, and (3) have a position marked to the market. These are all concepts option writers must become familiar with before beginning any trading.

In the world of futures and futures options, margin works very differently from margin on stocks. Assuming a stock is marginable (not all stocks are), stock traders can get a maximum leverage of two-to-one margin on stock positions. That is, for $1 in a trader's account, the trader can purchase $2 worth of stock. This is a 50 percent margin, as permitted by the Federal Reserve Board of the U.S. Federal Reserve Bank. The margin money, though, is actually a loan, and the trader is charged a rate of interest, which at best is the *broker's loan rate*, which is above prime. Under margin or performance bond regulations for futures and futures options, however, the trader not only *receives* interest on margin money instead of paying out interest (T-bills are a marginable equivalent to cash and are acceptable forms of margin), but there is also much more leverage. Margin has thus an entirely different meaning in the context of commodity markets.

There isn't any borrowing of money when one speaks of margin on futures, as there is with stocks. As we just explained, a stock trader typically can get a two-for-one margin when buying stocks. *A futures margin, on the other hand, is a required deposit posted with a futures brokerage house.* It is a good-faith deposit, in other words, representing only a fraction of the value of the futures contract being purchased. These margin levels are set by the exchanges, usually representing between 5 and 10 percent of the value of a futures contract.

Both the buyer and seller of a futures contract must post initial margin to open a position. Margin deposits are not the same for every commodity contract market. For example, currently, initial margin requirement to go long or short one S&P 500® futures contract is $21,563. In Exhibit 7.1, the CME's minimum initial margin requirements for other equity futures, as of February 10, 2001, are listed.

While margin amounts are subject to change, these figures give a good sense of the amount of money necessary to initiate outright futures positions. While these margin rates apply to

Futures Contracts	Initial Margin	Maintenance Margin
E-Mini S&P 500® (ES)	$4,688	$3,750
NASDAQ 100 Index® (ND)	$41,250	$33,000
E-Mini NASDAQ 100® (NQ)	$8,250	$6,600
NIKKEI 225 Index® (NK)	$6,750	$5,000
Russell 2000 Stock Index® (RL)	$26,325	$19,500

Exhibit 7.1   CME equity index futures margin requirements for outright positions (as of February 10, 2001).
Source: CME.

actual futures contracts, SPAN margin requirements apply to option contracts (or option and futures combinations in a total portfolio). Option buyers never have to post margin, it should be made clear, because there is limited loss in the form of the premium paid for the option. Margin is required only for short positions, or net short positions like credits spreads and other trade strategies involving combinations of short (call or put) options with short or long futures, or combinations of long and short options.

As the reader will see, however, with the examples that follow, the SPAN margin for a naked put option will be less than what it would cost to buy or sell an S&P 500 futures contract, even if the naked put is at the money. With our approach using S&P 500 credit spreads, furthermore, the initial margin requirement drops considerably, allowing trades to be established with much less capital. While the potential rewards are lower, the advantage can be seen in the limited risk and more efficient use of margin. That is, the percentage rate of profit based on SPAN margins is potentially much greater.

Initial margin demands for index futures tend to run relatively high compared with most commodity futures due to the higher value of the index contracts. Commodity futures markets can generally be traded with much less capital, which gets even lower when trading option positions. Even naked option strategies and ratio writes (which involve some degree of unlimited risk exposure due to partly uncovered short options used in ratio writing) can be put on with very little initial margin. Exhibit 7.2 lists the initial margin requirements for select CBOT commodity futures contracts, which should give some indication of how low margin requirements are for most commodities.

Margin demands on a trader's account will fluctuate throughout the life of the trade and are based on the level of the underlying futures as they are marked to the market at the close of each trading day.

By marked to the market, it is meant that a position is adjusted daily, based on settlement prices, for profit and loss in a trader's account. The exchange determines a settlement price at the close of the market each day, and then marks the positions based on that price. An account experiences either increased or decreased excess margin and liquidation value based on daily settlement prices.

Should maintenance levels be breached, meaning the account value falls below the maintenance margin level, a remargining is required to bring the account back up to the new initial margin level. This requires the timely deposit of additional funds, or an adjustment to any open trades in the form of either reducing exposure, or closing positions. It should also be noted that the exchanges can change the margin requirements for futures con-

Futures Contracts	Initial Margin	Mainenance Margin
Corn	$475	$350
Soybeans	$945	$700
Wheat	$540	$400
Oats	$270	$200
Rough rice	$675	$500
Soybean oil	$270	$200
Soybean meal	$810	$600

Exhibit 7.2   CBOT commodity futures margin requirements for outright positions (as of February 23, 2001).
Source: CBOT.

tracts without any prior notice. This is usually done after a dramatic change in volatility or in the value of the contract.

As the reader will see, one of the keys to making money with any type of net short options trades is having the ability to defend positions from excessive margin demands should they get into trouble. Forced closure of trades can result in unnecessary losses. However, through proper money management in the form of appropriate position sizing and by deploying effective follow-up action, losses can often be avoided. Of course, losses do and will occur. It is part of the trading game.

Now let's take our real examples of the June S&P naked and spread option positions presented in the previous chapter and illustrate these margin concepts given different assumptions about the time remaining until expiration and hypothetical movement of the underlying futures. We will be using S&P 500 futures options, deferring until a later chapter a discussion about commodity options. The same margin principles, however, apply to all commodity option trades.

Earlier, we saw the exchange-determined margin requirements for some equity index and commodity *futures* contracts. When constructing *option* trades, however, the margin determination gets more complicated, requiring sophisticated software to calculate, because often there are combinations of open futures and option contracts, both long and short, and across different markets in a *total portfolio of perhaps many different strategies and open positions.* Fortunately, we have an excellent software package to do most of the heavy lifting for us. We will present our examples using CME's Standard Portfolio Analysis of Risk software (PC-SPAN®, version 4.01a) for Windows. This software, by the way, is available for purchase directly from CME.

SPAN Margin Simulation

Let's take our first simulation: a naked put option on the June S&P 500 futures. We will set up a deep-out-of-the-money naked put using June S&P options. This position would exercise into the June S&P futures, and both the options on the June futures and the June futures themselves will expire on the third Friday of June based on the opening price of the S&P 500 index.

For our first example, we will use a naked June 950 put with the June S&P 500 futures settling at 1158.50 on March 16, 2001. SPAN can easily determine how much margin would be required to initiate this naked put trade. Using PC-SPAN, we can get the initial and maintenance margin requirements once we have the closing price for the June S&P 500 futures on March 16, 2000, which are included in the risk parameter files available from CME at the end of that day for downloading into PC-SPAN.

Combined with the risk arrays built into the SPAN algorithm, the latest risk parameter files are used by PC-SPAN to calculate the performance bond requirement for a naked S&P put option with a strike price of 950. In Exhibit 7.3, the trader

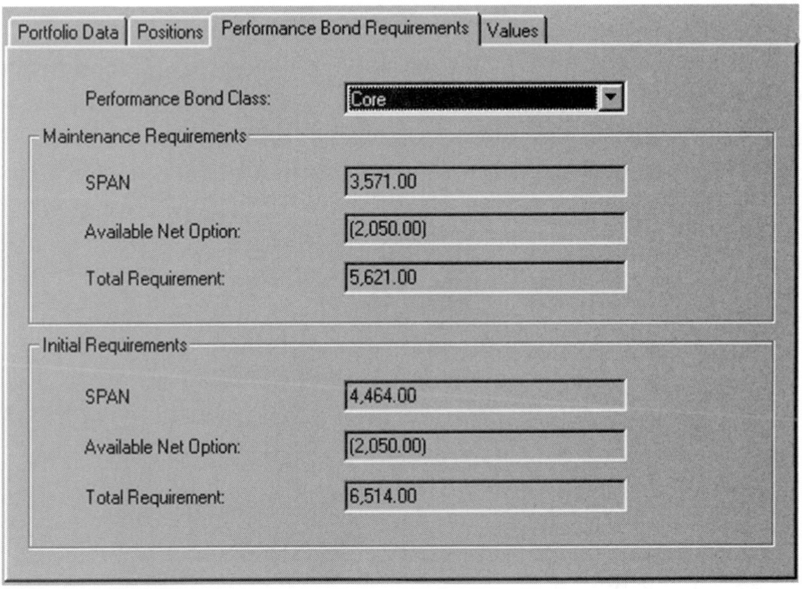

Exhibit 7.3   Initial margin requirement for naked June S&P put option with a strike of 950.
Created using PC-SPAN.

will see the amount required to open a naked S&P 500 June futures put at a strike price of 950 on this particular day with the futures having settled at 1158.50.

Since the underlying futures are over 16 percent away from the naked strike, or 208.5 points, the margin demand for the position is quite low. In this case, we would need to post only $4,464 in margin to open this naked put position, according to PC-SPAN. Now let's see how this requirement changes with a move lower by the S&P futures. A move lower or higher by the S&P futures will raise or lower this amount, respectively. For example, let's say the June S&P 500 futures moved 10 percent lower (assuming no change for now in the time remaining until expiration), from 1158.50 to approximately 1042. To simulate this change in the underlying, and again ignoring the impact of time decay (and changes in volatility), we simply set up the naked put trade 10 percent closer to the money using PC-SPAN.

For example, instead of the 950 strike, we would pick the 1050 strike in the software, which is very close to being 10 percent closer to the money. This is as if the S&P futures had moved 10 percent *lower*. To state this a different way, and assuming no change in volatility levels, to simulate the move of the underlying 10 percent lower, we are instead moving the strike of the June S&P naked put approximately 10 percent *higher* (closer to the money), which is essentially the same thing as a 10 percent price change lower. In Exhibit 7.4, the new initial margin and maintenance margin levels can be seen. We are simply looking at the requirements for a 1050 strike as a simulation of what would happen had the June S&P futures moved 10 percent lower.

As the reader can see, the initial margin now stands at $8,948, up from the initial $4,464 for one naked option contract, and maintenance margin now at $7,158. The price of the naked option, meanwhile, would now be $5,375, an increase in price of $3,325. If the position were now closed, there would be a loss of $3,325 for the naked put writer because we are still assuming no change in the value of the option due to time-value decay or a change in volatility. Nevertheless, note that while the naked put value increased by 160 percent, the margin requirement increased by only 100 percent. As the reader will see later, the spread easily

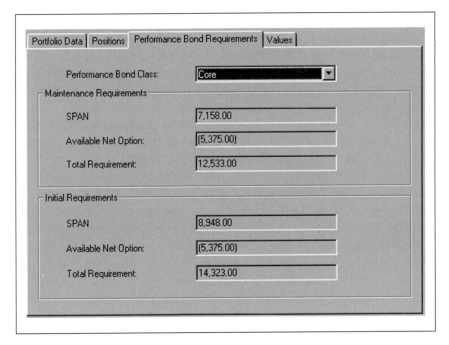

Exhibit 7.4   June S&P 500 naked put SPAN margin requirements for simulated move lower by 10 percent.
Created using PC-SPAN.

outperforms the naked put, given the same adverse percentage move lower by the underlying June S&P futures contract.

Let's now turn to an example of a June S&P put spread using the strike prices 950 × 850. We want to compare margin requirements both before and after an assumed 10 percent move of the underlying S&P futures. This is the same assumed move of the underlying futures as we simulated for the naked put option previously. We can then compare the performance of the two strategies. Therefore, first we will present the initial margin amount to write a put credit spread at the 950 and 850 strikes (selling one S&P June put option at the 950 strike and buying one at the 850 strike), which will be followed by the change in margin brought on by the same 10 percent move that we simulated earlier.

Based on settlement prices from March 16, 2000, of 1158.50, the initial margin required per spread (950 × 850) is $2,873, with a maintenance margin of $2,298. The credit received from writing this spread would be $1,325 ($250 × 5.3 = $1,325). This is about typical for a spread of this type in terms of the ratio of margin to premium. We like to get $1 in premium for every $2 in margin required. This trade comes in at slightly better than a 2-to-1 margin-to-premium ratio. These values can be seen in Exhibit 7.5, which were generated using PC-SPAN.

If the S&P 500 closes above 950 at expiration, this trade would end up a winner. To become a loser, the S&P futures would have to drop over 21 percent by expiration. Between establishing the put spread and expiration, however, there may be large moves that raise or lower margin considerably. If little or no time has elapsed since entering the position, we can assume, therefore, that the

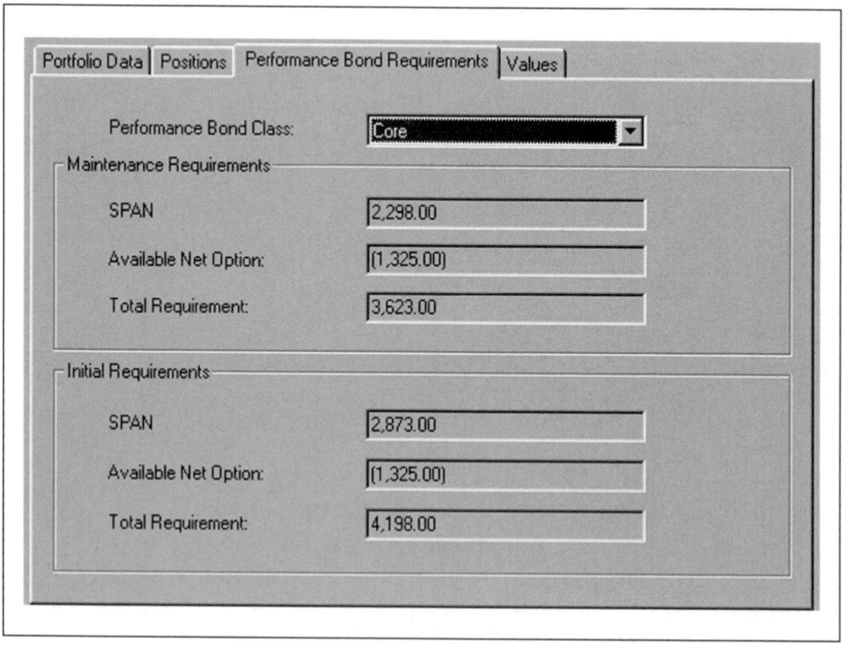

Exhibit 7.5   Initial and maintenance margin requirements for June S&P put spread at 950 × 850 strikes.
Created using PC-SPAN.

margin demand will increase if there is any downside for the S&P 500 futures. Indeed, the market was very bearish at this point, and considerable downside became a reality, as the reader will discover in the next chapter as we review our actual spread trades during this period. In fact, the trade record attests to the amazing flexibility of S&P spread trades that are established deep out of the money in the correct size relative to available risk capital.

Using PC-SPAN, we can approximate the margin demand at different *levels* of the underlying futures for this put spread example, and at different points before expiration (i.e., different number of days remaining until expiration). Let's start with how the margin demand might increase if we have first a 10 percent decline of the June S&P futures, assuming no changes in days remaining until expiration and no changes in volatility. To do this, we will follow the same method used previously, which involves building

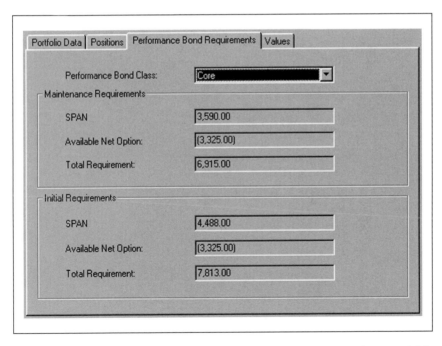

Exhibit 7.6   New margin requirements for June 950 × 850 credit spread following a simulated 10 percent adverse price move by the S&P futures.
Created using PC-SPAN.

a different position in PC-SPAN using new strikes (strikes 10 percent higher to simulate a price move 10 percent lower). Exhibit 7.6 contains the margin requirements we have discussed earlier for the June 950×850 put spread, with a simulated move lower of 10 percent by the June S&P futures. The spread has now widened to $3,325, an increase from the level at which we wrote this spread ($1,325), so we experienced an unrealized loss so far on the spread of $2,000. The spread has, therefore, increased by 159 percent (the change in the value of the difference in option prices for the two strikes). The net asset value is in parentheses in Exhibit 7.7, and is $3,325, which is what the spread is now worth. The new initial and maintenance margin values are also included. The new SPAN initial margin amount has increased to $4,488, with the new maintenance margin level now at $3,590, representing an increase of $1,615, or just 56 percent.

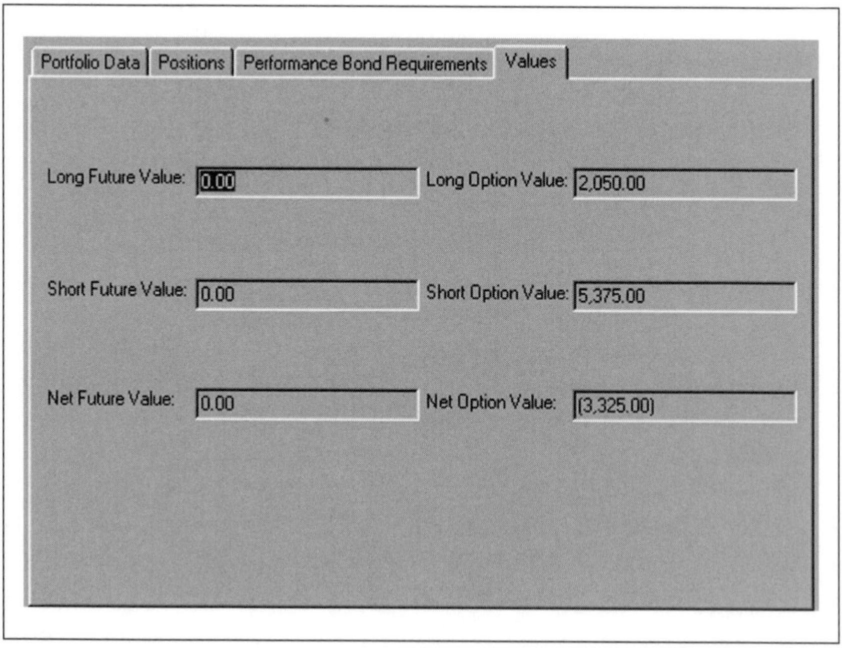

Portfolio Data	Positions	Performance Bond Requirements	Values

Long Future Value: 0.00   Long Option Value: 2,050.00

Short Future Value: 0.00   Short Option Value: 5,375.00

Net Future Value: 0.00   Net Option Value: (3,325.00)

Exhibit 7.7   June S&P 950×850 put spread long and short option values, and net option value at point $T + 0$ following an adverse move of 10 percent.
Created using PC-SPAN.

Note that the increase in initial margin was just 56 percent, while the spread widened by 159 percent. Recall that in our naked put example, the put value increased by 160 percent (nearly identical change in percentage terms to the change in the spread's value), yet the initial margin increased by 100 percent. In other words, the increase in margin for the spread is much lower, just 56 percent, indicating that the spread trades provide less exposure to adverse moves in terms of margin changes and thus provide more efficient use of margin. Another significant advantage not captured here but often a major factor in the functioning of the S&P futures market is volatility. The naked put option is subject to much more damage from a spike in volatility levels. In fact, as bearish conditions sharpen, volatility levels can climb quite high, pushing up the premium on the naked puts, and this can increase unrealized losses and margin requirements. The put spread, on the other hand, has a long leg as part of its construction. There-

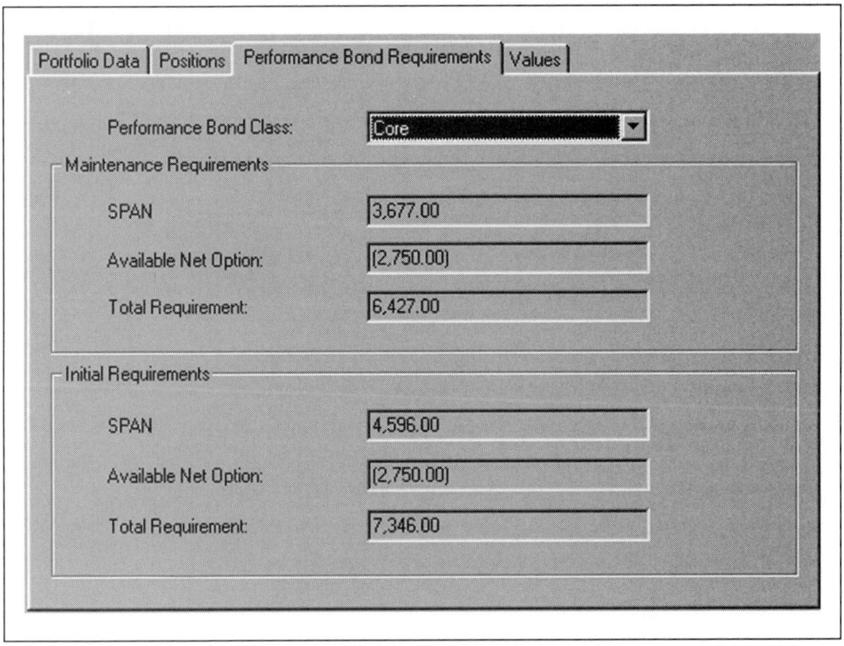

Exhibit 7.8 June S&P 950 × 850 put spread margin and net option value at $T + 30$ following a 10 percent adverse move.
Created using PC-SPAN.

fore, a spike in volatility is somewhat neutralized because the long side also gains from the increase.

Continuing our exercise, we can now relax our assumption about days remaining until expiration in order to simulate the impact on margin that a 10 percent decline would have under three assumptions about time remaining until expiration in this 90-day trade: (1) at $T + 0$, the opening date of the position; (2) at $T + 30$, 30 days into the trade; and (3) at $T + 60$, 60 days into the trade or 30 days prior to expiration. The values of the 950×850 S&P put spread legs separately at $T + 0$ are $2,050 and $725, respectively, for a net option value of $1,325. Now let's move to $T + 30$ to see what changes we get.

Exhibit 7.8 provides the new net option value, which is $2,750, with an initial margin requirement of $4,596 and the maintenance margin now at $3,677. While there is no significant

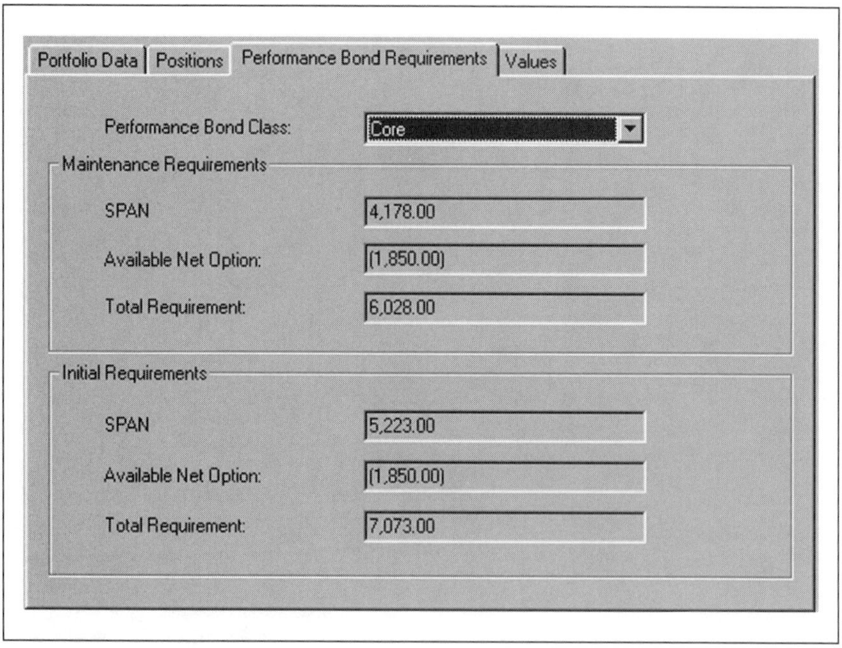

Portfolio Data	Positions	Performance Bond Requirements	Values

Performance Bond Class: Core

Maintenance Requirements

SPAN	4,178.00
Available Net Option:	(1,850.00)
Total Requirement:	6,028.00

Initial Requirements

SPAN	5,223.00
Available Net Option:	(1,850.00)
Total Requirement:	7,073.00

Exhibit 7.9   June S&P 950×850 put spread value at $T + 60$ point in time with 10 percent adverse move.
Created using PC-SPAN.

change in margin (actually a slight increase), the passage of 30 days has narrowed the value of the spread to $2,250, from $3,325. Had there *not* been a 10 percent move lower made by the underlying June contract (still an assumption in the model), the position would have shown a nice profit already. Instead, we have here a smaller unrealized loss due to the passage of 30 days and the consequent loss of time value.

Now we can move ahead another 30 days, but still holding with our assumption of an adverse move of 10 percent. In Exhibit 7.9, we can see that the margin requirement has increased slightly again, now at $5,223, but the spread has narrowed even more to $1,850, nearly back to breakeven. Had we seen a relatively stationary underlying futures contract, we would have witnessed instead a considerable narrowing of the spread at $T + 60$. For example, in Exhibit 7.10, we relax our assumption of a 10 percent

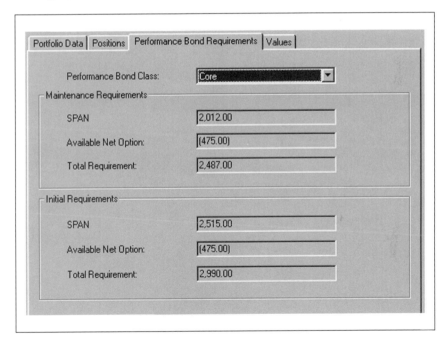

Exhibit 7.10   June S&P 950 × 850 put spread with stationary underlying assumption but keeping $T + 60$ assumption.
Created using PC-SPAN.

adverse move, but we keep the $T + 60$ assumption to see where the spread's value would be.

In Exhibit 7.10, we can see that the spread has narrowed by a considerable amount, to just $475, and initial margin has fallen to $2,515. The reader will recall that this is without any move of the underlying and one month before expiration of the spread. *At this point, it is possible to close the trade for a nice profit.* In this case, the profit on one spread would be $850 ($1,325 − $475 = $850), and the return on margin for this trade would thus be 30 percent ($850/$2,873 = 30 percent) over a 60-day period, an annualized return of 180 percent.

Finally, the most favorable condition would be a move higher of the June futures once we entered a June S&P put spread at the 950×850 strikes. This can be simulated, as well. Exhibit 7.11

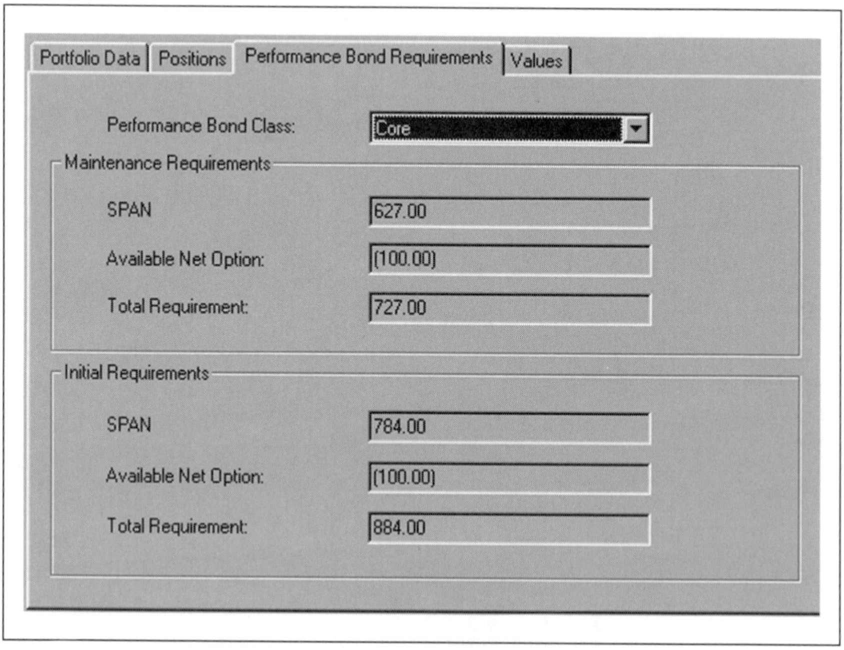

Exhibit 7.11   June S&P 950×850 put spread with simulated 10 percent favorable move by June futures at $T + 60$ time.
Created using PC-SPAN.

contains the new values in our model, which assumes a move higher by the June futures of slightly more than 10 percent and the passage of 60 days, leaving one month remaining in the life of the spread. As you can see, the net option value (the value of the spread) has collapsed to $100, or a profit of $1,225 if the spread were closed at this point. And the initial margin requirement has dropped to $784. The return on margin would have been 43 percent ($1,225/$2,873 = 43 percent) in just 60 days, or an annualized rate of return of 258 percent.

While there are many other simulations that one can do, we have shown first how a June put spread offers more efficient use of margin when compared with a naked put, and then demonstrated, by making different assumptions about time remaining and the position of the underlying, how the spread value and margin requirements would change and what sort of profits a spread trader can expect when trading S&P options. Having provided some simulated examples of S&P put spreads, we can now turn to our actual S&P put spreads, which should bring into clearer view the material we have presented up to this point.

Chapter 8

PARAMETERS OF PROFITABILITY OF S&P CREDIT SPREADS

In this chapter, we examine a number of actual S&P credit spreads that we did over a period of several years and during a mix of market conditions. We walk you through each of these trades and their setups, trying to breathe life into the S&P option characteristics, strategies, and margin concepts we have already touched on earlier in this book. As the reader will see, S&P spread trading offers flexibility and wide parameters of profitability if done correctly.

We prefer to sell S&P deep out-of-the-money credit spreads. Our experience in the past 10 years has been a good one, with most spreads ending as winners for the writers. *The key, however, is to manage the potential losers so that the few losers don't wipe out all your gains from the many winners.* It helps to trade with a trend, and most of our trades have been on the put side over the life of the 1990s bull market—with a historically bullish bias in equity markets, it makes sense to establish put spreads, also known as bull put spreads. These spreads tend to offer more premium for selling than do their call spread counterparts because there is a greater premium placed on puts as a result of investor fears of market crashes.

Just how much room these spreads have for profitability can be illustrated by the fact that our put spreads during the very

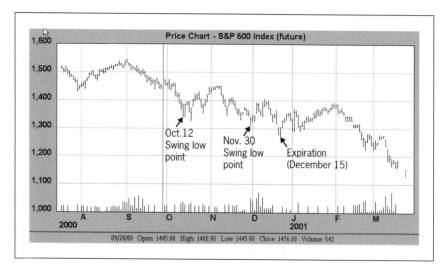

Exhibit 8.1   Daily bar chart of S&P futures for 2000 and 2001.
Created using OptionVue 5 Options Analysis Software.

bearish period of late 2000 and early 2001 managed to do quite well. The reader can see from the chart in Exhibit 8.1 just how severe the bearish conditions became for the S&P 500 as profitability concerns intensified for major technology and blue-chip companies.

Despite the harsh conditions, our credit spreads on the S&P 500 managed to survive, although one needed to be rolled to a later month. We established the following trades: two separate deep-out-of-the-money S&P 500 put spreads (December 1100 × 1000 and December 1250 × 1200), a dual credit spread (May call spread at 1650 × 1675 with a September put spread at 1100 × 1000), and a March 2001 put spread at 1225 × 1125 that needed to be rolled to a June 2001 put spread at 1050 × 950 to take it out of immediate danger during a severe bear attack. This trade ultimately ended up a winner, as well.

December 1250 × 1200 Put Spread

On September 28, 2000, the December S&P futures settled at 1440.50. On this day, we established an S&P December 2000

1250×1200 put credit spread. Exhibit 8.2 contains the price of the spread and the prices of the individual legs.

As the reader can see, we were able to sell this December spread for $800, or a credit of 3.2 points ($250/point). For the short leg, the December 1250 put, we received 8.20 points ($2,050). We paid 5.0 points ($1,250) for the long leg, the December 1200. We thus sold the higher strike (1250) and bought the lower strike (1200) to generate a credit. Before we examine this put spread at different stages of its life, let's take these prices and generate a profit-and-loss chart, which will provide a visual sense of the parameters for profit.

Exhibit 8.3 provides the profit-and-loss functions (showing profit and loss at different price and time intervals) given our entry prices seen in Exhibit 8.2, along with the possible levels of the underlying December S&P 500 futures contract on the horizontal axis. The reader should get a sense of the levels of the underlying futures that will result in losses or profits. The put spread would be at breakeven upon expiration of the December S&P futures at 1246.80. This represents a level nearly 14 percent below 1440.50, the level of the S&P futures when we established the trade. This is shown where the solid profit-and-loss function crosses the horizontal dashed (0) breakeven level. If we did nothing to defend this trade, should the S&P futures drop all the way to the 1200 strike, the maximum risk of this trade would be 46.8 points or $11,700. As the reader will see, however, we would try to close the trade or make adjustments to it long before getting this deep into trouble.

Over the next two months the S&P futures remained bearish, falling to a low of 1297 on November 30, yet this trade ended up

Short leg	Sold December 2000, 1250 put	Price: 8.20	Point value: $250	Short value: $2,050
Long leg	Bought December 2000, 1200 put	Price: 5.00	Point value: $250	Long value: $1,250
Date: 9/28/00; expired: 12/15/00			Net option value =	$800

Exhibit 8.2 Prices and strikes for December 2000 S&P 500 1250×1200 put spread.

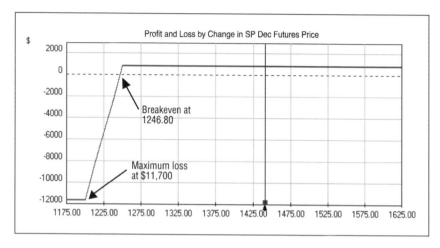

Exhibit 8.3   Profit-and-loss function for December S&P 500 1250 × 1200 put spread.
Created using OptionVue 5 Options Analysis Software.

being a winner, expiring Friday, December 15, 2000. Here was an instance where we were wrong about the market direction (if we thought the S&P 500 was going to fall, we would have recommended selling call spreads instead of put spreads), yet we still made a total profit on the trade since the market did not fall far or fast enough. At two swing-low pivots during October and November (see Exhibit 8.1), the spread looked in trouble as the market was moving against us. Follow-up action, however, was ultimately not necessary, and therefore not taken. Despite the underlying futures trading significantly lower, this trade ended profitable.

Exhibit 8.4 contains the net option value and the SPAN initial and maintenance requirements to open this trade. To do this spread, the exchange required a minimum initial margin deposit of $1,858. If the S&P traded in a bullish direction from here through to the expiration of the options, we would have kept the premium of $800 received from writing the spread with no additional margin demands. Ideally, therefore, the best scenario, as we saw from the last chapter, is for the underlying futures to

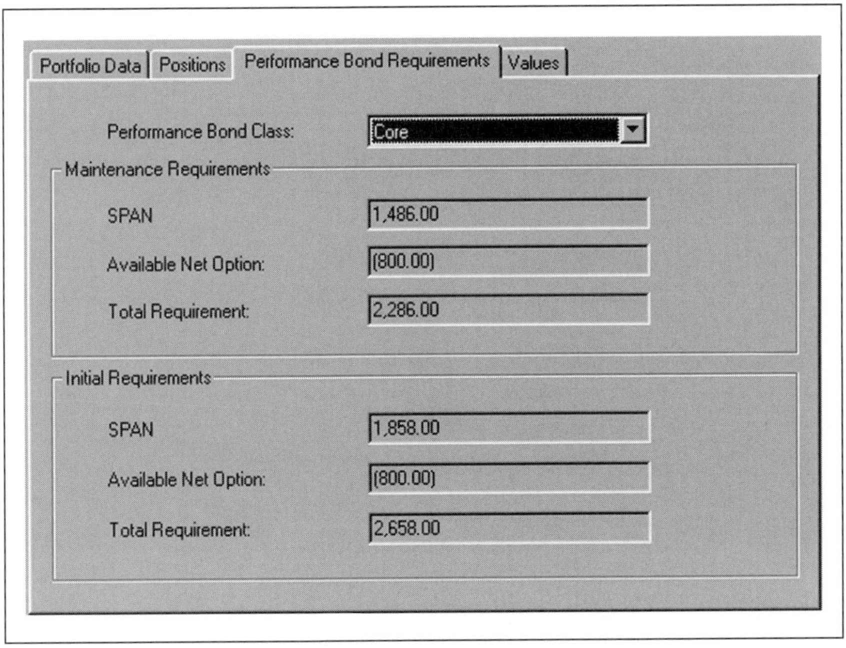

Exhibit 8.4   PC-SPAN performance margin requirements for a December S&P 500 futures options 1250 × 1200 put credit spread.
Created using PC-SPAN.

simply go higher if we are in a put spread. Had that been the case, we would have booked a 43 percent return on margin with this trade during a three-month period. Under these ideal conditions, the net option value, $800, would have simply dropped to zero as the market climbed higher. Yet, in this case we were wrong about market direction, and we faced bearish conditions once we got into the spread.

On October 12, the S&P hit a low point during this bearish period, as you can see in Exhibit 8.1. The December contract that day settled at 1361, a decline of 5.5 percent since initiating our spread trade. Despite this fall, the initial margin required for the spread increased to just $2,656, a 43 percent jump compared with a rise in the price of the spread by 121.8 percent. The new

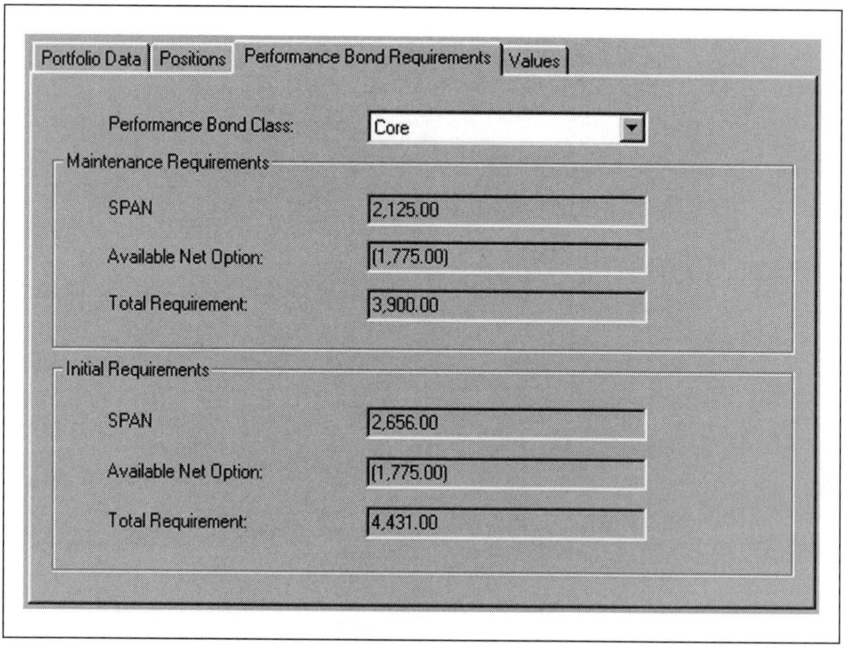

Exhibit 8.5 SPAN margins for December S&P 500 futures options 1250 × 1200 put credit spread on October 12, 2000.
Created using PC-SPAN.

maintenance margin increased from $1,486 to $2,125, as the reader can see in Exhibit 8.5.

Now let's look at the impact this temporary low had on the December 1250 × 1200 put spread value. Based on October 12 settlement prices, which are presented in Exhibit 8.6, the spread (net option value) had widened to $1,775 (7.1 points), brought about by the short leg increasing more than the long leg. The short option increased to $4,900, while the long leg premium increased to $3,125. Having a higher delta value, the short leg, therefore, increases more than the long leg given any decline in the underlying futures.

The S&P rallied through most of the rest of October (see Exhibit 8.1), but suffered another swing low that bottomed on November 30, settling that day at 1316, a further decline of 3.3

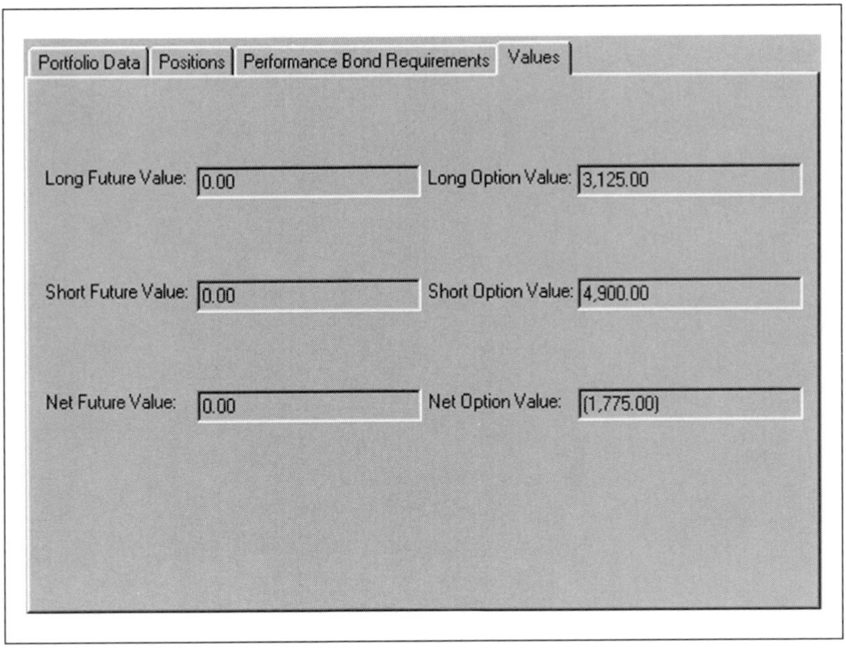

Exhibit 8.6   Short and long option value for December S&P 500 1250 × 1200 put credit spread at settlement on October 12, 2000.
Created using PC-SPAN.

percent and a total decline of 8.8 percent since opening the spread trade. As Exhibit 8.7 shows, the new SPAN margin had increased to $4,268. Meanwhile, net option value actually declined to $1,300 (5.2 points). Exhibit 8.8 contains the short and long option values, $2,200 and $900, respectively. Even though we were 8.8 percent lower, the spread was now experiencing the rapid decay of time value at the end of November, three weeks before expiration on December 15.

From this lowest of the swing lows, the S&P futures managed to trade sideways into December expiration. If we use the margin requirements of November 30 as our required capital for the entire trade (the most margin this trade required) the rate of return on this trade came in at 18.7 percent, an annualized return of 75 percent. Ideally, we could have made 43 percent had the

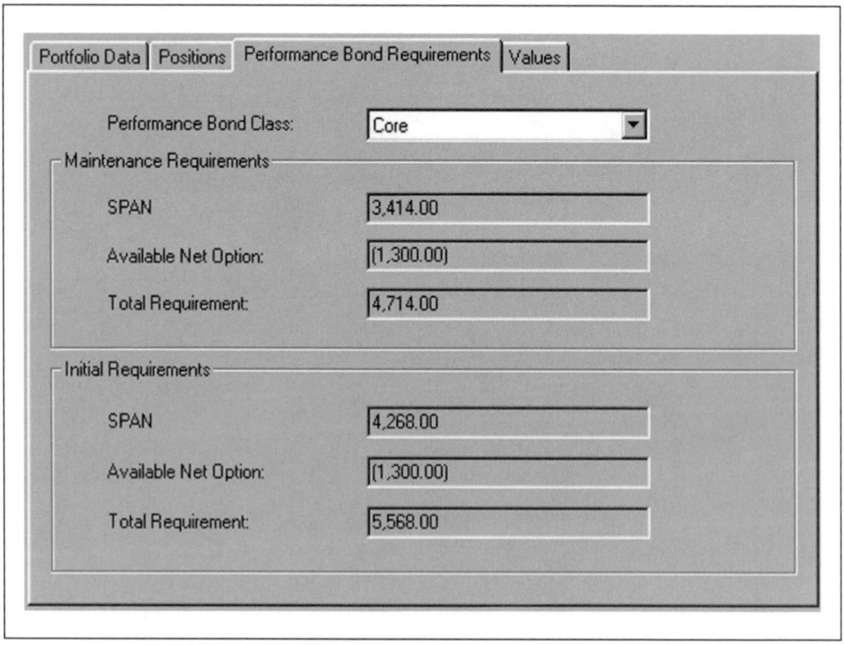

Exhibit 8.7   New margin levels for December S&P 500 1250 × 1200 put credit spread on November 30, 2000.
Created using PC-SPAN.

market been bullish during this period which offers a comparison with ideal conditions. The December futures ultimately settled upon expiration at 1338.40, 88.40 points above the short strike in our spread, and 102.1 points below where we entered the trade. The market had moved against us, yet we still made a profit. We were wrong about the market's direction, but our trade ended up a winner!

December S&P 1100 × 1000 Put Spread

Just like with the December 2000 S&P 500 futures option 1250 × 1200 put spread that we just reconstructed and examined, this

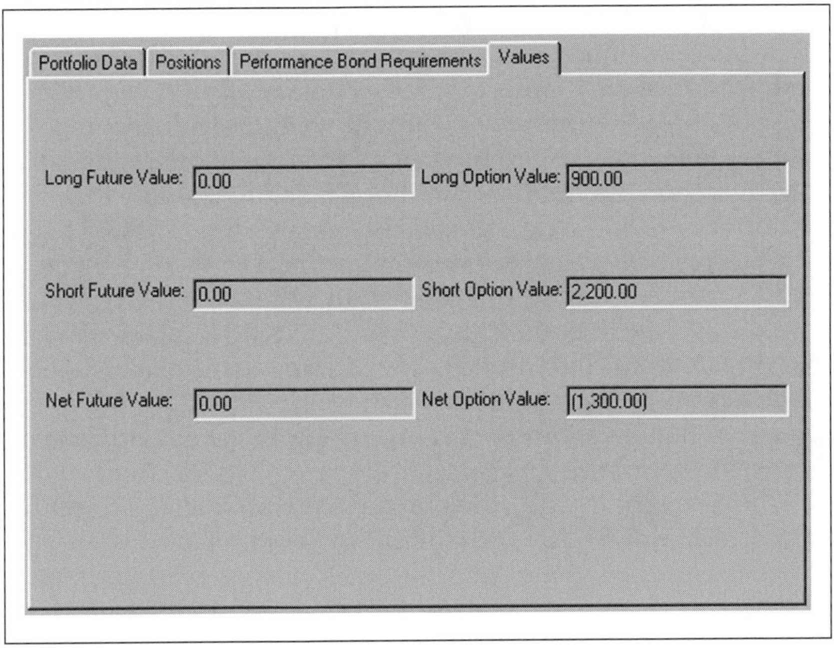

Exhibit 8.8   Long and short values for December S&P 500 1250 × 1200 put credit spread on November 30, 2000.
Created using PC-SPAN.

next put spread faced adverse conditions during its life. And once again, being wrong about market direction did not produce a loser. To the contrary, the spread weathered the bearish waters well enough to expire profitably without intervention.

When you consider the fact that this deep-out-of-the-money put spread (as well as the spread trade we presented earlier and one to follow) suffered severe bearish conditions yet ultimately were winners, it becomes clear that this strategy offers a high probability of success. With these trades you can be wrong about market direction and still win. The S&P suffered one of the worst bearish declines in its history, falling from just over 1550 at the end of August to just below 1100 in March, 2001, a 30 percent decline in a period of just seven months.

On June 6, 2000, we initiated a December S&P put spread when the September futures were trading at 1509.60. This was established three months prior to establishing the December S&P put spread we just reviewed and six months before expiration. We were thus able to book more premium dollars and write it farther from the money. As you can see in Exhibit 8.9, this farther-out-of-the-money spread was established at the 1100 × 1000 strikes, when the S&P was trading near 1500, slightly more than 27 percent out of the money. In other words, we would have to see a decline of 27 percent in the S&P 500 futures before the spread went into the money. Given that major support existed at the 1300 to 1350 levels, and at the 1100 to 1150 levels, it seemed that a decline of this magnitude was not in the offing during the life of the spread.

The net options value (net credit) for this spread, as seen in Exhibit 8.9, was $1,200 (4.8 points) when we opened the trade, with the short leg worth $2,275 (the December 1100 put strike) and the long leg worth $1,075 (the December 1000 put strike). The initial margin requirements for this deeper-out-of-the-money put spread were considerably lower than for our December 1250 × 1200 put spread, despite the fact that this spread was 100 points. Exhibit 8.10 shows the initial and maintenance SPAN margin levels, which were $1,970 and $1,578, respectively. Let's see how this spread did at the swing-low point (i.e., short-term bottom) on October 12, 2000 when the S&P futures settled at 1361, a decline of 148.6 points, or just over 11 percent as seen in Exhibit 8.1. The

Short leg	Sold December 2000 1100 put	Price: 9.10	Point value: $250	Short value: $2,275
Long leg	Bought December 2000 1000 put	Price: 4.30	Point value: $250	Long value: $1,075
Date: 6/6/00; expired: 12/15/00			Net option value =	$1,200

Exhibit 8.9 Prices and strikes for December S&P 1100 × 1000 put credit spread.

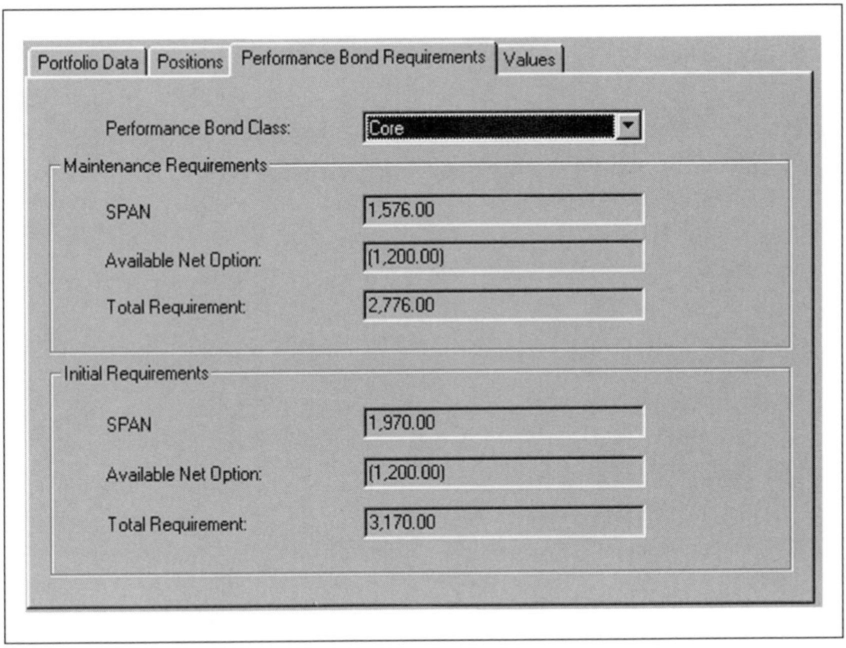

Exhibit 8.10   SPAN margin for December 1100 × 1000 S&P put credit spread
on October 12, 2000.
Created using PC-SPAN.

initial SPAN margin had increased to $2,274 from $1,970, a 15.4 percent jump. Yet the spread price declined from $1,200 to $975, an unrealized profit of $225, or 18.75 percent!

At the swing-low point of 1361 on October 12, 2000, therefore, we actually could have closed this spread with a decent profit. Exhibit 8.11 contains the short and long values of the December 1100 × 1000 put spread at the October 12 low.

On October 12, the short option at the 1100 strike had declined to $1,450, as seen in Exhibit 8.11, and the long option value at the 1000 strike had also declined to $475, falling less than the short option had declined. This differential decline in prices (i.e., the short put losing value faster than the long put)

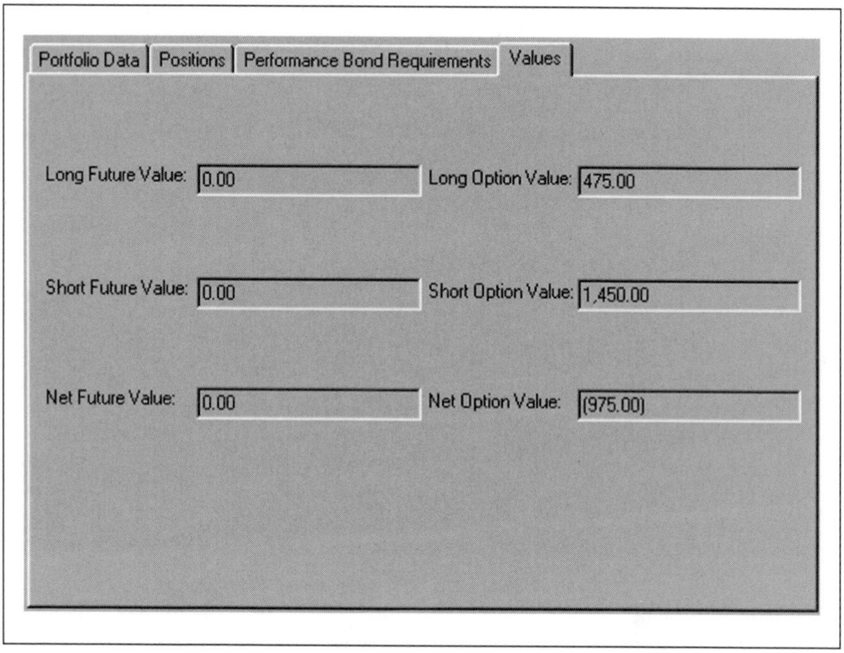

Exhibit 8.11 Short and long option values for December 1100 × 1000 S&P put credit spread on October 12, 2000.
Created using PC-SPAN.

produced a gain of $225 (with net option value at $975), which we already showed was a profit of 18.75 percent. Now let's see what happens as we approach the last month before expiration and suffer another swing-low point on November 30, 2000. The December futures settled at 1321.50 on November 30, yet this November 30 swing-low point for the S&P hardly affected the December 1100 × 1000 put spread, which now had a negligible net option value of $125, down from $975 on October 12. When the spread price gets this low, it is often worth closing it and booking the profits, especially given the potential for another swing low in these generally bearish conditions. Margin remained well behaved, meanwhile, with initial SPAN require-

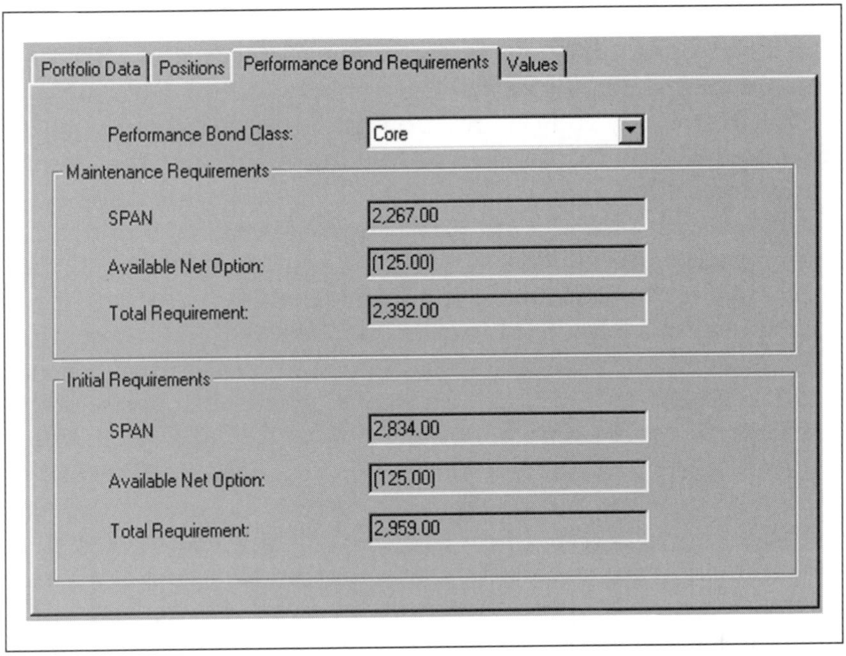

Exhibit 8.12 SPAN margin for the December 1100 × 1000 put credit spread when the December futures settled at 1316.00 on November 30, 2000. *Created using PC-SPAN.*

ments increasing to $2,834 from $1,450. The December 1100 × 1000 put spread expired worthless on December 15, 2000, as the S&P 500 held above 1300. Once again, despite this bear market, our neutral to bullish trade was a winner.

Dual Credit Spreads—May Call Spread with a September Put Spread

Before we turn to the last of our put spreads—a March 1225 × 1125 spread that suffered a sharp bear attack—we are going to back up to early 2000 to take a look at a combined September S&P 1100×1000 put spread and a May S&P 1650×1675 call spread established on March 27. Both were eventual winners.

On March 27, 2000, with the September futures trading at 1540, we sold the September 1100×1000 put spread for a net premium of 4.3 points (collecting $1,075), and at the same time we sold the May 1650×1675 call spread for a net premium 4.7 points (collecting $1,175). The total credit received was $2,250 for both spreads. Separately, the initial margin requirement for each spread was $1,876 (May call spread) and $1,663 (September put spread). The total margin came to $3,039 if taken as separate trades. When margined as a total portfolio, however, the SPAN initial margin requirement fell to $2,036 and maintenance margin to $1,629. This 33 percent decline in required margin resulted from the two credit spreads. As long as the risk of the second spread is not greater than the risk of the first spread, margin requirements should not increase. After all, the market can't go in both directions at once. If one loses, the other spread must win, so there is a lower margin requirement. Exhibit 8.13 contains the prices and related details of this dual credit spread.

September 1100 × 1000 S&P Put Credit Spread				
Short leg	Sold September 2000 1100 put	Price: 8.30	Point value: $250	Short value: $2,075
Long leg	Bought September 2000 1000 put	Price: 4.00	Point value: $250	Long value: $1,000
Date: 3/27/00; Expired: 9/15/00			Net option value =	$1,075
May 1650 × 1675 S&P Call Credit Spread				
Short leg	Sold May 2000 1650 put	Price: 12.50	Point value: $250	Short value: $3,125
Long leg	Bought May 2000 1675 put	Price: 7.8	Point value: $250	Long value: $1,950
Date: 3/27/00; Expired: 5/19/00			Net option value =	$1,175

Exhibit 8.13   S&P 500 dual credit-spread prices.

The short leg of the put spread was over 440 points out of the money, and was trading at more than twice its theoretical value (because implied volatility had jumped above historical volatility, thus adding additional premium for the spread), when we wrote it. The date of expiration for the September put spread, was September 15. The maximum risk on the trade was 96 points, or $24,000, if the S&P 500 was below 1000 on the expiration date and no adjustments were made. This would require a 35.7 percent drop in the S&P 500 index. However, we would have attempted to intervene earlier, as we would have to do with our March 1225 × 1125 put spread (as discussed later in this chapter), to initiate follow-up action should the trade have gotten into serious trouble.

Our S&P call spread with the 1675 × 1650 strikes was established after the S&P had rallied sharply. The rally was extended over 15 percent, from a low of 1347 to a high of 1562 at the time the trade was established. The expiration date was May 19, 2000, for the May call spread, which had a maximum risk of 20.3 points, or $5,075, under the condition that the S&P 500 is above 1675 upon expiration. Our expectation had been that the S&P 500 index would take a breather over the subsequent weeks, and that the out-of-the-money call spread would expire worthless on May 19, 2000. We were, as it turned out, correct in taking this view.

This dual credit spread went to term under generally favorable conditions as the S&P remained in a favorable trading range. As Exhibit 8.14 shows, the S&P 500 futures suffered a swing-low point at 1356.50. The impact of this drop in the S&P futures on our dual credit spread can be seen in Exhibit 8.15. The fall of 12 percent since initiating the dual spread resulted in the May call spread (which settles based on the June futures) price falling to 0.25, or $62.50 (0.25 × 250 points = $62.50), at which point we recommended that the position be closed, taking the $1,112.50 in profit, the difference between the opening value of the spread and value of $62.50. Meanwhile, the September put spread, which settles daily based on the September futures, had widened to $2,750, an unrealized loss of $1,675. The reader will recall we opened this spread at a value of $1,075. Margin requirements increased to $2,853.

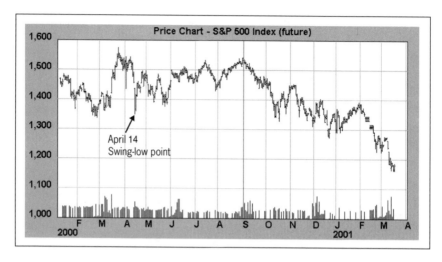

Exhibit 8.14   Daily bar chart of S&P futures.
Created using OptionVue 5 Options Analysis Software.

The put spread was allowed to go to term and we kept the full credit. Since the S&P futures remained bullish going into the summer and early September, trading in an approximate 100-point range above 1400, our September 2000 1100 × 1000 put spread never got into any trouble. With the S&P 500 staying

September 1100 × 1000 S&P Put Credit Spread (4/14/00)				
Short leg	Sold September 2000 1100 put	Price: 20.4	Point value: $250	Short value: $5,100
Long leg	Bought September 2000 1000 put	Price: 9.4	Point value: $250	Long value: $2,350
Date: 4/14/00; expired: 9/15/00			Net option value =	$2,750
May 1650 × 1675 S&P Call Credit Spread				
Short leg	Sold May 2000 1650 put	Price: .40	Point value: $250	Short value: $100.00
Long leg	Bought May 2000 1675 put	Price: .15	Point value: $250	Long value: $37.50
Date: 4/14/00; expired: 6/19/00			Net option value =	$62.50

Exhibit 8.15   Dual credit-spread prices at April 14, 2000, swing-low point.

in a relatively narrow range, not rising too high and not falling too low, time worked to our advantage eroding premium on our put spread. This deep-out-of-the-money put spread produced a full profit of $1,075 on a maximum margin of $2,853. This is a 38 percent profit, or an annualized rate of return of 76 percent.

Rolling Our S&P March 1225 × 1125 Put Spread

As the reader will see, we established an S&P March 1225 × 1125 put spread on September 5, 2000, when the S&P futures were trading near 1440 (just ahead of a selloff, as it turned out). Unlike the other spreads reviewed in this chapter, however, this one would require intervention in the form of a roll to a more distant month and strike price. Before getting into the details of this trade, we will discuss first what we mean by rolling a position.

By rolling, we are closing an open trade and opening another for additional credit large enough to cover losses on the initial trade, sometimes adjusting the size of the new position to generate the necessary credit. Rolling out in time allows for selling more time premium and moving the trade out of immediate trouble. This move took the March 2001 put spread we established, as seen in Exhibit 8.16, and rewrote it for more time premium in a different month and thus allowed for it to become an ultimate winner. When we rolled the March put spread to June, besides generating a net credit, which required a doubling of the position size from one spread to two, the margin per spread was reduced as a result of the roll. Let's now take a closer look at the details of this interesting trade.

Our March put spread was originally sold for a $1,200 credit (4.8 points). We sold the March 1225 put for $2,250 and bought the March 1125 put for $1,050. Initial margin for this trade was $2,423 and maintenance margin $1,938. The March S&P futures continued to remain bearish during this period, trading down to just above the short strike (1225) of this spread in late February.

Some traders in this spread opted to exit on a short-term countertrend rally that took March S&P futures up to 1374 on January

Short leg	Sold March 2001 1225 put	Price: 9.00	Point value: $250	Short value: $2,250
Long leg	Bought March 2001 1125 put	Price: 4.20	Point value: $250	Long value: $1,050
Date: 9/5/00; rolled to June: 2/22/01			Net option value =	$1,200

Exhibit 8.16   Prices and strikes for March 2001 1225 × 1125 S&P put credit spread on September 5, 2000.

31, 2001. The value of the spread had narrowed to $875, an unrealized gain of $325. Had traders remained in the March put spread, on the other hand, another swing-low point was registered on February 22, when March futures settled at 1254.50, which saw the net option value (spread) rising to $3,750 (15 points), up from the opening spread value of $1,200 (4.8 points). Initial margin increased to $5,185 with an unrealized loss of $2,550 (10.2 points). It was at this juncture that we recommended a roll to a June spread, as seen in Exhibit 8.17.

Closed March 2001 1225 × 1125 S&P Put Credit Spread				
Short leg	Bought September 2001 1225 put	Price: 19.00	Point value: $250	Short value: $4,750
Long leg	Sold September 2001 1125 put	Price: 4.00	Point value: $250	Long value: $1,000
Date: 2/22/01; Rolled to June 2/22/01			Net option value =	$3,750
Opened 2 June 2001 1050 × 950 S&P Put Credit Spread				
Short leg	Sold 2 June 2001 1050 put	Price: 13.20	Point value: $250	Short value: $6,600
Long leg	Bought 2 May 2001 950 put	Price: 4.30	Point value: $250	Long value: $2,150
Date: 2/22/01; expired: 6/15/01			Net option value =	$4,450

Exhibit 8.17   June S&P 1050 × 950 put spread prices and prices of S&P March 1225 × 1125 put spread at time of roll on February 22, 2001.

First of all, it is worth noting that had our March put spread been permitted to go to term, it would have produced a large loss, with the short option settling deep in the money. At expiration, for instance, the 1225 strike expired 51.7 points in the money, while the long strike at 1125 expired worthless. In terms of the overall risk-and-reward profile of this type of trading, this level of loss would be unacceptable. Intervention to move the spread out of danger, therefore even if it means reducing our profit potential and extending the time on the trade, is far better than suffering large losses. Generally, we do not like to let the short strike of a spread get in the money. As the reader will see, by rolling from March to June, the put spread eventually expired profitably.

This kind of remedial follow-up action makes sense in light of statistical data. Between 1982 and 2000, the S&P futures contract traded lower by 15 percent or more just 9 percent of the quarters. In other words, a strike placed more than 15 percent out of the money had a 91 percent chance of expiring worthless if allowed to go to term. Even more revealing, 77 percent of the swings low measured 5 percent or less. Given the historical bullish bias of stock prices, these probabilities are to be expected to some extent. Meanwhile, 83 percent of the quarterly periods had swings low measuring 10 percent or less. Trading quarterly spreads 15 percent out of the money, therefore, makes great trading sense. Knowing about these range probabilities helps when establishing and, if need be, when rolling these spreads out of trouble.

As the reader will see, this trade suffered a 10.2-point loss, or $2,550, when it was rolled on February 22, 2001, to a June spread and down to new strikes at 1050×950. By closing the 1225×1125 put spread, and writing two new June put spreads lower at the 1050×950 strikes, we generated a net credit of 2.8 points, or $700. In other words, the credit on the new put spreads was enough to cover the losses on the closed March put spread, and still leave us with a small net credit. The details of this March-to-June roll are included in Exhibit 8.17.

In addition to generating a net credit of $700, the total margin increased to $6,158 (for two spreads). The March spread lost

$2,550, but the two new June put spreads led to a net credit of $4,450 (8.9 points × $250 × 2 spreads = $4,450). Of course, our total risk increases by going to two spreads, but we felt confident that the S&P had little chance of falling an additional 14 percent before expiration. To be sure, this follow-up action is only possible provided sufficient capital is available to handle the increased total margin.

The worst point for this new trade came on March 23, 2001, when the S&P made another swing low, bouncing by the close to settle at 1147.50. The intraday low took the June futures contract just below 1100, but not down to the short strike of the spread. Exhibit 8.18 contains the prices of this spread as of the close that day.

The total margin cost for the new trade, based on initial requirements, had risen to $9,322 ($4,661.00 per spread) and the net option value (spread) of the two spreads rose to $3,800, or $7,600 for the two. Following this swing-low point on March 23, however, the S&P managed a countertrend rally that took it out of trouble through expiration in June, when it expired worthless, and thus profitable. The profit rate on this trade was just 7.5 percent which is lower than previous trades but not a loser.

In this chapter we have presented a number of S&P credit-spread trades done during 2000 and 2001. By examining dynamically how margin requirements and each spread's net option value (the value of the spread) changed with movement of the underlying futures and the passage of time, we have demonstrated how wide the parameters of profitability are for these S&P credit

Short leg	March 2001 1225 put	Price: 23.50	Point value: $250	Short value: $5,875
Long leg	March 2001 1125 put	Price: 8.30	Point value: $250	Long value: $2,075
Date: 3/23/01; Rolled to June: 2/22/01			Net option value =	$3,800

Exhibit 8.18   S&P June 1050 × 950 put spread at settlement on March 23, 2001.

spreads. While no holy grail of trading, it is clear from the few case studies here, most under extreme duress, that deep-out-of-the-money put and call credit spreads on the S&P 500 futures offer a viable method of trading options on futures, providing timely follow-up actions are taken and appropriate money management techniques are applied.

Chapter 9

COMMODITY FUTURES AND OPTIONS CHARACTERISTICS

Until now, we have kept the focus on S&P 500 stock index futures and futures options, addressing key characteristics, strategies, and actual trades. Now we turn the reader's attention to commodity futures and options. Commodity futures, unlike the S&P futures and options and other cash-based stock index futures and options, have an actual physical commodity (e.g., soybeans, orange juice, etc.) as the underlying.

As the reader will see, commodity futures trade based on a physical commodity, not a cash index. Recall that the S&P futures trade on the S&P 500 cash index. Except for the currencies and cattle commodity futures, settlement is made with a transfer of the commodity itself. Aside from this key difference, however, most of the characteristics of S&P futures and futures options readily carry over to commodity futures and futures options.

Unlike stocks, which trade in shares, and stock options, which all trade in 100-share blocks, each commodity market has its own set of contract specifications. In this chapter, we cover basic characteristics and properties of commodity futures and options, for which we present actual trades later in this book.

Commodity futures and option contract specifications may appear daunting to traders new to these markets. Take the following expiration statement from the Chicago Mercantile Exchange (CME) regarding heating oil, natural gas, and crude expiration dates.

Expiration occurs on the Friday immediately preceding the expiration of the underlying futures contract; provided, however, that in the event that such Friday is an Exchange holiday, such options shall expire on the second business day prior to the Exchange holiday; and in the event that such Friday does not precede the expiration of the underlying futures contract by three (3) or more trading days, such options shall expire on the second Friday preceding the expiration of the underlying futures contract.

Whew! With statements like this, it is easy to understand why some traders new to commodity options may get discouraged at first. But with today's trading software and a good broker, this is a nonissue. With one click of the mouse, or a call to your broker, you have the expiration date for any commodity option. The fact is that today's software tools can easily carry out all option calculations, such as finding expiration dates, as well as converting option premium into money terms, making these a snap for even the beginner.

When setting up a trade strategy using one of the leading option trading software packages, for instance, you can input desired positions and then get the expiration date(s) of the options and convert premiums into dollar terms. In other words, the preceding statement from the CME, which reads more like a brain twister than a method for figuring out when a commodity option expires, is an unnecessary turnoff. With computer power today, these markets remain accessible to anyone willing to extend basic option knowledge into new arenas and acquire the latest trading tools.

Futures on Physicals

The grain futures, such as soybeans, which are traded on the Chicago Board of Trade (CBOT), offer an excellent jump-off point to begin the transition from S&P futures and futures options to commodity options and futures. First, let's quickly review the basic properties of options and futures, before we take a look at the particular characteristics of soybeans.

Remember, all options and futures are similar hedging and speculative instruments. Specifications are uniform for each particular market. A key difference between futures and options, however, can be seen in the form of the obligations incumbent upon a holder of each one of these instruments. Option contracts do not carry the same contractual obligation as the futures. *The option buyer has the right, but is not obligated, to exercise the contract into a futures any time ahead of or on the expiration date.*

There are two primary functions served by options and futures: hedging and speculating. Generally, hedgers look to use options or futures to establish a worst-case pricing structure so that business decisions regarding the use of the physical commodity, like soybeans, can be made with relative security.

For example, let's take the example of a hedger. A soybean grower must plan production based on some idea of a market price. There are, however, no guarantees against a decline of soybean prices once planting has begun. If prices drop once production is under way, future sale proceeds of soybeans may not be enough to cover the production costs, thus putting in jeopardy the financial health of the grower. Hedging can protect the farmer against this type of price uncertainty.

In the example of the soybean grower, by locking in a floor price through the purchase of a soybean put option, the grower would, for example, at least know that no matter where the future market price of soybeans is at harvest time, he or she will be able to sell the soybeans at the strike price. Of course, to establish this future price floor, the grower must pay a premium to purchase the put options, but this cost can be priced into production at the outset like any other cost of production.

The key here is the removal of uncertainty, whether it is on the downside as in this soybean case, or the upside in the case of a cattle farmer that needs to buy soybeans or a producer that needs soy to make a product.

To get more familiar with commodity options, we need to get more familiar with the futures upon which they trade, and the cash market upon which the futures trade. Futures on physicals, which are the most common form of futures (and therefore futures options), have appeared in greater and greater numbers since the first futures contracts were introduced as standardized contracts.

Futures on physicals can be lumped into six groups. These groups include grains, softs (e.g., exotics like coffee, cocoa, etc.), metals, meats, energy, and interest rate products. Let's take an example to illustrate the speculative use of futures on physicals. We alluded earlier to the economic function of hedging, so we will not go into this dimension in any more detail given that we are speculators.

Speculating on Commodity Futures

As can be seen in Exhibit 9.1 soybeans trade in contract sizes of 5,000 bushels and are priced in dollars and cents per bushel. Let's say that July soybeans are trading at $4.45. This price, which refers to the price per bushel, can be used to calculate the total value of a July soybean contract. To arrive at this value, we would multiply the July per-bushel price ($4.45) by 5,000 (the total number of bushels represented by one contract). The value is thus $22,250.

The advantage of futures and, as you will see, of futures option strategies is that a trader can get much lower margin (and thus better leverage) than with stocks, which typically are limited to a two-to-one margin ratio. This leverage really pays off when we combine futures contracts with option contracts, such as ratio writing or synthetic call buying strategies. To construct the same positions on a stock would require going long or short the stock, which ties up loads of capital. With options on futures strategies, which often require being long or short futures, we can go long or short the underlying futures for a mere fraction of the total value of the contract.

We can illustrate the leverage power of futures by continuing with our case of soybean futures. To go long or short one $22,250 soybean contract, we need only put up a fraction of that amount. Currently, initial margin requirement (in effect as of March 23, 2001) for one soybean contract is $945, with maintenance margin set at $700. Initial margin, therefore, comes to 4.25 percent of the value of the July contract. In other words, with just $945 in margin deposited in a futures account, a trader can control $22,250 worth of soybean futures.

If a trader decides to purchase a July soybean contract, it would be necessary to put up $945 in initial margin. If the price of July soybeans goes to $4.50 from $4.45, an increase of 5 cents, the value of the contract increases by $250 (+1.12 percent). If the trader sells (offsets) the July soybean contract, the percentage gain from the trade would be greater than the increased value of the contract. For example, the trader would instead have gained 26.4 percent ($50 × 5 cents = $250/$945 = 26.4 percent) from the trade. As the reader can see in Exhibit 9.2, therefore, a 1.12 percent move of July soybeans results in a 26.4 percent profit! This is the power of leverage.

Since futures positions are marked to the market based on daily settlement prices, a decline of 5 cents would trigger a

Contract Size	Exchange	Months	Tick Size	Point Value
5,000 bushels	CBOT	January, March, May, July, August, September, November	$.025 cent = $12.50	$.01 cent = $50

Exhibit 9.1   Soybean futures contract specifications.
Source: CBOT.

Contract Size	July Soybeans Price	Contract Value	Change in Price	Change in Contract Value
5,000 bushels	$4.50	$22,250	+$.05 cents ($250)	$22,500 (+1.12%)

Initial Margin for Long Futures	Purchase Price of Long Futures	Change in Price	Change in Futures Contract	Percentage Gain in Long Futures
$945	$4.50	+$.05 cents	+$250	$250/$945 = +26.4%

Exhibit 9.2   July soybean futures margin leverage.

maintenance margin call in this soybean trade, assuming we are operating with a $945 account. To remain in the position, therefore, would require reposting margin to bring the account value back up to the original margin requirement of $945. This is because the maintenance margin level of $700 would have been breached (5 cents × $50 = $250; $945 − $250 = $695). In other words, a decline in the price of soybean futures would have lowered the value of the account to below maintenance margin levels of $700. The trader would be required to deposit enough funds to bring the account back up to the initial requirement of $945.

When marked to the market, in other words, following the close of trading after a day during which the July soybeans settled at $4.40 (assuming the trader entered the trade at $4.45), the trader would be asked by his or her broker to post an additional sum of money ($250) in order to keep the position open. If the funds were not available, the broker would have the power to liquidate the trade at whatever price is available once it was clear that the account holder was not able to meet a margin call.

By presenting this soybean example to the reader, we want to illustrate the inherent risks and leverage power encountered in futures markets. While this example is based on exchange minimum margins, it may not be the case with all brokers that a trader will be allowed to trade at these minimum levels. Traders looking to trade commodity futures and options should find a broker who offers exchange minimum margin requirements, which allows a trader to get the best leverage.

Let's now turn to some other aspects of commodity futures and options, after which in Chapter 10, we will examine some commodity option trading strategies.

Speculators and First Notice Day

As speculators, first notice day is only a concern if a trader is long. This is because holding past this date can result in getting assigned a delivery notice. Commercial hedgers, or those involved with the cash commodity, make up most or all of the trading volume following first notice day. Speculators, meanwhile, will typically roll long positions to the next contract month before first notice day, or close their positions.

Unlike options, futures contracts cannot be assigned ahead of first notice day, which is what makes speculating in futures possible. If a speculator had to worry about an assignment and delivery, margin requirements would be higher, and the powerful leverage we demonstrated earlier would be lost.

In an assignment, the long futures contract holder would be required to take delivery of the full contract, which in the case of July soybeans that we saw previously, would require $22,250 on hand to fulfill.

Because this can only happen on or after first notice day, speculators are not subject to such an onerous expense. While it can happen after first notice day if a speculator fails to offset a position, the broker can just retender the contract, charging the trader a fee and commission costs, with no movement of the commodity. The trader would not receive actual delivery, just a warehouse receipt that can be retendered at a rate of about $100.

Some of the initial confusion with options on commodity futures centers on the rule of the *last trading day*, which varies according to each futures contract. In other words, December wheat futures do not expire on the same day of the month as December S&P 500 futures. December wheat futures options, for example, would expire in late November, and December S&P

futures options would expire the third Friday in December. We will leave this question aside for now and pick it up again in a subsequent chapter covering specific examples of commodity options and futures on physicals (e.g., corn, wheat, sugar, etc.) where it will become much more tangible. Suffice it to say that the option trader needs to pay extra attention to each market. *Futures* magazine publishes expiration dates for most options on futures contracts. Specifications for commodity futures and futures option contracts are provided at the websites of the major exchanges.

Commodity Futures Terms and Specifications

Just like with stock options, all listed futures have standardized contract terms. What does this mean? By standardization, exchanges have established one set of terms and conditions for the listed contract so that one market price will prevail for the commodity and option. Without standardized terms, a trader would have much more difficulty determining the fair price of a futures contract, or any contract for that matter. For instance, all gold contracts are quoted in quantities of 100 ounces. This allows for one price to be quoted, not many different prices reflecting arbitrary contract specifications. Each commodity market, therefore, has its own set of terms.

As we saw in the example of soybeans, different quantities and unit measures of the product (5,000 bushels) are represented by each futures contract. Here, we have bushels for soybeans as the unit of measurement. Most of these terms are determined by customs particular to each commodity market, shaped by the patterns that are prevalent in the trading of the cash commodity on the spot market, or by producers delivering the product to market, with a few exceptions. Lumber, for instance, is measured in number of board feet, and gasoline is priced in gallons.

In addition to uncommon expiration dates, commodity futures have different contract point values (i.e., corn is worth $50 per penny while cotton is $500 per penny). However, the basic premise of futures trading remains the same across all of these markets. The contract details become second nature once a trader gets familiar with each market. We don't trade all markets, for instance, but we have ones that we prefer. In the next several chapters, we will focus on orange juice, soybeans, natural gas, cocoa, and coffee. While not the only markets we follow, these are excellent markets for the kinds of strategies we employ.

Options on Commodity Futures

Armed with some concrete knowledge of commodity futures markets, let's now begin to look at the commodity options that trade on these and other markets.

Looking again at our previous example where a hypothetical trader has bought soybean futures in anticipation of a bullish move, we can now bring options into the picture. Perhaps the trader fears that an impending government report could send soybean prices considerably lower, leading the trader to fear an unlimited risk scenario in the wake of the report. Even though futures have what are called *daily price limits*, a trader can get caught in what is called a *limit move* (i.e., where a futures contract price moves up or down by the exchange set daily limit); this may happen for consecutive days before a trade can be offset. The reason for this is that the cash commodity does not have price limits, and can trade wherever it happens to go based on supply and demand. If the futures are limited to the approximate margin amounts on a daily basis, the futures contract may cease to trade because the spot market is out of line with the futures market. Similar to circuit breakers in the equity markets, daily limits on movement of the futures markets attempt to provide some stability.

This can be disastrous for the holder of a futures contract, or somebody in a futures position following a news event. However, if a speculator purchases a put option to protect a soybean futures position instead of holding a soybean futures contract outright ahead of a big government news report, the risk will be limited.

To illustrate how this works, let's say we are long July soybeans using the example from earlier. Recall in the previous example that we got long July soybeans at $4.45 on March 28. Hoping to gain from a big upside move, but not wanting to face ruin on the downside, we could have purchased a July $4.40 put for 8 cents, or $400. The margin required for this combined position would be much lower than the $945 initial margin for an outright futures position in soybeans because the purchase of the put limits the risk on the trade. The July soybean put options with a $4.40 strike (5 cents out of the money) would keep losses on the downside limited to $650 ($400 for the option and $250 maximum loss on the futures position should a large drop occur). Yet, there is still potential for unlimited gains on the upside, with much less initial margin required up front (see Exhibit 9.3).

When we combine a long futures position with a put, we call this a *synthetic call,* and it can provide a trader an excellent way to capture unlimited profits on the upside with limited risk on the downside. This is known as a synthetic call because, like a simple long call, there is unlimited profit potential with limited risk. A key advantage of the synthetic call over an outright purchase of a call option is that a trader can get long the underlying without paying inflated call premiums. Often the call premiums are inflated when a big upside move has begun.

Buy 1 July soybean futures contract Price = $4.45	Buy 1 July $4.40 soybean put price Price = $.08	July $4.40 soybean put cost $400	Maximum loss for entire position $650

Note: The put cost + difference between futures price and $4.40 (.05) strike is the maximum loss.

Exhibit 9.3　July soybean synthetic call.
Source: CBOT.

Commodity Option Terms and Specifications

The soybean commodity option synthetic call we reviewed is only one example of the ways that futures and options can be combined into a trading strategy. Given the high leverage available with futures contracts, when combined with options, the same trading strategies that are used with stocks and options on stocks will have even more power. Before we move into commodity option trading strategies, however, let's tackle some more terms and specifications of these instruments.

Through the first half of this book, we introduced the reader to the S&P futures and futures options. Even though the reader should now know that these are cash-based futures and options, most of the essential trading principles carry over to commodity options. By having some familiarity with the S&P stock futures and options, therefore, the reader should have very little trouble grasping the practical aspects of commodity futures and options.

We are repeating somewhat here, but we want to make sure this principle is well understood. The first basic concept pertaining to all commodity options is that the underlying is not a cash commodity (or a stock index). *The futures contract is the underlying.* A trader holding a July soybean call contract will acquire a July soybean futures contract if he or she chooses to exercise that contract on or before expiration.

A second important concept is that commodity option specifications are always identical to the futures contracts on which they trade. That is, if you learn how soybeans futures trade, you can easily figure out the option specifications. For example, one call contract for July soybeans is always equivalent to one July soybean futures contract. The price terms match, as well, with few exceptions. A 5-cent move in the soybean futures, for example, equals $250. This is the same for a 5-cent move of a soybean option.

If we sell a naked July $4.40 soybean put contract for 8 cents, converting the premium into dollars is simple once you know the quotation protocol for soybean futures. Aside from a few exceptions to this rule, commodity option price terms are identical to futures price terms. For example, if we bought the July

$4.40 soybean put contract for 8 cents, we know the value of this contract is $400. In other words, one penny on a soybean futures contract is always equivalent to $50, as it is with a soybean futures option contract. The only difference is in minimum tick size, which is ⅛ of a cent for soybean options and ¼ of a cent for soybean futures. This makes understanding options an uncomplicated task once you have developed an operational awareness of the underlying futures market.

Strike Prices and Contract Months

Each commodity option has its own unique strike price chains, usually set at intervals generally reflecting the degree of volatility of a market or contract and the price level of the commodity in question. For example, May orange juice option strikes are 5 cents apart, or $750 (each penny = $150) in value. Exhibit 9.4 illustrates the May call and put strike chain for orange juice.

Just as with strike prices, contract months can differ across the major commodity markets. Some, such as interest rates currency and stock index options on futures, have four main expiration months. These are March, June, September, and December. Others (e.g., heating oil, natural gas, unleaded gas, and crude oil) have contracts expiring in every month. The rest of the major futures contracts have a mix of different months, some with five (corn, oats, and wheat), six (gold, silver, and live cattle), and seven (lean hogs, soybeans, soybean oil, and soybean meal) months.

In between the months that match the delivery months for the underlying futures contracts, there are what is known as *serial option contracts*. The underlying futures contract is the *nearest* futures contract after the option expires. April S&P options, which we mention later, expire into June futures contracts. This same principle applies to all commodity options for which there are serial options. Another important aspect of exercise to keep in mind is that commodity options are automatically exercised when in the money at expiration, whether a trader issues an exercise notice prior to expiration or not.

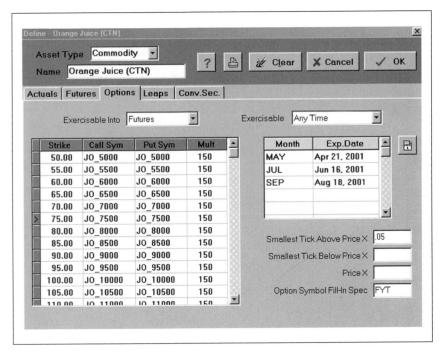

Exhibit 9.4   May orange juice call and put option chain.
Created using OptionVue 5 Options Analysis Software.

The value of the intervals between strikes on commodity options can differ for each commodity option, and can vary during the life of the option series depending on the current price of the futures and time remaining until expiration. Also, months nearer to the front-month futures contract may have more strike prices than deferred months.

We saw how orange juice strike price intervals are equal to 5 cents. Heating oil, for example, has even smaller intervals. As Exhibit 9.5 shows, the strike intervals for heating oil are set at 1 cent. Heating oil trades in minimum tick sizes of 0.01 cent per gallon, which is equivalent to $4.20. So a 1-cent move is worth $420. With 1-cent strike intervals, therefore, the value between strikes is $420. Finally, take a look at the S&P 500 futures in

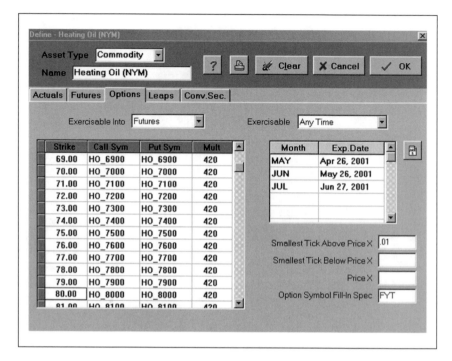

Exhibit 9.5   Heating oil option strikes.
Created using OptionVue 5 Options Analysis Software.

Exhibit 9.6 for comparative purposes. Here we see strikes set at 5-point intervals. Now we know that the S&P futures and their options have a value of $250 per point. Therefore, each one of the strike intervals represents $1,250, quite a bit larger, reflecting the larger contract value.

Expiration of Commodity Options

One important aspect of commodity options as opposed to stock index futures options to keep in mind pertains to the expiration cycle. We know that each commodity market has different option months, corresponding generally to the futures delivery months

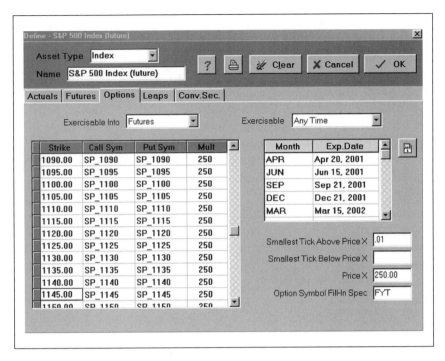

Exhibit 9.6 S&P 500 futures option chain.
Created using OptionVue 5 Options Analysis Software.

(serial months also differ). Even if they have the same contract expiration months, however, this does not mean that the options on commodities or stock index futures will expire on the same day of that month.

If you look at Exhibit 9.4 containing the orange juice strike intervals, on the right side of the figure the reader will note the list of expiration months and dates. The May orange juice options expire April 21, 2001. In Exhibit 9.5 containing the delivery months for May heating oil options, even though we are talking about the same expiration month, the expiration date for May heating oil options is April 26, 2001. Exhibit 9.6, containing the delivery months and expiration dates for S&P 500 options, shows that April options expire April 20, 2001.

If these were June S&P options, they would expire at the end of the third week of June (the June futures expiration date), which happens with all cash-based options on futures (i.e., they expire on the same day as the futures contract with the same expiration month). Commodity futures options, however, as you can see from these two examples (heating oil and orange juice), usually expire the month before the named futures contract month (May options expire in April, for example). Actually, commodity options expire usually well ahead of first notice, allowing traders plenty of time to offset positions and avoid the risk of assignment.

In this chapter, we have highlighted the main characteristics of commodity options and the futures on which they trade. We have shown that while each market must be taken as a separate set of standardized terms and specifications, there are some simple rules that allow for easy interpretation of all commodity option contracts once a trader understands the underlying futures markets (with few exceptions). In the next chapter, we will construct hypothetical commodity option trading strategies, models that will assist the reader further in getting familiar with these instruments.

Chapter 10

SELLING STRATEGIES FOR COMMODITY OPTIONS

In the previous chapter, we emphasized the most important features of options on commodity futures. Rather than stressing the differences between each one of these diverse markets we outlined the common thread running between them. That is, while each of these contract markets must be studied and learned separately, it was shown that most option rules and characteristics (e.g., calculating the value of a contract, exercise protocol, and pricing fundamentals) are universal to all. We also noted how the power of today's relatively low-cost option trading software has removed most of the traditional obstacles in the way of traders who might want to learn how to trade these markets. It also helps to have a good broker who has worked for many years with these markets.

In this chapter, we apply what we have learned about commodities and options to strategies for selling commodity futures options. We do not offer a compendium of all option strategies. This would only be repeating what has been produced countless times in a seemingly endless series of books presenting static option models. *Instead, we center the reader's attention on what has worked for us.*

Over the past several years, we have recommended essentially six types of trades:

1. S&P 500 credit spreads.
2. Commodity options credit spreads.
3. Call and put ratio writes.
4. Call and put ratio spreads.
5. Synthetic calls and puts.
6. Naked put and call trades.

The first of these we have already covered in great detail in the first half of the book. Now, we will turn to the other option writing strategies, providing a basic blueprint for constructing each of these option trades, along with a discussion of each setup's hypothetical profit-and-loss parameters. Following our presentation in this chapter of our featured setups, in Chapter 11 we will jump into a blow-by-blow analysis of some actual trades, based on these trading strategies.

Naked Option Trades

The term *naked*, whether referring to puts or calls, implies exposure to unlimited risk. When a trader sells a put (or a call), as opposed to buying a put (or a call), she or he faces unlimited risk, along with the potential for limited profit. Buyers of puts or calls, on the other hand, always acquire the potential for unlimited profit, with limited risk. On the surface, the typical beginning trader would jump at the long trade (buying, not selling puts or calls), since the profit-and-loss and risk-and-reward profile appear so much more tolerable (limited loss) and desirable (unlimited profit). However, as with most anything in life, appearances don't always match reality, as we showed with our illustration of the buyer's dilemma covered in Chapter 1.

Let's begin by looking at a naked commodity option, and what is involved in setting up this type of trade. We saw in Chapter 6 that a naked option involves selling (getting short), also known as writing, an option for a certain amount of premium. This can be done at, in, or out of the money, depending on one's trading style and outlook on the market. We only recommend selling out-of-the-money options. In Chapter 6, we explained naked option writing as a stepping-stone to building our credit spread, which is not a naked trade, but a covered trade, because we are simultaneously buying an option on the same underlying futures farther away from the money. This is a covered, as opposed to a naked, position because our losses are limited to the size of the spread between the two strikes, minus the premium received when writing the spread. But what happens if we remove the covered side of the spread? Now we have an uncovered position, AKA a *naked option position.*

We know that a naked trade involves selling an option for a certain amount of premium. For example, we could sell a $4.00 September soybean put for 10 cents in premium when the September futures are trading at $4.20. If the option expires out of the money, the writer keeps the 10 cents (or $500) in premium as profit. Breakeven would be at $3.90 ($4.00 – 10 cents = $3.90). Ideally, a naked option writer should sell premium that is inflated (a situation that arises when the actual option price is greater than the theoretical price). It also helps to have both volatility measures (implied and historical) at relative extremes (i.e., in the top percentile of historical ranges for both). This gives the writer an extra edge because option premium tends to move back to the historical norm rather quickly, helping the position to profit even before the loss of time value.

When in an uncovered put option position like the soybean example, a sharp fall of the underlying soybean futures will result in mounting losses on the naked put unless the trade is offset by a purchase of the put (to buy back the short put, in other words). There are other ways to limit losses, such as shorting the futures or creating a spread position. Typically, an option writer will have a predetermined price (i.e., mental stop loss) to exit the position if a trade gets into too much trouble. We often put an actual stop-loss GTC order to buy back the option if it doubles in value. While there is no guarantee that a position can be closed exactly at that stop-loss target price (due to price gaps), provided the option market is sufficiently liquid, a trader generally can get out, which means losses in practice are not unlimited. They are limited by the amount the trader is willing to risk plus slippage before closing the position. The bottom line is that a trader should have a game plan going into each trade.

More option premium can be collected when selling naked options versus spreads. Naked positions, as opposed to hedged positions such as credit spreads, therefore, offer a more aggressive option writing strategy. Naked selling involves greater reward along with greater risk.

However, because the value of many commodity futures contracts is relatively small compared with index futures, naked option margin requirements for commodities tends to be more tolerable for the average trader, especially if the brokerage allows exchange minimum margins to be computed based on the SPAN performance bond system. While naked put options on grains are generally considered safer because of the upside surprise potential caused by freezes, flooding, drought, and other planting- and harvest-related problems (causing price spikes), we will take the example of a naked call written on July corn to better illustrate the idea of selling naked options. As Exhibit 10.1 shows, the July

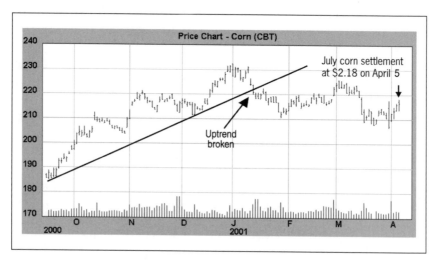

Exhibit 10.1   Daily price bar chart for corn futures.
Created using OptionVue 5 Options Analysis Software.

corn futures last settled at $2.18 on April 5. As the reader can see, July corn had broken its uptrend and appeared to be forming a bearish pattern ahead of a bigger move lower, which would warrant selling calls. If we wanted to trade based on this neutral to bearish outlook, we could sell naked July $2.30 calls that expire on June 23.

Let's say we determined $2.30 as a resistance level, so that if July corn breaks out above $2.30, we would close the trade. The July $2.30 calls were selling for 6 cents, and each cent is equivalent to $50 ($6 \times \$50 = \$300$) in premium. Therefore, the sale of July $2.30 calls, as the prices in Exhibit 10.2 show, would have generated a credit of $300.00. We will assume that the theoretical price

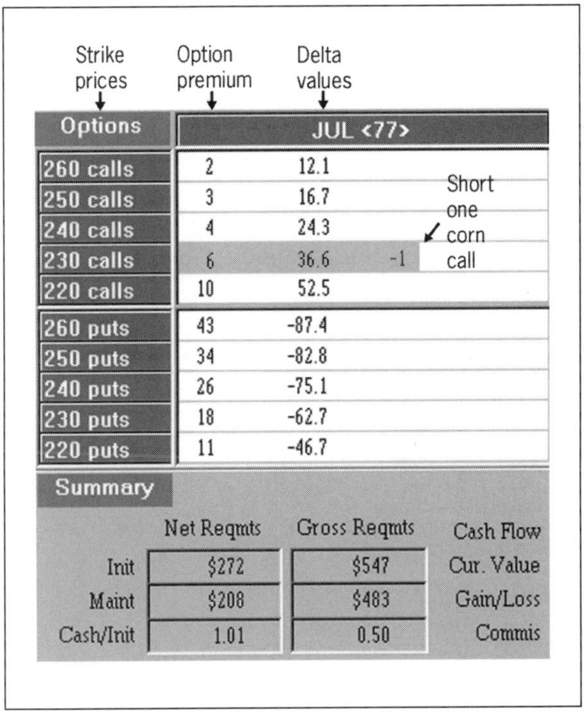

Strike prices	Option premium	Delta values		
Options			JUL <77>	
260 calls	2	12.1		Short
250 calls	3	16.7		one
240 calls	4	24.3		corn
230 calls	6	36.6	-1	call
220 calls	10	52.5		
260 puts	43	-87.4		
250 puts	34	-82.8		
240 puts	26	-75.1		
230 puts	18	-62.7		
220 puts	11	-46.7		

Summary				
	Net Reqmts	Gross Reqmts	Cash Flow	
Init	$272	$547	Cur. Value	
Maint	$208	$483	Gain/Loss	
Cash/Init	1.01	0.50	Commis	

Exhibit 10.2   July corn option prices.
Created using OptionVue 5 Options Analysis Software.

is less than the actual price, which means we are selling overvalued call options. These are conditions that an option writer should try to find when considering a trade.

We can see from the table of premium prices for the other strikes in Exhibit 10.2, a move up by 10 cents would cause the premium to increase to about 10 cents from 6 cents (moving from the $2.30 strike to the $2.20 strike). This assumes an instant move with no erosion of the premium due to a change in time value, and no decrease in value due to a decrease in volatility. We might want to set a stop-loss point, or plan to exit the trade, should the July call option premium double in price. This would represent a 100 percent loss on the amount of money we might have gained if the position worked in our favor. In terms of a graphical view of this profit-and-loss scenario, Exhibit 10.3 presents a profit-and-loss function for this naked July $2.30 call.

The horizontal line to the left of the kink represents the limited profits we spoke about earlier. This chart shows that if July corn futures remain below $2.30 on expiration (on June 23, 2001), the $300 would be retained in the account, and thus the trade would be a full winner. If, on the other hand, July corn rises

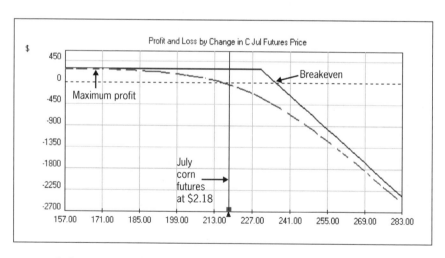

Exhibit 10.3   July corn naked call option profit-and-loss function.
Created using OptionVue 5 Options Analysis Software.

above $2.30, we would try to exit at a loss of $300. Potential for unlimited losses exists on the upside should corn continue to rise and the trader holds the short option.

On expiration, the breakeven on this trade would be at $2.36, which is equal to the strike of the naked call option plus the premium received from selling the option. The July corn futures, therefore, would need to be trading above $2.36 in order to cause a loss upon the expiration date. Keep in mind that when this option was sold, it was out of the money (July corn options strike = $2.30, July futures = $2.18; thus 12 cents out of the money), which increases the odds that it will expire worthless, and means that the premium received (6 cents $\times$ $50 = $300) is pure time value.

The option writer is always interested in the passage of time to bring about decay of time value. If July corn futures trade sideways, down, or even moderately higher (by less than 5.5 percent), then at expiration all the time value will have decayed producing a maximum profit. In other words, if July futures don't expire above the strike of the naked call option, the options ends up worthless and the entire premium is retained in the account of the option writer.

A partial profit may arise when the option expires in the money. The solid profit-and-loss function line represents the level of July corn at expiration. As Exhibit 10.3 shows, if we have July corn at $2.34½ at expiration, we would still have a winner. The July $2.30 calls would have 4.5 cents intrinsic value, but we sold these call options for 6 cents in time value. We would still profit, with a gain of 1.5 cents, or $75.

In terms of defensive actions, a simple offsetting trade is perhaps the best approach, especially if July corn experienced a technical breakout. If a trader is placing a lot of short-term naked positions on commodity markets, it is in our view best to take the small loss (which will free up margin to use on another trade), rather than risk a larger loss.

The bottom line, from our experience, is to know where you want to get out of a trade before getting into the position, and allow only a small degree of subjective judgment about this rule. With options on futures, fortunately, traders can place stop-loss orders on the premium to exit a position.

Before moving on to our next commodity option trading strategy, a few words about margin requirements are in order. For the corn trade we have just illustrated, the margin required to write a single naked call option would have been $272. If margin requirements did not increase, this position has the potential to produce an approximately 110 percent profit rate ($300/$272 = 110 percent) over the life of the trade (about 3 months).

As the reader will see in the next chapter, margin requirements for writing naked options on many of the markets we trade are relatively small. This permits an option writer, even one with a small account, to devise a diversification plan across many markets.

Partially Naked Trading: The Ratio Spread

Our second featured trading strategy is known as a *ratio spread*. Here, we usually have some partially naked positions (technically, there are always some uncovered positions in a ratio spread) because we are creating a ratio of fewer long options relative to short options in the strategy. We say *partially* because there is a long option side in the strategy that partially offsets losses (up to a point) if the underlying makes a large move after the trade is initiated. Let's put together a simple ratio spread, one that we can construct out of our naked July corn call option position. We will then look at the profit-and-loss functions and the amount of margin required for doing this type of net premium selling trade.

Let's start where we left off with our preceding naked position. There is a natural segue going from naked calls to a ratio spread. Constructing a ratio spread entails some uncovered positions. To be more specific, to put together such a strategy we simply add a bull spread to our naked position, the result of which is a *call ratio spread*. The same design can be applied to a naked put with a put spread if the outlook is bearish. This offers a sort of broad-stroke view of a ratio spread, so let's get a closer look at the mechanics of this type of option writing strategy.

The reader will recall that July corn futures were trading at $2.18 cents when we established the July $2.30 naked corn call position. If we now add a bull call spread, we end up with a ratio spread. We will have two short calls and one long call. In other words, we will buy one $2.15 call and sell two $2.30 calls. Recall that a bull call spread, which we touched on in a previous chapter, has one long call and one short call, with the short call being the higher strike in the spread. Since we are now long one call at a lower strike, one of the short calls at the $2.30 strike is covered and one remains naked. Since we are selling two calls at the $2.30 strike, and buying one July call at the $2.15 strike, we have constructed a 1×2 ratio spread. The reader should note that both nickel and dime strikes (i.e., $2.15, $2.10) are now available on corn options. In 2000, the Chicago Board of Trade (CBOT) added a two-tiered strike structure for options (serial and nonserial) for the two nearby futures contracts. Previously, only dime intervals were available.

While corn futures don't offer the best ratio writing market (we will present our actual trades in Chapter 11 covering natural gas and orange juice, which tend to get more inflated premiums), we want to stay with our corn example for consistency to help the reader understand the structure of this option writing strategy. Also, with this example of a 1×2 ratio there is no credit generated. Generally, by selling enough calls (or puts if a put spread) a credit can be established. We will now look at the implications of such a strategy.

Exhibit 10.4 provides theoretical prices for July corn call options that expire on June 23, 2001 (the expiration date for the July corn futures options). Recall that we sold the $2.30 call option at 6 cents (or $300) when setting up our naked call trade.

We are now going to sell another July $2.30 call for 6 cents ($300) and buy a July $2.15 call for 12 cents. We have, therefore, received $600 from the sale of the two July $2.30 calls, and we paid $600 for the purchase of the one July $2.15 call. The net result of this addition of a bull call spread is that we have no net debit or credit to the account ($600 − $600 = 0). By selling the additional call, we generated just enough premium to cover the cost of the bull call spread, which means that the downside risk has been eliminated completely should July corn drop below $2.15, and the $2.15 call expire worthless. Often, by selling over-

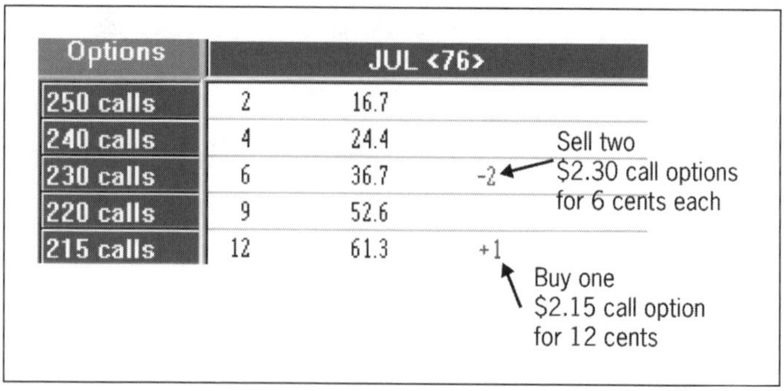

Options		JUL <76>		
250 calls	2	16.7		
240 calls	4	24.4		Sell two
230 calls	6	36.7	-2	$2.30 call options for 6 cents each
220 calls	9	52.6		
215 calls	12	61.3	+1	

Buy one
$2.15 call option
for 12 cents

Exhibit 10.4 Theoretical prices of July corn call options.

valued options, usually deeper out of the money in greater numbers, we can generate a credit. This allows a profit even if the market for the underlying futures heads lower.

The reason for a risk-free downside in this case is due to the fact that the premium received from two short July $2.30 calls (+$600) pays for the loss incurred if the $2.15 call expires worthless (–$600). Had we just employed a simple bull call spread (buying the $2.15 and selling the $2.30) in this trade to bet on a move higher, we could have lost a maximum of $300 ($600 – $300 = –$300).

It is often possible with prices that are trading away from theoretical values (i.e., overvalued call options) to generate a credit with a ratio spread using a 1×3 structure. However, a trader is not limited to a 1×3 ratio, and can thus build a ratio spread with any number of possible long or short call combinations, 1×3, 2×5, or 3×7. This would ultimately depend on (1) how much capital is available, (2) how much implied volatility exists in the call premium, (3) how far out of the money the strikes are, (4) time to expiration, and (5) how aggressive a trader decides to be in a particular trade. The same criteria would apply to put ratio spreads should the trader be bearish, or neutral to bearish. We discuss selection criteria in more detail later.

In the next chapter, we will present an actual call ratio spread that we did on natural gas, which established a 2×8 ratio for a nice credit. For now, let's stick to a downside breakeven structure to simplify the analysis; later, we can alter the ratio for a net credit. We have seen the downside risk potential is zero so far. Now let's look at the possible profit to the upside, and the potential for losses, which reside at a point above the two short strikes once the long call no longer covers the losses of the one partially naked call. This is partially uncovered because the gains on the July call with a strike price of $2.15 would offset the losses on the naked $2.30 call option up to a certain point. Technically speaking, however, this is a naked, or uncovered, call because above $2.43 the gains from the long call no longer offset losses on the short call. There is unlimited loss potential on the one extra short call on the upside should July corn continue to rise above $2.43. It is possible to lose more money than a trader has in his or her account if underlying futures rise high enough and no defensive action is taken.

As the reader can see in Exhibit 10.5, should July corn rise from the settlement price of $2.18 (where we established the

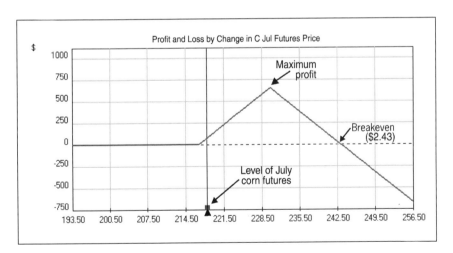

Exhibit 10.5 Profit-and-loss function for July corn call ratio write with upside breakeven at $2.43.
Created using OptionVue 5 Options Analysis Software.

trade) we would realize a profit on this trade as long as the July corn options expired above $2.18 and below $2.43. Above $2.43, we see that profits turn to losses. Above $2.43, losses from the naked July $2.30 call overwhelm the gains from the long July $2.15 call. Now we can move from this static (at-expiration analysis) to one that allows for the passing of time, and thus the impact of time decay (which benefits the spreader), and volatility declines since we are net short volatility (and benefit from declines in volatility) with the two short calls versus the one long call.

Our previous figures of profit and loss have not incorporated changes in time value during the trade. They are based solely on expiration with no time value left. Next we will look at how profit-and-loss scenarios are impacted as time value decay wears on the position. As Exhibit 10.6 shows, before expiration (shown by the solid line) if the underlying July futures move toward the short strike of $2.30, we would have different profit-and-loss functions depending on the time that has elapsed since entering the position. In Exhibit 10.6, the vertical marker is set at the short

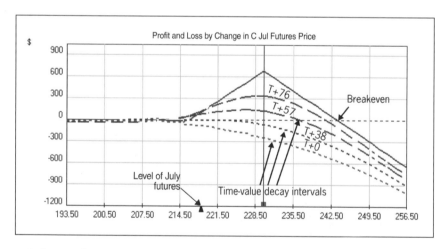

Exhibit 10.6   Profit-and-loss function for July corn call ratio write with impact of time-value decay.
Created using OptionVue 5 Options Analysis Software.

strike of $2.30 as a reference point. As the reader can see, at each time interval (represented by the profit-and-loss functions with dashed lines), the longer the trade has been open (i.e., closer to expiration), the higher the profit-and-loss function. Each profit-and-loss function thus captures the change in the option prices brought about by the erosion of time value at any *given* level of the underlying futures.

In fact, as the reader can see in Exhibit 10.6, the position could be closed at a profit at the short strike of $2.30 if we were at $T + 38$ days into the trade (T = the start date; thus $T + 38$ is 38 days in the trade). There would be a smaller profit at the short strike even before $T + 38$. The total trade time is $T + 76$, or a total of 76 days in the trade. The reader can see that a profit rate of greater than 100 percent could be obtained even if the underlying were trading near the short strike at $T + 57$ days into the trade. The profit would be $333, which, if divided by the initial margin requirement, would give a profit rate of 148 percent. The initial margin for this trade was $225.

Finally, we can look at this strategy from the perspective of volatility. When considering these types of trades (and ratio writes, which we will look at next), it helps to establish positions when the implied volatility is relatively high—that is, high relative to historical volatility and high in terms of absolute extremes of implied and historical volatility in the past. Essentially, since the trade has more short calls than long calls, a trader can establish an edge by selling the high-implied volatility, since more calls are sold than bought. Here, the trader becomes a net seller of *overvalued* premium. While we have not priced into this model overvalued option prices, we can nonetheless show the impact of declining volatility on the profitability of this ratio write, which, when added to the erosion of time value that we saw earlier, can help set up a very profitable exit point.

Exhibit 10.7, which abstracts from the impact of time decay, shows the impact on profitability given incremental decreases (in intervals of 5 percent) of implied volatility. While this drop in implied volatility works best when starting from overvalued options, here we are attempting to demonstrate how the principle of declining volatility, regardless of how high from the outset, benefits a net short trade. Obviously, the higher the implied volatility at initiation of a call ratio write, the better off the option writer will be. As the reader can see in Exhibit 10.7, with each 5 percent decline in volatility, the profitability function gets pushed higher at any given price of the underlying futures.

With the underlying futures assumed stationary at $2.35½, the collapsing volatility pushes the profit-and-loss function into the positive, from −$358 ($V - 0$) to +$230 ($V - 20$). At $V - 20$, we have had a 20 percent drop in volatility. Moreover, in between $V - 0$ and $V - 20$ there are levels at which a profit would be generated by drops in volatility. Often, market selection for these types of strategies begins with a search for overvalued options so that the position has a built-in edge in terms of being short volatility should a drop in volatility occur. Combined with time-value decay illustrated earlier, a drop in volatility can assist the position in reaching a target profit zone so that it can be closed ahead of expiration—a nice advantage.

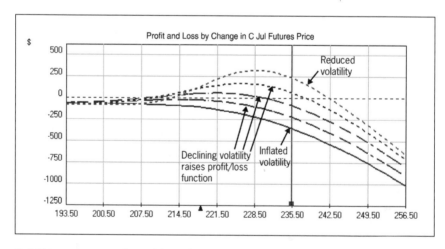

Exhibit 10.7   Profit-and-loss function showing impact of declining implied volatility.

Created using OptionVue 5 Options Analysis Software.

Generally, most ratio spreaders are looking to establish positions for an initial credit. In our earlier example using July corn futures and call options, we did not generate a credit with the ratio spread (1×2). Instead, we sold just enough premium with the two July $2.30 calls to pay for the one July $2.15 call. This would be considered a slightly bullish spread because we would need a move higher by the underlying futures to profit. This trade could be constructed with a more neutral bias (or changed to a have a more neutral bias once established) by adjusting the ratio of short to long calls.

For example, we could have set this up initially as a 1×3 ratio spread. This would have produced an initial credit of $300 $(3 \times \$300 = \$900$ for short calls and $\$600 \times 1 = \$600$ for the long call). This construction would profit if July corn declined, stayed the same, or moved up to the breakeven point on the trade, which would be located above the short strike of $2.30 by 10.5 cents. At expiration, should the July futures settle at $2.30, all the calls would expire worthless and the July $2.15 call option would have 15 cents in premium (only intrinsic value). The ratio trader would keep the premium from selling the short calls ($900) and gain $150 ($750 − $600 = $150) on the July $2.15 call for a total profit of $1,050 (maximum profit).

Of course, just as with the 1×2 spread, but even more so, a strong move higher could produce unlimited losses unless effective follow-up action is taken to adjust the position, or close it altogether. We will return to follow-up action and adjustment measures later. First, let's turn to our third and final commodity option writing strategy—the ratio write.

Substituting a Long Futures Position to Make a Ratio Write

We can continue to build upon our two previous models. First, we saw how a naked corn call would work in terms of profit-and-loss functions. Next, we added a bull call spread to the naked call to make a ratio spread. Now we can turn this ratio spread into a ratio write by substituting for the long call a long futures position. Because of the high leverage available with futures trading, ratio spreads have a special advantage over the same option setup using stocks. With a stock position as the underlying in a ratio write, it would be costly in terms of the amount of capital it ties up. With futures margins leverage, however, as we have already demonstrated, only a fraction of the value of the contract is required to be posted in the form of initial margin requirements to go long or short the underlying. This makes ratio writing an ideal strategy for options on futures.

The shape of the profit-and-loss function for a ratio write is different from the ratio spread. The ratio spread, the reader will recall, had limited downside risk because the long side of the spread was constructed using a call option. With a ratio write we have substituted the underlying futures for the call option on the long side. While this exchange will increase the risk on the downside, it will also increase our maximum profit on the trade, at $2.30, and raise the upside breakeven level substantially.

As Exhibit 10.8 shows, if the ratio writer is long July corn *futures* instead of a July corn *call*, the downside has no limit in terms of losses. As the reader will see, furthermore, there is theoretically no limit to the potential upside losses, as well, which we will turn to in a moment. The downside risk in this July corn call ratio write, however, is cushioned (lowered) by the amount of premium received from selling the two July $2.30 corn calls. Recall that the July $2.30 corn calls were sold for 6 cents each, so we would have a $600 cushion underneath the July futures, which were bought at $2.18 (i.e., breakeven at $2.06). The profit-and-loss function in Exhibit 10.8 incorporates a loss if the underlying futures fell below $2.06 ($2.18 − 12 cents = $2.06) on expiration. Upside breakeven at expiration would be found at $2.54 ($2.30 + 24 cents = $2.54). The underlying futures profit up to $2.30 (+ 12 cents) and the premium received from writing the two $2.30 calls (12 cents) adds a total of 24 cents to the strike price ($2.30) to establish breakeven.

Having looked at this ratio write from a static perspective, let's introduce now the influence of time decay, just as we did previously for the ratio spread strategy. It is important to remember that ratio writes and ratio spread strategies are better off established when there is high-implied volatility in the options. The higher the implied volatility of the options in relation to historical volatility, the more premium available to sell, and thus the more probability the trade will be a success. We will turn to the implied volatility factor shortly. For now, let's look at how time decay, which we have already seen from the call ratio spread example earlier, works in our favor throughout the life of the trade.

As the reader can see in Exhibit 10.8, at any given level of the underlying, as time passes, the profit-and-loss function moves higher. If the level of the July corn futures, for example, is $2.35½, there would be a loss (if the trade were closed). The first profit-and-loss function (the one sitting below breakeven) shows the position with a loss at $2.35½. However, by $T + 38$ days into the trade (T = the start date), given the same level of July corn futures, we now have a point at which we can exit the trade with a profit. Our $T + 38$ day's profit-and-loss function, just above the profit-and-loss function at point $T + 0$, now would give us a pos-

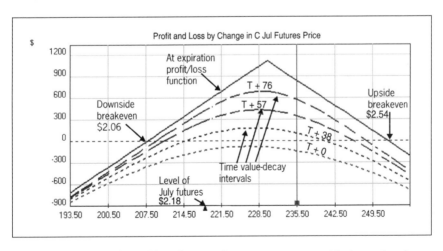

Exhibit 10.8   Profit-and-loss function for corn ratio write with time-value decay.
Created using OptionVue 5 Options Analysis Software.

itive return if the trade were closed. And at each of the other points of time into the trade ($T + 57$, $T + 76$) and at expiration (the solid line), we would have a profit at $2.35½. The trade thus profits in spite of an unfavorable move of the underlying futures because time is on our side. This means we do not need to predict the direction of the underlying futures to win.

Nevertheless, regardless of how much time decay we have during this type of trade, if the underlying continues to move higher or lower, losses would begin to appear in the account if no follow-up action were taken. Follow-up action, which we will discuss later, essentially involves altering either the ratio of calls to the underlying (i.e., buying back one of the calls to minimize losses and possibly selling more calls at higher strikes), or adding another July futures contract. This will help limit losses on the position. Other types of follow-up action are available, such as rolling the calls higher and in greater number, or going long another futures contract at a predetermined point, where a good-till-canceled (GTC) stop order could be placed. Let's complete the analysis of profit and loss for a ratio write first, now allowing for changes in volatility.

We saw how time-value decay can lead to a profitable exit point during the life of a ratio write, even with little or no movement of the underlying futures. Additionally, changes in volatility, while a two-way street (unlike time-value decay, which always works in an option writer's favor), can produce profits immediately on this type of strategy. Recall that we look for option premium that is overvalued as a selection criteria for setting up one of these kinds of trades. Therefore, we are looking for options with a high level of implied volatility (and an actual price greater than the theoretical price). Therefore, with spikes in absolute implied volatility, and implied volatility greater than historical volatility, we have a nice writing opportunity. Given this overvalued condition, we have a definite edge when establishing a ratio write. Let's return to our July corn call ratio write to see how this helps a ratio writer.

Since the long side is built with July futures, we don't have to pay for overvalued call options on that side of the trade (remember that high implied volatility is likely to pump up the price of all the calls), which is the nice feature to a ratio write. Meanwhile, the overvalued calls can be sold. Exhibit 10.9 assumes a drop of implied volatility in 5 percent increments. As the reader can see, at each level of lower implied volatility (represented by higher profit-and-loss functions), we have a greater profit potential at any point in time and any level of the underlying.

The five profit-and-loss functions represent different levels of volatility ($V - 0$, $V - 5$, $V - 10$, $V - 15$, and $V - 20$); $V - 0$, the lowest (solid) line represents no change in implied volatility. We should point out that these functions do not incorporate time-value decay. Therefore, we are looking only at the role of implied volatility here. As we drop volatility to level $V - 5$ (a 5 percent decline), which is shown by a dashed line above the solid function, we begin to get into a profitable zone even with the level of the underlying higher at $2.35½. Further reductions in volatility (which translate into falling premiums on our short calls) allow

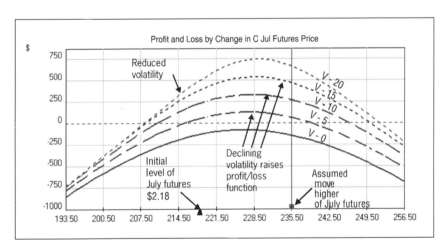

Exhibit 10.9   Profit-and-loss function for corn ratio write with volatility declines.
Created using OptionVue 5 Options Analysis Software.

for higher and higher profit points along our profit-and-loss functions still holding the price of the underlying futures constant.

Ideally, once in a ratio spread or a ratio write, the trader looks for profitable preexpiration exit points brought about by time-value decay, or collapsing implied volatility, and or gradual movement toward the short option strike. Both can occur together, and this will reduce the premium on the short calls, and thus bring about a profitable point to close the trade. If the position is kept delta neutral through much of its life (we explain this later), then these trades can be very easily closed well ahead of expiration at a profit. The beauty of these trade strategies, therefore, lies in the ability to remove them with a nice profit without the need for a change in the underlying futures. Indeed, an adverse move that is not too large can be neutralized in the short term. As the reader will see in the next chapter, actual trades that we have done using ratio writes and spreads were closed ahead of expiration with a profit.

Selection Criteria

Given what the reader now knows about a ratio write or a ratio spread, how do we identify potentially profitable trading opportunities? First of all, there are never any guarantees, which is why traders should always keep positions small and diversified, preferably never risking more than 20 percent of account value on any one trade. These kinds of trades offer substantial profits when they work out, so it pays to keep losses to a minimum on those that go against the ratio trader.

We already mentioned previously that commodity options offer lots of volatility, which makes them excellent candidates for ratio trading. Most competent brokers today can identify commodities with high implied (relative to historical) volatility, along with percentile rankings (how high is the volatility, in other words, in terms of past levels). This is an excellent starting point for selecting ratio trades.

Software can help, as well. Exhibit 10.10 contains search results showing gold at the top of the list with the highest implied volatility relative to historical volatility (referred to in Exhibit 10.10 as *statistical volatility*). As the reader can see, the current implied volatility is 14.7 percent, and the statistical or historical volatility is 9.8 percent. Since it is the statistical volatility that is used in option pricing models, the options are likely to be overvalued. This we could then confirm by comparing the actual prices of any gold option with its theoretical value to see which are the most overvalued. It helps to have a broker review these screens, however. Many commodity option chains, moreover, have a volatility skew, with call option prices getting more overvalued as you move farther away from the money. This skew can be used to aid in constructing ratio trades.

A spread ratio writer, for instance, would want the skew to be such that the options farther away from the underlying futures (i.e., the $2.30 July corn calls) have higher implied volatility and thus are more overvalued than the July $2.15 calls. Recall that the ratio spread trader is buying the July $2.15 calls and selling a larger number of the $2.30 calls (1 × 2 or 1 × 3 in our examples). By selling the more overvalued and buying the less overvalued, the trader can take advantage of not just overvalued options, but the volatility skew, selling the *most* overvalued options.

Report based on data as of 04/06/01
List the best 50 futures assets in terms of high IV/SV ratio

	Symbol	Name	DVO	Statistical Volty		Implied Volty	
				Current	Pctl	Current	Pctl
1.	GC	Gold (CEC)	1,577	9.8%	56	14.7%	71
2.	HG	Copper (CEC)	41	12.1%	10	17.9%	2
3.	KC	Coffee (CSCE)	2,076	27.1%	4	39.6%	33
4.	HU	Gasoline (NYM)	4,749	27.3%	48	39.0%	92
5.	SI	Silver (CEC)	572	12.9%	35	18.3%	16
6.	DM	Deutsche Mark (CME)	0	9.5%	69	13.3%	66

Exhibit 10.10 Survey results of OptionsVue 5 scan for high-implied volatility relative to historical volatility. The implied volatility percentile ranking (71) is also indicated at far right.
Created using OptionVue 5 Options Analysis Software.

Once a trader has found the highest implied (relative to historical or statistical) volatility conditions, and determined which of those have the best possible volatility skews, the next step is to select the strikes that would provide the best possible odds for profitability. Here, we can offer a few tricks that combine statistical and technical analysis.

It helps when an option writer knows the historical ranges that a commodity has demonstrated. In Appendix C, we have provided quarterly range data for the most liquid futures contracts. While no guarantee, these data give a trader a good sense of past ranges of major commodity markets, thus offering a sort of statistical road map. While some commodities are more volatile than others, and certain quarterly periods more likely to experience greater price shocks, much of the data are well behaved. Ambitious traders with a knack for numbers might want to make a seasonal adjustment to these data (i.e., break out the quarters with the most volatility and run statistical tests on the other quarters in search of normal distributions).

How can these data be put to practical use? For example, when constructing a ratio trade, it would help to know how likely is a 10 percent move higher (if in a call spread or write) by the underlying in any given quarter. We referred to this in a previous chapter when explaining how we select the strike prices for our S&P credit spreads. A ratio trader might look to construct a call ratio spread trade three months out that has a breakeven point that is located, for example, 10 percent away from the current price if the quarterly statistical data in Appendix C show that only 5 percent of the time this particular market swings high 10 percent or more. It may sound crude, but it does give the option writer some parameters of profitability to work with.

Another tip for finding the best ratio spread and ratio writing constructions would involve trying to set the breakeven points above major highs and below major lows, in addition to within a reasonable trading range probability distribution. Often, these areas provide friction in the form of support (key lows) or resistance (key highs), which can provide a ratio trader enough time (i.e., hopefully congestion results around these areas) to remove the position for a profit, or at least adjust the position to minimize losses.

In this chapter, we have reviewed three types of option writing strategies: (1) naked calls, (2) call ratio spreads, and (3) call ratio writes. We now turn to our actual trades in Chapters 11 and 12.

Chapter 11

PUTTING THEORY INTO PRACTICE

Here is where the tire meets the road, where theory meets reality. We have devoted the last two chapters to preparing the reader for this chapter. Here, we present our actual commodity trades, reconstructed with attention paid to all of the concepts that we have covered regarding futures and option mechanics and the strategies that we have outlined. We could fill an entire book with real trades that we have done over the past 10 years, but this would be impractical.

The purpose of this chapter, therefore, is to illustrate the ideas contained in the previous chapters covering commodities so that the reader truly understands it. There is nothing like real-world experience to drive home the point. Here, you will see how we selected and constructed the trades and deployed any necessary follow-up action.

We will start with two orange juice trades—first, a naked call position and then a call ratio write—followed by a ratio spread on natural gas. In Chapter 12, we present our final strategy—the synthetic call—and some real trade examples of this net long strategy, or net buying approach.

In 1998, we made a trade in orange juice that involved selling $1.40 calls naked. At the time when the naked orange juice call was initiated, the March 1999 orange juice futures were trading at approximately $1.10. The market had rallied to as high as

157

$1.28 in October 1998 on the heels of a bullish USDA crop report, and then fell back to lower levels, well off its highs. Our expectation at the time had been that with increasing Brazilian production and without a cold-weather threat, the price of orange juice would continue to move lower (or at least not significantly higher) into the new year. To take advantage of this outlook, we ended up selling very overvalued out-of-the-money March $1.40 call options. These call options would expire worthless on February 19, 1999.

As can be seen in Exhibit 11.1, orange juice had not been above $1.25 in the past year, and it had a major congestion or resistance zone in the $1.25 area, so we thought that we had a nice cushion for profitability with this trade, especially given the high implied volatility (i.e., overvalued options) of the options. As Exhibit 11.1 shows, the implied volatility was near an extreme, and the implied volatility was greater than historical volatility. The implied volatility at the time was 41.4 percent, and the statistical or historical volatility was only 25.9 percent. So we had

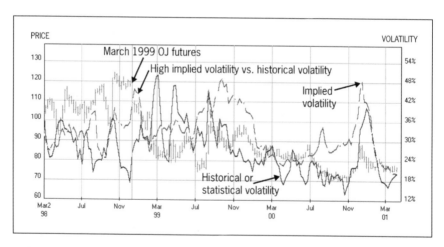

Exhibit 11.1   Implied and statistical volatility with orange juice futures bar chart. The dashed line represents implied volatility.
Created using OptionVue 5 Options Analysis Software.

significantly overvalued options prices (15.5% overvalued) and levels of volatility were in the top percentiles.

When we sold the March 1999 $1.40 call options, we were able to collect 4 cents, or $600 (4 × $150 = $600), despite the fact that they were more than 27 percent out of the money with the underlying futures trading at $1.10. The fact that there was so much volatility in the price of the premium allowed for this wide profitability zone and thus a reasonably good chance of success with this trade, especially given the technical picture. To sell these naked March 1999 $1.40 call options, a trader would have needed $600 in initial margin per contract (each 1 cent is equal to $150 and contract sizes are 15,000 pounds of frozen concentrated orange juice). As the reader can see from Exhibit 11.1, orange juice continued to trade lower going into 1999, and the March 1999 options expired worthless on February 19, 1999. This resulted in a profit of $600, or a 100 percent gain on initial margin required.

An Orange Juice Call Ratio Trade with Numerous Adjustments

We initiated our next orange juice trade in late November 2000. This was a trade that started out as a ratio write but then became more complex as a series of adjustments were made to the initial setup. The adjustments were made as precautionary measures, essentially defensive follow-up action, or to take profits as the trade began to wind down. While some of the adjustments may appear at first a little difficult to comprehend, they all follow the logic presented in the previous chapter about intervention to either minimize potential losses or take profits before giving them back.

Often, when using a call ratio writing strategy, we go long a commodity futures contract and sell a greater number of calls that are overvalued. The calls we sell are very far away from the money. These deep-out-of-the-money calls generally have the same expiration month as the underlying futures. This is your standard call ratio write (i.e., long one futures/short two or more calls). In the following trade, however, we have actually added short options underneath the futures. We combined selling March calls *and* puts while going long March orange juice futures. If we look just at the options in the position, we have a short strangle (short puts and short calls, simultaneously). However, because of the ratios used in this trade, which we will get to, the trade in effect is a ratio write.

When the orange juice ratio write trade was established on November 17, 2000, the March orange juice futures were trading at 78.7 cents per pound. At that time, orange juice was at a relatively low level historically, with overhead resistance likely to be encountered between 80 cents and $1.00, a major congestion area on the weekly bar charts. As Exhibit 11.2 shows, orange juice was trading just below this congestion area, well off the highs of 1998. While a freeze can cause a spike higher in orange juice futures, especially in the month of December or January (which we actually did get while in the trade), we felt the congestion zone would provide some measure of protection against

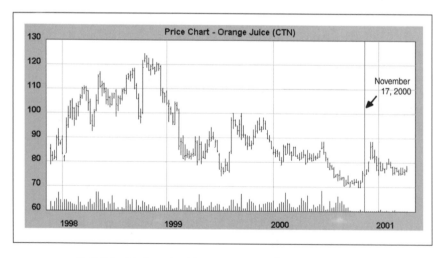

Exhibit 11.2   Weekly orange juice futures bar chart.
Created using OptionVue 5 Options Analysis Software.

a runaway train, at least enough time to make the necessary adjustments to the trade.

Given the technical picture to which we just alluded, we felt that given the significantly overvalued March call options we had the necessary conditions for a call ratio write with a reasonably good chance of success.

To establish our call ratio write, we went long two March orange juice futures at 78.7 cents and simultaneously sold 10 March $1.00 calls (1 × 5 ratio). At the same time, we wrote two March 75-cent puts. As the reader can see, we constructed this entire position in the March expiration month. The options for this position expire on February 16, 2001. The overvalued call options were 27 percent out of the money and had three months left in their contract life. The initial Standard Portfolio Analysis of Risk (SPAN) margin requirement for this trade was just $1,484, a mere fraction of the value of an orange juice contract, which was $11,805. Yet, at no point in the trade did the account suffer enough unrealized losses to trigger a margin call. Breakeven on the original setup would have been just over $1.05 on the upside on the March orange juice futures—the level at which gains in the underlying futures, in addition to the credit received from writing the puts and calls—would stop covering losses on the short $1.00 calls as they moved deeper into the money. The underlying futures, however, would fall far short of this breakeven level, and the 10 short calls lost most of their premium one full month before expiration. On the downside, losses were possible if the underlying futures moved below 70 cents at expiration. Here the two 75-cent puts and the long futures position would have incurred losses greater than the premium received from selling the 10 calls.

First, let's quickly review the setup for this ratio write, including entry prices for the options. We bought our two March orange juice contracts at 78.7 cents, and sold 10 $1.00 calls at 2.10 cents each. Each penny of an orange juice option contract, as with a futures contract, is worth $150.00. Therefore, since we sold 10 of the $1.00 calls at 2.10, we received a credit of $315 per contract to our account, or a total credit of $3,150. The March 75-cent puts, meanwhile, were sold for 3.90 cents, or a credit of

$1,170 ($585 each). Exhibit 11.3 contains all of the components of the trade, including the prices and short option value.

The total credit value of the options came to $4,320, which was collected when establishing this ratio write. All of this premium was potentially retainable. For example, if March orange juice futures were to have settled at expiration below $1.00 and above 75 cents, the entire $4,320 would have been retained on February 16. If orange juice had settled at 78.7 cents exactly (meaning no losses or gains on the underlying futures), based on initial margin, the profit rate on this trade would have come to 550 percent (in a period of just three months). As it turned out, the position required a number of adjustments during its life, to which we will now turn.

As the reader can see in Exhibit 11.4, immediately following the setup of this trade, March orange juice futures began a bullish move that would eventually spike in early December upon news of a freeze. While orange juice moved higher in the first two weeks of the trade, it was in a relatively stable manner. For example, by December 1, March orange juice had moved up to 82.50 cents. Despite the move higher, however, the trade was profitable by $140 as the two long futures and short puts produced gains greater than the losses on the 10 short calls. The initial setup of the trade had a slightly bullish delta to it. Therefore, gains in the futures would produce a small, unrealized profit in the account.

Futures	Options	Price	Value
Bought two March orange juice futures		$78.70	
	Sold 10 $1.00 calls	$2.10	$3,150.00
	Sold two $75 cent puts	$3.90	$1,170.00
Date opened: 11/17/00		Credit	+$4,320.00

Exhibit 11.3   Orange juice call option ratio write prices.

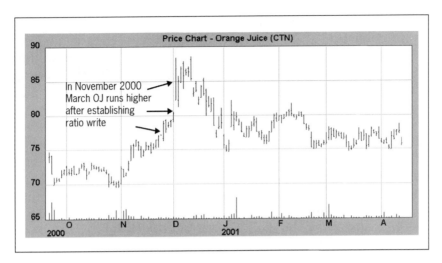

Exhibit 11.4 Orange juice futures daily bar chart.
Created using OptionVue 5 Options Analysis Software.

Our two March orange juice futures traded up to $82.50, producing a gain of $1,140 while the March $1.00 calls had increased to 3.05, a rise in price of each option by .95 cents, or a total loss of $1,425 on the 10 short calls. Meanwhile, the two 75-cent puts had lost $435 in value (1.45 cents × 2 = 2.9 × $150 = +$435). Since the trade had been close to delta neutral from the start, the move by March futures was mostly offset by changes in value of the short calls and puts.

In the beginning of December, however, there was a freeze in Florida resulting in a spike higher in the price of orange juice. This would temporarily put this trade at a loss because we were behind more on the short calls than we were ahead on the futures and short puts. This led us to make our first adjustment to the trade, as we feared a possible move higher. On December 7, orange juice had rallied to approximately 88 cents. At this point we decided it was prudent to take some precautionary measures, especially with the total delta of the $1.00 calls having increased to 2.7 from 0.9 at the initiation of the trade, and especially since we had moved quite a bit closer to the short call strike price. We therefore added a third futures contract at 87.7 cents and sold two additional calls at the strike of $1.15 for 2.25 cents, or an additional collection of $675.00 in premium. The calls were still very overvalued and this brought in some additional cash to help in the event of a whip lower by the futures contracts, while bringing our position delta back in line. By keeping a position delta that was close to neutral, we were hoping to keep the position relatively safe from movements of the underlying futures as we waited for option premium to decay on our short options.

As we would later realize, the price of orange juice would peak on December 12 at $90.50, which means that all of the short calls that we had sold would never even get in the money, and would eventually expire worthless. To be cautious, we would still need to make adjustments as we saw the need to either further defend the position or take profits before we finally closed down the trade.

With the March futures hovering around 85 cents in the middle of December, and having rallied fast on the freeze news, we were concerned, given that we had added a third futures contract to hedge the upside risk, we might experience some big losses should the March contract whip lower on us. Therefore, we decided on December 14 to protect the downside against such a scenario by making a trade on the put side. To do this, we purchased a put ratio spread (which would gain on a move lower to a point), buying two March at-the-money 85-cent puts and selling six March 75-cent puts.

The March put spread would cost us 1.5 cents to establish (we collected 13.5 cents for selling the six puts at the 75-cent strike, and we paid out 15 cents for the two puts at the strike of 85-cents). While this trade would keep us protected down to 75 cents, it would begin to take a bite if March orange juice fell significantly below 75 cents due to the extra short puts we had added to our two original 75-cent puts. By the end of December, in fact, March orange juice was back to 80 cents from its peak, which resulted in a loss of 7.7 cents on the third futures contract we had purchased at 87.7 cents. We ended up selling two more March $1.00 calls for 2.5 cents apiece, adding another $750 dollars to the account.

Going into January, we decided to exit one of the futures contracts at $75.80 when there was no freeze in the extended forecast. It was unlikely, we concluded, that another significant rally would occur. In fact, nearly certain that another rally would not push March orange juice futures up near our short call strikes before expiration, we sold two more 85-cent calls, collecting an additional $600 in premium.

We were wrong—a sharp rally on January 5 would scare us enough to put us back into the third futures contract we had dropped just two days before. While we may have overreacted, as March futures ended up not moving very far, it is always better to play good defense than to not take protective action. As it turned out, on January 17, with less than 30 days to go and March orange juice trading below 80 cents, we were able to exit two of the three futures contracts and buy back the two $1.15 calls and the ten $1.00 calls all at a profit. This was the beginning of our effort to close down the trade, which had already become a winner. At this point, we had only one long futures contract, two short 85-cent calls, and the 85-cent (long) and 75-cent (short) puts. Finally, on January 26, with time decay having stripped much of the premium from the short calls and puts, we exited the rest of the trade, satisfied with the profit, and knowing the risk and reward of waiting until the expiration for additional gains was not worth it.

Taking into account all of the aforementioned adjustments done to our orange juice trade, the net result was a profit of $3,400. This was achieved during a period of two and one-half months. Based on an initial margin requirement of less than $1,500, the profit rate came to 227 percent.

As the reader can see from this example, while numerous adjustments were made throughout the life of this trade, the overall thrust was to keep the position from suffering any significant unrealized losses by adding futures, shorting more calls, and adding a put ratio spread, among the other follow-up actions. We made these adjustments in an attempt to keep the overall trade from getting too exposed to delta and a sudden adverse move of the underlying futures while we waited for the overvalued short options in the position to lose their extrinsic value (time and implied volatility). We made some wrong moves but still ended up winning. The short options did end up doing well ahead of expiration. Generally, the approach here is to watch position delta (the delta on the overall position) and keep it from becoming too positive or negative. We had an initial bullish bias in this trade, so we kept delta close to +1.0, sometimes a little higher, at times a little lower. This kept the position from suffering losses on the upside as March orange juice futures rallied strongly in December.

A Simple Natural Gas Ratio Spread

In August 2000, natural gas options were very overvalued following concerns over supplies and a sharp rally in the price of natural gas futures. This created an excellent opportunity for setting up a ratio trade. Generally, deep-out-of-the-money options become more overvalued than closer-to-the-money options in the commodities markets. In this case, we decided to put on a call ratio spread, which would profit if the market turned bearish, remained neutral, or continued bullish to a point. The only risk was if the market became too bullish too fast for us to take the appropriate follow-up actions. Exhibit 11.5 presents a daily bar chart for nat-

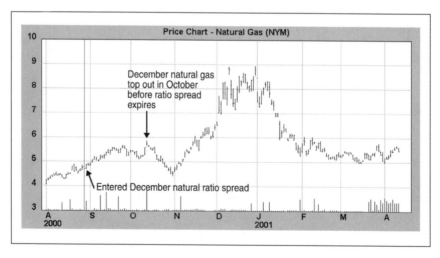

Exhibit 11.5   Daily bar chart of natural gas futures.
Created using OptionVue 5 Options Analysis Software.

ural gas futures showing how bullish the market had become during the life of the trade.

We initiated this trade on August 29, 2000, by purchasing two December 2000 natural gas call options with a strike price of $5.50 at a price of 31.5 cents each. With natural gas futures trading at about $4.80, we simultaneously sold 10 of the December 2000 natural gas calls with a strike price of $7.00 at a price of 10.5 cents each. This initial position had a negative delta of 0.9, which means it had a slightly bearish bias to it. But the aim really is to keep the position delta within a neutral range to keep the trade from getting away from us. Generally, position delta that is greater than -1.0 and less than 1.0 allows for reasonable management of the trade in terms of keeping the potential losses from an adverse move of the underlying. Of course, if the position delta becomes too negative, adjustments need to be made to bring it back to a tolerable range. But if a large move occurs in a short period of time, it is possible to get into trouble with the trade.

Writing this December ratio spread generated a credit to the account of 42 cents, or a dollar amount of $4,200. Each cent is worth $100 on the natural gas contracts (42 cents $\times$ $100 = $4,200). The initial SPAN margin requirement for this trade was $8,756.00. The expiration date for this call ratio spread was November 27, 2000. If the December natural gas futures settled below the long strike of the ratio spread at expiration (less than the $5.50 strike), we would just keep the entire initial credit on the trade for a profit of $4,200. Between $5.50 and $7.00, we get extra profit in the form of value of the long call. With the December natural gas futures trading at about 48 cents the day we established this trade, we felt comfortable with this trade; the strike prices of the short strikes were 47 percent out of the money and the two long calls with strikes at $5.50 would provide a buffer should a rally ensue. As can be seen in Exhibit 11.6, breakeven at expiration would be just below $7.50 for the December natural gas futures. A profit would be made on any price below this level.

Eventually, in fact, natural gas futures would rocket up to just shy of the $7.00 mark in the last week of November as supply problems caused the market to go wildly higher. However, as it

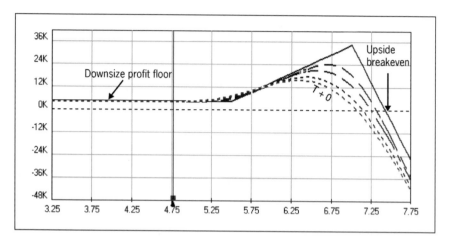

Exhibit 11.6   Profit-and-loss function for natural gas ratio spread.
Created using OptionVue 5 Options Analysis Software.

turned out, we exited the trade in October when the market traded back down below the level at which we had entered the position, as the short calls lost nearly all of their value. Even though a strong, but relatively controlled, rally took place right after establishing the position, as can be seen in Exhibit 11.5. the short calls never got into trouble, and the margin requirements did not change significantly. On September 19, 2000, for example, at the peak of the rally with the underlying December futures reaching $5.55, and after entering this trade when the December natural gas futures were at $4.70, the position was showing an unrealized loss of $2,260. The two long calls had gained $5,240, and the 10 short calls had lost $7,500. We could have added more long calls to adjust the delta during this run-up, but chose not to intervene.

Once December natural gas futures began a retreat, the short $7.00 strike calls began to lose a lot of their value. The total value of the call options fell to as low as $1000 on October 31, offering a nice opportunity to close the position. The short side of the trade lost more premium than the long side of the trade, and there was a net profit of $3,980, at which point we decided to take profit.

Despite the month of November's rally, the $7.00 December calls expired worthless on November 27, 2000. If we take the initial margin as capital required for this trade, and a profit of $3,980, this strategy generated a 45 percent return over a two-month period, not quite as good as our orange juice trade, but still a solid winner.

In this chapter, we illustrated three trades: (1) a naked orange juice call, (2) an orange juice call ratio write, and (3) a natural gas call ratio spread. All of these trades are based on the idea that deep-out-of-the-money calls tend to become overvalued and thus offer a nice writing opportunity. By selling an uneven ratio of calls to either the underlying futures (in the case of a ratio write) or long calls (in the case of a ratio spread), we can usually eliminate or minimize the downside risk (and even profit in some cases from a decline). The goal of these trades is to try to keep the trades close to delta neutral while we profit from time-value decay on the short calls.

Chapter 12

SYNTHETIC CALL STRATEGIES FOR COMMODITIES

Our last strategy to review in this book is the synthetic call strategy. Until this point, we have emphasized net selling strategies. The synthetic call (or put), however, is actually a net buying approach, and can be an excellent way to speculate on potentially large moves by commodities.

After reviewing the strategy, we will present two actual trades that were done with synthetic calls on commodity markets. We deploy synthetic call strategies when we feel that a particular market has some immediate or near-term potential to run higher. The synthetic call works best as a bullish strategy (or bearish if constructed using calls) when a trader feels that a particular market is likely to experience a very big move higher, or an explosion in volatility. It is termed a *synthetic* call because it acts like a long call, having limited loss yet unlimited profit potential. It offers an alternative, however, to the purchase of call options, which can be expensive and often require a large move just to get to breakeven. As option writers, primarily, we prefer to avoid buying expensive options for reasons we have outlined earlier in this book. Instead of buying calls, which can often be overpriced just when you really want to buy them, to bet on a move higher, the trader establishes a synthetic call, using long futures (thus getting around inflated premiums) and long puts. Following is an explanation of why we buy puts.

Constructing a Synthetic Call Trade

By going long a futures contract and buying a put to protect the downside in the same expiration month, we are establishing a synthetic call. The trader buys a put to hedge the downside risk of holding a long futures position, while preserving the unlimited upside profit potential of a long futures contract. If the upside move is expected to be big, a synthetic call will capture the potential profits of such a price spike.

As the reader will see, if priced correctly, the synthetic call can reduce downside risk to a tiny amount. Let's take a look at an example of a basic synthetic call using a real trade that we did in November 2000 on cocoa futures.

This particular trade was entered on November 17, 2000. With the March cocoa futures trading at $744 per metric ton (contracts are 10 metric tons in size), we bought a March cocoa futures contract and hedged it by purchasing a March $800 put for $750. The maximum loss on this position was $190 if the futures ended below $800 at expiration. The put option had very little time premium in it. We can calculate the time premium by first subtracting the amount that the futures contract is below the strike price of the put option, which gives us the amount that the option is in the money (800 − 744 = 56 ticks). The dollar amount of intrinsic value that this represents is thus $560 ($10 × 56 = $560). Since the option actually cost $750, we now know that $190 is time premium ($750 − $560 = $190).

If the position expired right where we opened it, the put option would have a value of $560 (its intrinsic value). Stated another way, the futures contract would have settled in the money by 56 ticks. Since we paid $750 for the option, we would have lost just $190 ($750 − $560 = $190), the share of the put purchase price attributed to time value. By loading as little time value into this trade as possible, therefore, we reduced our maximum risk. However, this would require a bigger move just to get to breakeven, which was at $819 (the strike of the option plus the 19 ticks we paid for time value). In other words, we needed enough of a move of the March futures to cover the time-value ($190) cost of the put. (See Exhibit 12.1.)

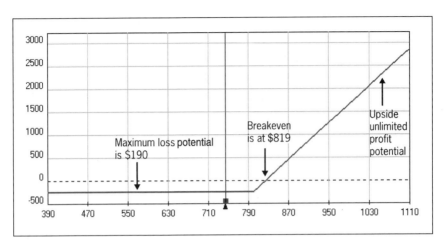

Exhibit 12.1 Profit-and-loss function for March 2000 synthetic call position on cocoa.
Created using OptionVue 5 Options Analysis Software.

Let us explain this again to make this clear. When we subtract from the price of the option ($75 \times \$10.00 = \$750$) the amount of intrinsic value on the option (strike price minus futures price for puts), we are left with time value in the option price. In our cocoa trade, we had just $190 in time value. This is also our maximum loss figure.

When the March futures rallied once we entered this trade, and before expiration on February 2, we had a nice possibility to take profits well ahead of expiration. With 79 days to expiration from the start date of the trade, we had lots of time to see a rally.

The March cocoa futures contract had traded to new lows on November 16 just before we entered the position.

We exited this trade January 11, 2001, yet more profit was available to those who stayed with the trade. We exited the March cocoa futures contract at $837 (+$930), and we sold to close our March $800 put at 140 (−$610). The overall profit on the trade was $320.

This is about as close as a trader can get to a free trade. We risked $190 and made $320 profit (and potentially more because profit could be unlimited), when we closed the trade on January

11, 2001. For traders who decided to stay in longer, however, there was even more upside to ride as Exhibit 12.2 reveals. The March cocoa futures continued to run through December and into January, ahead of expiration of the March put in February. Typically, a trader would enter this type of trade with more than one futures position and put hedge. Since their is low and limited risk with this strategy applied to this market, even a small account can manage at least a couple of lots (two long futures and two puts). By having two contracts, the trader can take profits at a predetermined target, and let the second contract serve as a runner to capture any more possible upside, while placing a stop loss at breakeven.

While we could present many examples of this type of trade, we believe this cocoa trade illustrates very well the basic mechanics of the synthetic call. A good way to look for trades with good potential to run are those with low volatility readings, which can be found by doing scans using search criteria for lowest implied volatility percentile rankings and lowest implied volatility relative to statistical volatility. Often extremely low volatility leads to volatility breakouts and big moves of the underlying.

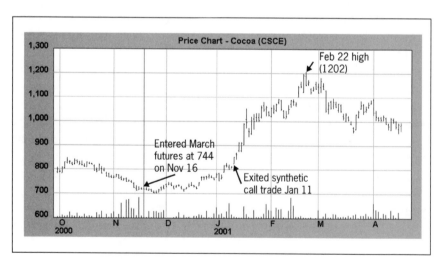

Exhibit 12.2   Cocoa futures daily bar chart.
Created using OptionVue 5 Options Analysis Software.

The cocoa synthetic call provides an excellent example of the potential profits to be made using a synthetic. We saw how a big upside move of the underlying futures led to a triple-digit rate of profit while never risking more than the amount of time value on the put position. The synthetic call strategy should be one of many trading strategies in an option writer's arsenal. Used effectively, it can provide windfall profits with limited risk. It is the only buying strategy we like.

Chapter 13

USING PUT-CALL RATIO ANALYSIS TO FIND TIMELY ENTRIES

Combined with finding the right pricing for option selling, some relatively simple technical analysis can go a long way toward adding statistical probabilities to your S&P credit spread trading setups. While charts may tell you where to *exit* such a position should it get into trouble, correct use of put-call ratios offers an excellent way of determining just when to *enter* a credit spread like the ones we reviewed in Chapter 8.

One approach that works well and that can be adapted to naked writing strategies as well as ratio writes incorporates a conventional approach to interpreting put-call ratios and combines it with our own unique volume-weighted, put-call ratio oscillator. This indicator can help pinpoint or, at worst, approximate a zone where an intermediate market top or bottom exists—just where you would want to establish an option position such as an out-of-the-money credit spread.

During any intermediate bull or bear trend, investor moods tend to remain slanted in one direction or the other—either hopeful or worried, driven by greed on the one hand and by fear on the other. When either of these two sentiments becomes too prevalent, a contrarian analysis suggests that the trend is ready for a change. This is based on the long-held view by technicians that the crowd, or the majority of the investing public, is usually wrong just when everything seems right. Historical data support this view, and it is possible to construct sentiment parameters that indicate when the crowd has gone too far toward one pole or the other, where conditions tend to be ripe for a reversal.

By attempting to use the crowd's psychology to locate over-bought and oversold conditions, we are using what is called *contrarian sentiment*, a branch of technical analysis. Indeed, put-call ratios have been, and remain, very effective contrarian sentiment tools, particularly since the speculative use of options by the public has exploded with the online investing revolution.

Using contrarian sentiment (i.e., put-call ratios) as a position trading *signal*, however, is not necessarily a good idea. While put-call ratios can tell what the general market mood is, these sentiment indicators don't tell you when exactly to go long or short futures outright. While conventional use of put-call ratios can be helpful, it nevertheless is often very difficult to know just when excessive bearishness or bullishness has become too much in terms of making a trading decision to get into a straight long or short position. But when combined with writing credit spreads, these indicators can be very useful.

Determining overbought and oversold market conditions for making trades with any indicator can be very tricky, as over-bought or oversold conditions can often remain for much longer than your indicators suggest—leaving you flattened by another bull stampede or bear attack—a problem known all too well by many traders.

However, by combining a standard put-call ratio measure with our unique volume-weighted put-call oscillator, we can reasonably attempt to approximate intermediate-term tops and bottoms, a way to determine at least whether the trend has nearly run its course. While not always reliable, when it is used to assist with timing the writing of deep-out-of-the-money S&P credit spreads, for example, put-call ratio analysis can help tip the scales of probability more in your favor, increasing the chances for success.

The oscillator approach presented here, therefore, offers an excellent and simple-to-follow broad market-timing tool for S&P 500 spread traders. This approach, moreover, can be readily adapted to many other commodity markets.

Building and Using Put-Call Ratios

There are many ways to use put-call ratios, and there are many put-call ratios to use. Most popular is the total equity-only put-call ratio, which is the purest representation of the speculative crowd. The once popular Standard & Poor's 100 stock index (OEX) put-call ratio no longer works as a contrarian indicator, in our view, due to the heavy use of OEX stock index options for hedging purposes by institutional investors. In fact, we have found that the OEX tends to offer a more effective leading indicator—a sudden surge in put buying or call buying often precedes a big market move in the direction of the bet, especially if it is contrary to the direction that the crowd is betting.

The daily total equity put-call ratio is simply the total put volume divided by the total call volume on all option exchanges. To construct your exponential moving average in a spreadsheet, you will need to take a few steps. First, any spreadsheet will easily make a 10-day moving average. Once you have 10 data points (i.e., 10 daily total equity-only put-call ratio values), you simply add and then divide by 10, which gives you your first 10-day moving average (10DMA) value, from which you can build your 10-day exponential moving average (10DEMA). The 10DEMA is constructed from the 10DMA and new daily values of total equity call volume and put volume. Following are the two formulas that we use:

$$\text{(Yesterday's 10DMA} \times 0.80) + (\text{today's put-call ratio} \times 0.20) = \text{(today's) 10DEMA}$$

Then you will need to use the first 10DEMA value to compute the next 10DEMA value, so the formula becomes:

$$\text{(Yesterday's 10DEMA} \times 0.80) + (\text{today's put-call ratio} \times 0.20) = \text{(today's) 10DEMA}$$

This can be written in spreadsheet cell formula language for instant crunching as you update the new daily values column (i.e., the new daily total put and call volume columns). You will want to create both daily equity put and call volume columns along with a total volume column because we need the total volume when computing the oscillator value. Essentially, then, all you need to do is insert daily call and put volume and total volume numbers each day and the spreadsheet will update the rest for you. You don't need to be an Excel guru to do this. Only basic spreadsheet knowledge is required.

Based on recent experience, we have found a 10DEMA less than 0.39 to be a good bearish parameter value, and a 10DEMA greater than 0.47 a good bullish-level parameter value. That is, if the 10DEMA is greater than 0.47, it would be flashing too much bearishness. If the 10DEMA is less than 0.39, it would be flashing too much bullishness. These are not signals, per se. For that we need to combine the 10DEMA with our volume-weighted total equity put-call ratio oscillator spikes, and of course it helps to filter these signals with confirming price and volume action. So let's now turn our put-call ratios into a volume-weighted daily oscillator.

Constructing a Put-Call Ratio Oscillator

To construct our oscillator, we will need daily total equity call and put volume, and total daily total equity options volume. Here is the basic formula:

[(Daily put-call ratio − 0.44) × total options volume]/1,000
= daily put-call oscillator

By subtracting 0.44 (a neutral sentiment middle point), we are attaching either negative or positive signs to our daily put-call ratio, and creating a value that is a certain amount under or over our neutral value of 0.44. And by multiplying by total daily equity options volume, we are attaching a weight to the day's nonweighted oscillator value. We divide by 1,000 to shift the decimal so that the oscillator value is in hundreds.

When we have two consecutive spikes (either above +100 or below −100), and the 10DEMA flashing bullish or bearish, respectively, then we have an ideal point to write a deep-out-of-the-money credit spread—a well-stretched market that offers a nice, low-risk entry point. Ideally, one of the spikes should be above +200 or below –200.

As the reader can see in Exhibit 13.1, the 10DEMA combined with oscillator spikes provides rather good entry points, indicating an overly bullish market with limited upside or downside, and a possible imminent intermediate turn of the market (which is when you should be thinking of writing your credit spreads). It is best to have the put-call ratio oscillator give a double spike (back-to-back). As Exhibit 13.1 shows, there are a number of these double spikes, which effectively signified excessive sentiment and thus a turn of the market.

Remember, an oscillator value below –100 is considered very bearish (i.e., too much bullishness), suggesting that the market is near a top if it occurs when the 10DEMA is flashing too much bullishness. An oscillator value above +100 (i.e., too much bear-

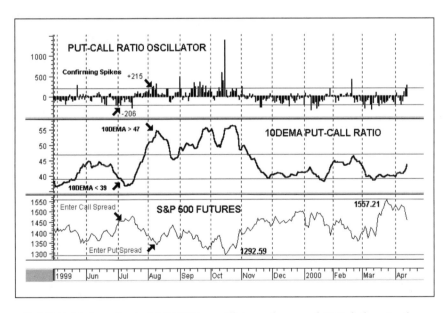

Exhibit 13.1   Chart of 10DEMA, oscillator values, and S&P daily price bar.
Created using MetaStock Professional.

ishness), on the other hand, is considered bullish and the market, therefore, is near a bottom. Again, we like to see consecutive spikes, confirmed by the 10DEMA into bearish or bullish territory at least by the second spike day. It also helps to have one of those spikes above +200 or below −200.

Typically, you will get a turn in the broad market (see Exhibit 13.1) when the 10DEMA is flashing too much bullishness (i.e., 10DEMA < 0.39 and the oscillator consecutively spikes below −100) or too much bearishness (i.e., 10DEMA > 0.47 and the oscillator consecutively spikes above +100). Sometimes, it is only a temporary retracement; however, it often provides a correct signal of an intermediate-term market bottom or top. At the very least, we have a market that is stretched far enough that we have a better chance of our deep-out-of-the-money credit spreads remaining profitable by expiration. And this same technique can be used to assist with timing and setup of ratio writes, or other net short strategies. A limited upside or downside once entering a trade can help by putting the brakes on a large move against a position, at least providing some cushioning effect. That is all we care about—stacking odds in our favor by whatever means possible.

In this chapter, we have provided the basic formulas for building a put-call ratio moving average indicator and daily oscillator value. While this chapter is limited to using equity put-call ratios to find timely entries for our S&P credit spreads, it can be adapted to other markets. This would require additional back-testing and forward-testing of oscillator values and put-call ratio moving averages to see if they are effective predictors of commodity futures price behavior.

Chapter 14

THE COULDA-WOULDA-SHOULDA APPROACH IS NOT GOING TO MAKE YOU ANY MONEY

We have all been through it—the one that got away from us and cost us a pretty penny. Had we done something differently, it obviously (now) *coulda* been a small loss, or no loss at all, and maybe even a winner. In other words, all of us have at one time or another been caught saying we *shoulda* done what in hindsight *woulda* saved us from losing on a trade. Or we *coulda* made a ton of money if we had just done something differently. You get the point.

Coulda-woulda-shoulda tales abound in chat rooms and, no doubt, around many office watercoolers. But they won't make you any money. It is the perfect 20-20 hindsight trading method, as the joke goes. Above all, though, this postmortem thinking represents a large part of the central problem that most traders face—a failure to act according to an objective set of rules to eliminate most emotions from day-to-day trading decisions, thus eliminating most of the "couldas," "wouldas," and "shouldas" in trading, although it may still not guarantee profits.

Through many years of interacting with traders, we have experienced both the joy of winning and despair of losing. In this

183

chapter, we present some valuable trading wisdom, basic guidelines that hopefully can minimize the despair and maximize the joy of trading.

Stick to Your Trading Plan

If you have developed a trading plan, and are using it, make sure you stick to the rules when trading. Too often traders suffer from the subjective versus objective battle that ultimately undermines what might otherwise have been a good system. For example, let's say a trader has thought of a trading approach, or maybe is deploying some of the ideas learned in this book. Whatever the case, the trader should always know ahead of doing a trade just what action should be taken and when, based on a set of rules (the objective factors). The problem arises in the heat of battle, when subjective forces easily overrun the objective forces, crippling the trader with fear and/or greed. The trader rationalizes breaking a rule only to learn later that had the rules been followed, instead of losing on the trade, it might have been a success. While we know that trading systems can fail, the sure-fire way to have them fail fast is for the trader to fail to stick to trading rules.

Don't Overtrade

Another pitfall is to overtrade. Our experience shows that traders who trade less generally trade better. You don't need to be trading every day or every week. Let trades come to you according to a well-thought-out trade selection criteria. The correlation between numbers of trades a trader does and performance is not very good. Even just four credit spreads on the S&P 500 stock index futures per year can yield an eye-opening profit if all goes moderately well. It may seem boring to wait for a credit spread to expire worthless every three months (thus producing a profit), but boring is better than broke. Have a trade selection methodology that tries to minimize the number of trades, and stick to it.

Diversify Across Markets

We can't stress enough the importance of diversification. Many novice traders fail to develop a disciplined plan to trade across many uncorrelated markets, and across many systems or methods. The ideal trading plan should involve trading setups that work on many markets and across many time frames. In our book, we combine different types of strategies across different markets to get the most out of the versatile world of futures options. We deploy primarily ratio writes, credit spreads, and naked options, with occasional synthetic call or put positions. These trade setups can be applied to many commodity markets, provided they have sufficient liquidity and implied volatility.

Avoid the Deer-in-the-Headlights Syndrome

Easily the Achilles' heel of trading, seat-of-the-pants trading decisions are a sure-fire way to always get it wrong. For example, let's say fear is mounting as the market is selling off day after day, as your out-of-the-money S&P 500 put credit spread is getting closer and closer to the money and the spread is widening. What should you do? The question should have been answered before you entered the trade. You should know when to close the trade before opening it. Deciding in the heat of battle too often results in a decision that you regret later. And worse, many traders tend to get trapped in the deer-in-the-headlights syndrome—frozen and not being able to act while their account is wracked with bigger and bigger losses.

Don't Buy Options

Buying options is a loser's game with worse odds than encountered in a casino. The psychology of the buyer often works as a trap. Let's say that after buying a near-term corn futures option for

6 cents, two weeks have gone by and the option is now worth 4 cents. The question then arises, should you sell it now for only a 2-cent loss, or should you hold on, hoping for a move of the underlying in the remaining two weeks? It is a double-edged sword. If you sell the option you lose for sure, and if you wait and it doesn't rise fast enough in sufficient magnitude you also lose. Let's say you decide to wait another week. With one week remaining, maybe the underlying has made a move in your favor, but the time value has decayed sharply as expiration nears, erasing most if not all of the gains resulting from the move of the underlying you had hoped for. But since you are closer to a profit you hold on, only to watch the market reverse as the premium evaporates to a negligible level, and you end up losing. A few of these episodes and it will be more than your account that is drained.

Take Advantage of Chances to Sell Options

Selling options gives traders an edge because predicting the market's direction or correctly timing the market is not a necessary condition to win. When selling options, a trader can profit in all but one scenario for the underlying. Let's say a trader were to short June S&P 500 futures call options with a strike of 1500 with the June futures trading at 1400. She will profit if the underlying (1) goes nowhere, (2) trades moderately higher but not above 1500, or (3) drops by any magnitude. The trader would *not* profit only if the June futures rose sharply. Buyers of call options, on the other hand, profit only if the June futures trade higher. And the move must be big enough to cover the premium just to get to breakeven. It is often akin to the feeling of trying to walk up a down escalator.

Sell Overvalued Options and Buy Undervalued Options

If you were going to buy a car, would you make a purchase without checking into the fair market value of that vehicle? Would you consider buying a home without an appraisal of the value of the real estate? Not likely. Yet many novice option traders never even bother to determine the fair value of an option before buying it. Of course, sellers of options tend to know more about this because selling overpriced options is an essential trading criterion. Buyers who are too often blinded by a quest for unlimited profits from owning options rarely bother to consider the fair value of an option. But by using implied and historical volatility levels, a trader can determine if an option is overvalued or undervalued. If implied volatility is out of line with historical volatility, then options can be either overpriced or underpriced. The bottom line is this: Always look to sell options that are overpriced, and if buying, avoid options that are overpriced and look for options that are undervalued.

Beware of the Illusion of Limited Loss

Without a very well developed trading system or plan, buying call and put options can be a recipe for psychological pain that most cannot stomach. To win at buying options you must be able to endure a slow but savage treatment by the market in the hopes that one day you will hit the grand slam, which will more than make up for the many small losses incurred along the way. It is not something that most beginning traders can stomach or afford. And many don't realize that losses may be limited when buying options, but the number of losing trades you may incur is not limited. This is the illusion of so-called limited loss. Indeed, *unlimited limited losses* can put a big hole in your account. Hitting the "big one" then becomes even more tempting since it is the only way to make back what you have lost. Many traders simply quit before they actually have enough time to finally make a nice profit on one play that more than compensates them for their losses.

Avoid Overuse of Technical Indicators

Our approach to trading options does not employ too many technical indicators. Often, traders who have just discovered the world of technical analysis think that learning advanced charting and using technical studies will give them an edge in trading. Our experience has shown that traders tend to suffer from information overload, often resulting in paralysis. Too many indicators can lead a trader to always find a reason not to do a trade because one indicator is still not confirming. Instead, we prefer simple support and resistance-level charting techniques, combined with using both historical and implied volatility levels to guide us in the selection of trades. We also like to use contrarian sentiment analysis, such as put-call ratios, for determination of oversold and overbought regions, which can be combined with volatility and support and resistance zones for better trade identification and management. Since the selling of options does not totally depend on correct market timing, many of our trades don't rely heavily on market indicators.

Learn Your Markets Well before Attempting to Trade

It takes time to master a market, so don't rush into new markets until you have become comfortable with them. It is often best to select just one market, such as the S&P 500, or perhaps one area, such as the grains or metals, to focus on. It is nice to be able to diversify across many of the commodity markets available to traders, but this should only be done once a solid understanding of the nature of each of these markets has been attained. It is a good idea to read as much as you can about a particular futures market, study the daily price movements, especially in relationship to options that trade on the futures, making sure there is sufficient liquidity before attempting any trades. Also, not all trade setups work well in all markets. One trading strategy may work well in one market and not in another for a variety of reasons. Only by careful observation of each market can a trader determine what the best approach should be.

Practice Sound Money Management

The operating phrase here should be to *learn to play good defense, not offense.* Once a trade has been identified, it is then necessary to determine just how much capital will be put at risk in any one trade. Most beginning traders too frequently bet the farm looking for a grand slam, risking too much in a single trade. To survive as a trader in the futures and futures option markets, it is important to maintain sufficient excess margin in your account (or risk capital availability) in the event that a position needs to be defended. There are numerous ways to follow up a trade that gets into trouble, but having enough margin is often the decisive factor in keeping yourself in the game and not having to exit at a premature point with losses when the trade might otherwise have been a winner.

Make the Trade

If you have done your homework and understand the risks and rewards of a potential trade, then don't be afraid to "do it." You can never know the absolutely perfect entry point, so don't try for it. Don't get caught up in timing or bid/asks. Too many times you will miss the trade. Don't trip over pennies, it might cost you dollars.

GLOSSARY OF OPTIONS ON FUTURES TERMS

assignment   Notice to an option writer that an option has been exercised. For instance, if an option writer sold January S&P 500 call options with a strike price of 1360, and March futures then traded up to 1380, if assigned the writer would get a short futures contract at the price of 1360 (the strike price of the option).

bearish   A market condition where prices are falling and investors are pessimistic.

bullish   A market condition where prices are rising and investors are optimistic.

call option   Contract giving the holder the right to buy a futures contract at a set price for a set period of time.

call spread   Simultaneous purchase and sale of call options on the same underlying, which can be in the same month or different months. *See credit spread.*

credit   The money that a trader receives into an account as a result of selling an option contract, or being a net seller of options. The money received from selling options is thus greater than the money paid out to purchase options. For example, deep-out-of-the-money call credit spreads will produce a net credit because the short options are more expensive than the long options. This is due to the short options being closer to the money.

credit spread   The simultaneous purchase and sale of option contracts for the same commodity or other instrument with expiration either in the same months or different months. For example, a put credit spread involves the simultaneous sale and purchase of put options at different strike prices. The higher strike price is sold and the lower strike price is purchased, resulting in a credit to the account. Because the higher strike for puts (opposite for calls) has more time value, and the lower strike has less, a simultaneous purchase of both establishes a credit in the account.

debit spread The net change in a trader's account from simultaneous purchase and sale of options. For example, a typical debit situation is created when a trader buys a call option nearer the underlying futures and sells another call option farther away from the underlying futures. This vertical bull spread results in a debit to the trader's account because the farther-away (more out of the money) call option is less expensive than the one that is purchased.

delta The amount that an option's premium will change following a change in the underlying futures expressed as a positive or negative number between zero and one. If, for example, the S&P 500 futures rise 10 points, and the premium on a call option increases by 5 points, we know the delta is a positive 0.5 (we get a one-half-point increase in premium for each one-point increase in the underlying futures). Delta, however, is not a constant and is affected by the passage of time and how close to the money the option strike is. As an option gets deeper in the money, its delta will approach 1.0 or −1.0 with a put. As it gets farther away from the money, its delta will approach zero. A zero delta would mean that a change in the underlying would have little or no impact on an option's price. A delta at 1.0 would mean that a change in the underlying would result in a one-for-one change in the option price.

delta neutral By combining positions, using either options only, or a combination of options and futures, a trader can create a neutral-position delta trade. For example, in a call ratio write, a trader can buy a futures contract and sell enough out-of-the-money calls to create a delta neutral position, where the combined deltas of the short calls would be −1.0 (or very near to −1.0). This means that a positive change in the underlying will have little or no change in the value of the option position because the short calls taken together will lose the same as the futures contract gains, assuming all other things equal (such as implied volatility levels). In this situation, a move higher by the underlying futures to a point would be offset by a loss on the calls. Position delta neutral trades can also be set up with call-and-put combinations.

early exercise The exercise of a call or put option before the expiration of the contract. Options on futures contracts are American style, which means they can be exercised at any time before expiration.

equity option An option that has common stock as the underlying.

exercise The action taken by an option holder to exchange an option contract for an underlying futures contract. This decision might arise should an option lose all its time value and the option is in the money. A call holder would exercise to acquire the underlying futures contract, and a put holder would exercise to short an underlying futures contract or offset a long futures. The exercise takes place at the strike price of the option.

exercise price This is the same as the strike price, and it is the price at which an option holder, or buyer, has the right to acquire (call holder) or sell (put holder) a futures contract.

expiration date For options, this is the last day for exercising option contracts into the underlying futures. For futures, it is the last day that a futures contract trades. For the S&P 500 futures, for instance, the last day of trading for each contract is the third Friday of the delivery month (i.e., the June S&P futures expire on the third Friday of June, based on the opening quotation price of the S&P 500 index for that day). The last day of trading would therefore be the day before, Thursday.

fair value Of an option, this is often used to describe the value of an option based on a mathematical model such as the Black-Scholes Option Pricing Model. The black model, a version of the Black-Scholes model, is used to determine fair value of options on futures. Key variables in these models include historical volatility, short-term interest rates, price of the underlying, and time remaining until expiration. Fair value is also referred to as *theoretical value,* and this value can differ from the actual market value of an option. The difference between the theoretical value of an option and the market value represents the level of implied volatility in the option's price.

first notice day Usually several weeks before the last trading day of a futures contract. At this date the holder of a futures contract may be served notice of a delivery intent of the underlying commodity (e.g., soybeans).

follow-up action Any adjustments made to an open option position. This action typically is defensive in nature, usually involving the adjustment of ratios by adding or removing contracts, or rolling the position out of immediate danger. For example, a credit spreader may close a spread at a loss and write it again further out in time and farther away from the money. Or, for example, a ratio spreader may decide to go long more futures contracts to adjust the delta of the ratio spread to keep it near delta neutral following a move of the underlying futures.

futures contract An agreement between two parties to buy or sell a commodity at a future date. This contract is standardized and traded on a futures exchange, specifying the quality and quantity as well as the delivery date and location. Some contracts, such as index futures, settle in cash.

gamma The rate at which an option's delta changes as the underlying futures change. Gamma is calculated by dividing the change in delta by the change in the underlying futures price. It measures the change in delta caused by a change in the underlying futures.

good until canceled (GTC) An order that remains active until it is canceled, filled, or the option or futures contract expires. For example, a trader can tell his broker to put in place a GTC order to go long a futures contract at a specified price below the current market level. If the price of the futures contract on which the GTC order is placed falls below the designated price, known as a limit price, the trader automatically gets long the futures at the limit price or better.

implied volatility The amount the market price is implying that the real price of an option should be. Implied volatility arises if the theoretical value of an option is less than the market price of the option. The difference between the two prices reflects implied volatility.

in-the-money option When a call option's strike price is less than the price of the underlying futures, the call option is in the money. When a put option's strike price is greater than the price of the underlying futures, the put option is in the money.

intrinsic value The portion of the price of an option determined by how much an option is in the money. If the underlying futures price is greater than the strike price of a call option, the call option will have intrinsic value equal to the futures price minus the strike price. If, for example, S&P 500 futures settled at 1300 and the call options have a 1290 strike price, then the option would have 10 points of intrinsic value or would be said to be 10 points in the money. Of course, the option will be worth more than 10 points if it is before expiration due to the influence of time value. A put option, on the other hand, would have intrinsic value if the underlying futures price is less than the strike price of the put option. For example, if the S&P 500 futures settled at 1290 and the strike price for the put option is 1300, then the put option would be 10 points in the money.

long Buying a futures or option contract.

long call A position taken by the buyer of an option. A buyer of an option purchases a call and is thus long a call option. Call option buyers may profit if the underlying futures are bullish.

margin The funds required by the exchange and broker to be deposited in a trader's account to open a futures or short option position. Also known as a performance bond, the deposit is required to maintain the smooth functioning of the brokerage and clearing systems, and the exchanges where they do business.

naked option The sale of an option in exchange for premium by an option writer without any corresponding hedge position. Naked options theoretically face unlimited losses with limited profitability.

net option value The value of options that are combined as long and short positions. Net option value can be positive or negative, depending on whether the options create a net debit or net credit to an account.

offset The closing out of a futures or option position.

open interest The number of futures or option contracts that have not been offset or fulfilled for delivery.

option buyer Any trader who purchases an option contract by paying premium. For example, a call option buyer generally has a bullish outlook and expects the underlying to move higher. An option buyer profits if the price of an option rises and the position is offset with a gain. Option buyers face unlimited profit potential with limited losses.

option leg This refers to one side of an option trade, such as the short or long side of a credit spread.

option seller *See option writer.*

option writer Anyone who sells an option and collects premium, as opposed to buying an option and paying premium. For example, a put option writer expects the underlying to move higher, resulting in the decline in premium on the put that was sold. If the writer offsets the position, and the price of the option has declined, the trader realizes a profit. An option writer faces the possibility of unlimited losses with limited profit and is subject to exercise notices at any time, especially if the option is deep in the money and no longer has time premium in its price. At this point the option is said to be at parity, and the holder would have an incentive to exercise it because no time premium would be forfeited in the exercise.

out-of-the-money option   An option with no intrinsic value. When a call option has no intrinsic value, its strike price is above the price of the underlying futures, and is thus out of the money. When a put option has no intrinsic value, its strike price is below the price of the underlying futures, and is thus out of the money.

overvalued options   Options with prices that are greater than the theoretical price of the option. *See implied volatility.*

parity   Parity pricing for an option is reached when the price of an option is equal to the amount of intrinsic value only. In other words, an in-the-money option's price would equal the intrinsic value (the difference between the strike and the premium) and contain no time value.

premium   The amount of money for which an option contract is bought or sold. A buyer and seller exchange options in a marketplace. The seller receives premium from the buyer for the sale of the option.

put option   A contract giving the holder the right to sell a futures contract at a set price for a set period of time.

put spread   The simultaneous sale and purchase of a put option on the same underlying in the same or different contract months.

ratio spread   The simultaneous sale and purchase of options on the same underlying but in different combinations, preferably with the short leg selling above theoretical prices. For example, a put ratio spread might involve buying 2 July soybean puts near the money and selling 10 deep-out-of-the-money soybean puts. The aim of the ratio spreader is to generate a credit on the spread and to have the underlying be neutral or moderately bearish for a profit. *See ratio write and credit spread.*

ratio write   The simultaneous sale and purchase of the underlying futures and out-of-the-money options. The ratio writer looks to sell overvalued options that are hedged by the long or short futures, which can be in different combinations, such as two long futures and eight short calls, or two short futures and eight short puts. The idea is to generate a credit, and hope for a neutral to bearish (put ratio write) or neutral to bullish (call ratio write) move of the underlying futures.

resistance   A price level where selling pressure increases, which results in a barrier to higher prices. This level may be a zone where previously many buyers took positions who had expected a market move higher but suffered losses instead. As the market approaches this area again, often a congestion region, those buyers step up to sell resulting in downward pressure. Resistance is broken when enough buyers maintain upward pressure until all sellers have been exhausted.

rolling options Closing an option trade either at a loss or gain and repositioning the trade higher or lower in relation to the underlying preferably for a net credit if a net short position. Options can be rolled out in time to capture more time value in addition to being rolled down or up the option chain.

serial options Options that expire in months between listed futures contract delivery months. A serial option, therefore, would have the next nearby futures contract as the underlying and exercise into that contract.

short Selling an option or futures contract to open a position.

standard portfolio analysis of risk (SPAN) This is a risk-based, portfolio approach for calculating margin requirements for options on futures. Futures contracts are examined over a range of price and volatility changes to determine the potential gains and losses, which become the basis for calculating margin requirements for options positions.

strike price Also known as the exercise price of an option, the strike price is the contract specified price of an option where the option buyer has the right to purchase (call) or sell (put) the underlying.

support An area where buying pressure increases, which thus keeps prices from falling below that point. *See resistance.*

synthetic call The simultaneous purchase of a long futures contract with a protective long put hedge.

synthetic put The simultaneous sale of a futures contract and purchase of a protective long call hedge.

technical analysis The study of historical chart patterns, such as support and resistance points, along with the use of technical indicators, such as those showing changes in volume, open interest, moving averages, stochastic levels, and momentum.

theta This Greek letter is used to measure the change in an option premium caused by an erosion of time. In other words, theta measures the rate of time value decay, and it accelerates as the expiration date nears.

time value The amount of an option premium that reflects the amount of time remaining before expiration. Essentially, the price of an option can be reduced to two major factors, intrinsic value and time value.

vega This measures the rate of change of an option's premium for an equivalent change in volatility in percentage terms. In other words, vega tells you how much an option's value changes given a 1 percent change in volatility. If implied volatility falls by 1 percent, then vega is the percentage drop in an option premium value. The formula to compute vega is the percentage change in premium divided by the percentage change in volatility.

volatility There are two types of volatility: historical and implied. Essentially, historical volatility measures the extent of price changes over a historical time period. Implied volatility is a measure of value the market is placing on the option above what the historical volatility would suggest.

Appendix A

HISTORICAL COMMODITY CHARTS (MONTHLY)*

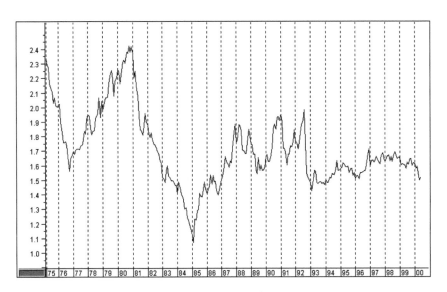

British Pound

---

*All monthly charts created using MetaStock Professional.

199

Cocoa

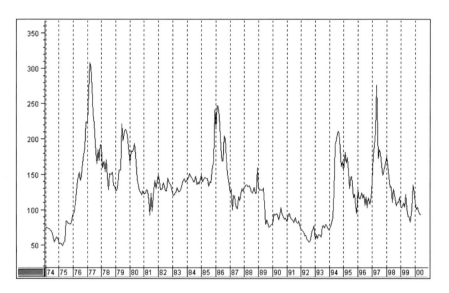

Coffee

200

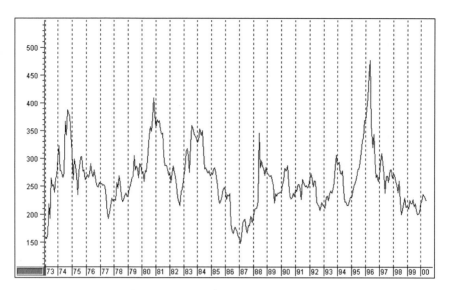

Corn

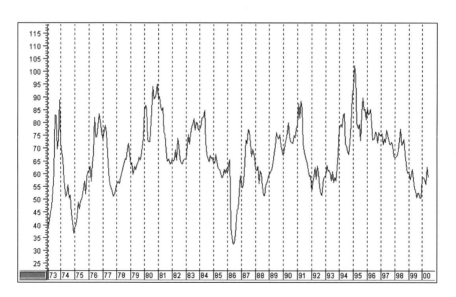

Cotton

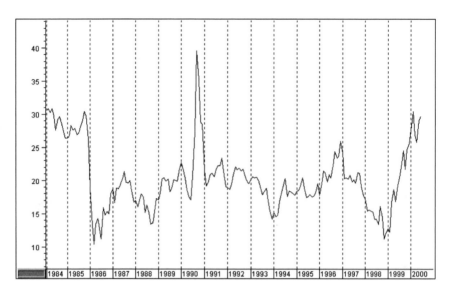

Crude Oil

Eurodollars

202

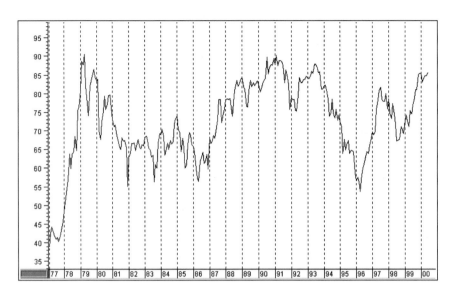

Feeder Cattle

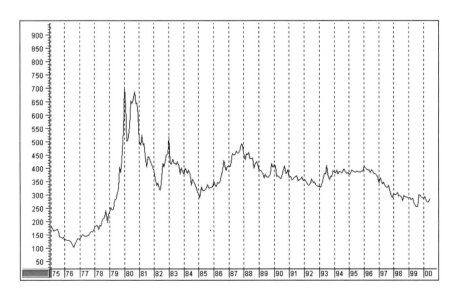

Gold

203

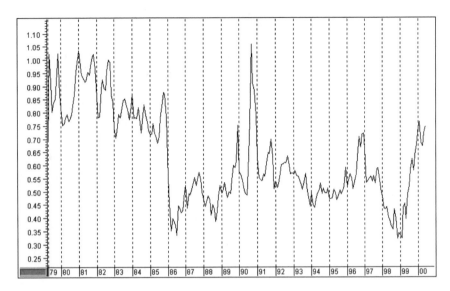

Heating Oil

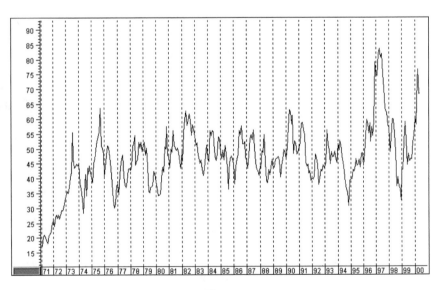

Hogs

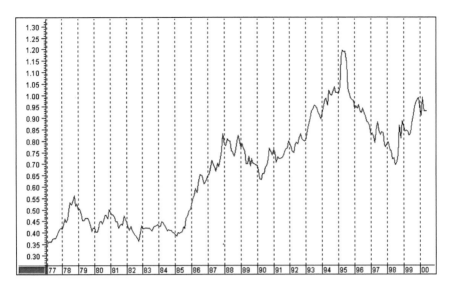

Japanese Yen

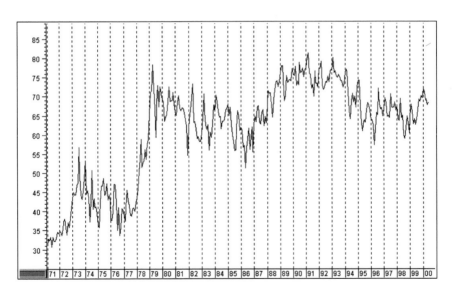

Live Cattle

205

Lumber

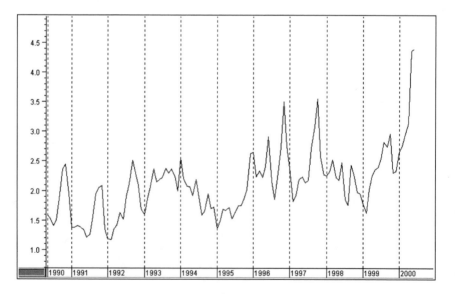

Natural Gas

206

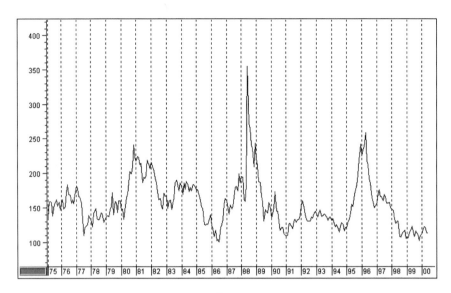

Oats

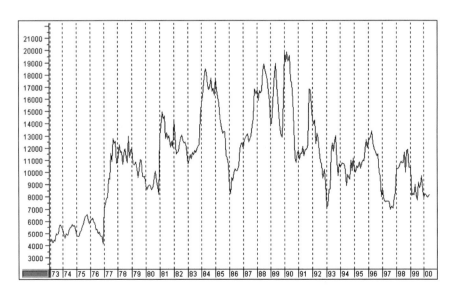

Orange Juice

207

Platinum

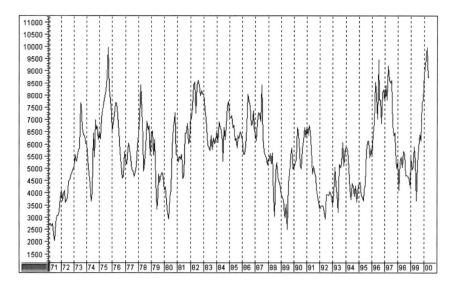

Pork Bellies

208

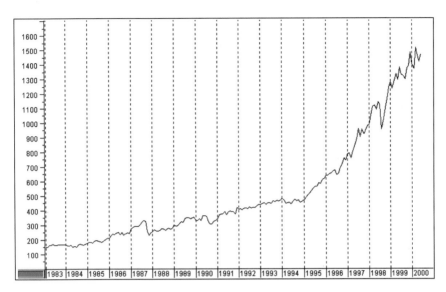

S&P 500

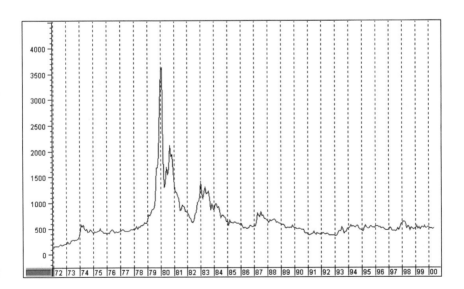

Silver

209

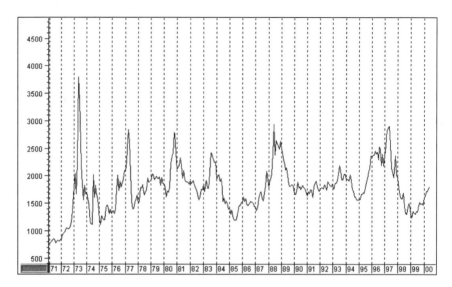

Soybean Meal

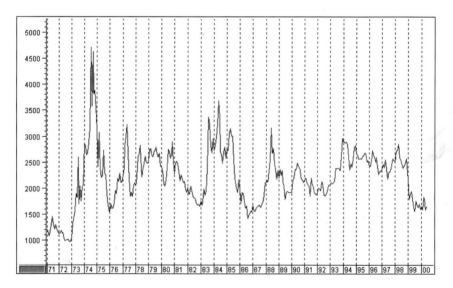

Soybean Oil

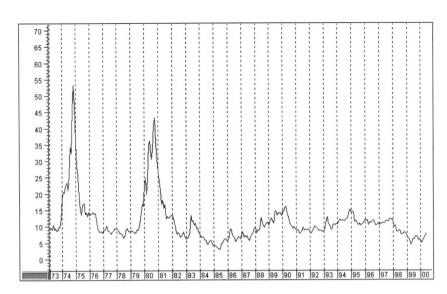

Sugar

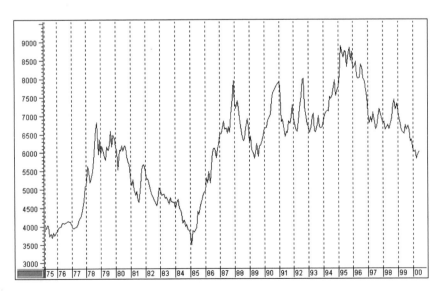

Swiss Franc

211

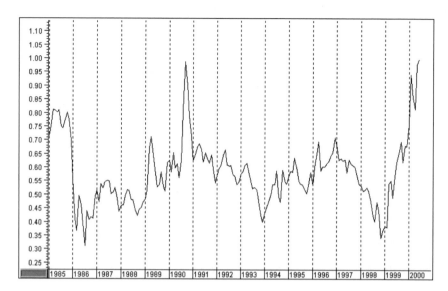

Unleaded Gasoline

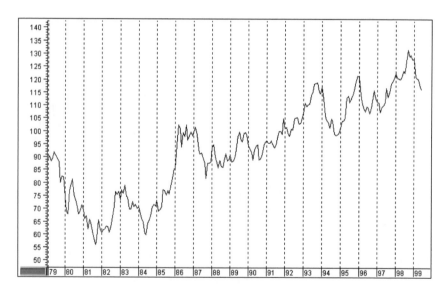

U.S. 30-Year Bond

212

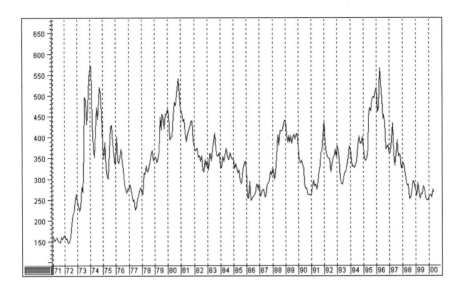

Wheat

Appendix B

HISTORICAL COMMODITY CHARTS (DAILY)*

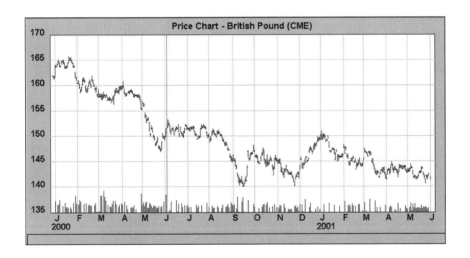

*All daily charts created using OptionVue 5 Options Analysis Software.

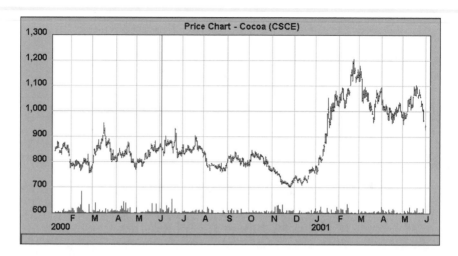

Price Chart - Cocoa (CSCE)

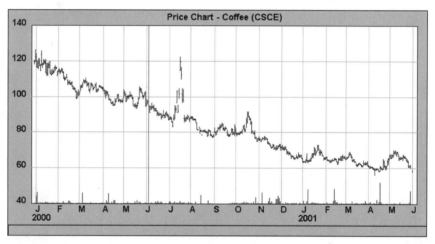

Price Chart - Coffee (CSCE)

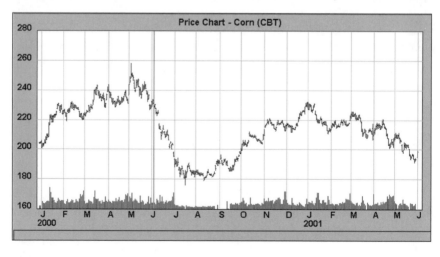

Price Chart - Corn (CBT)

216

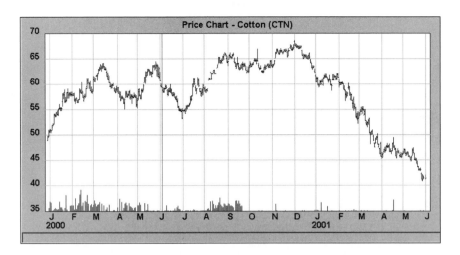

Price Chart - Cotton (CTN)

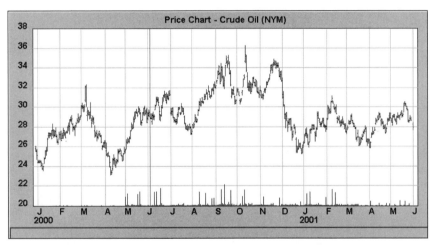

Price Chart - Crude Oil (NYM)

Price Chart - Eurodollar (IMM)

217

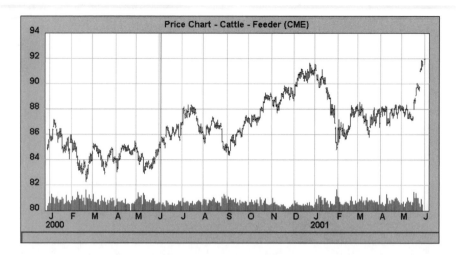

Price Chart - Cattle - Feeder (CME)

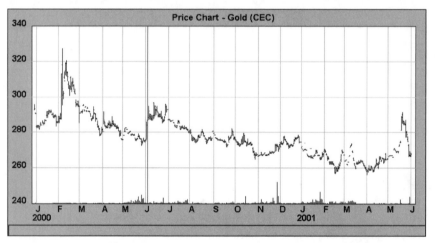

Price Chart - Gold (CEC)

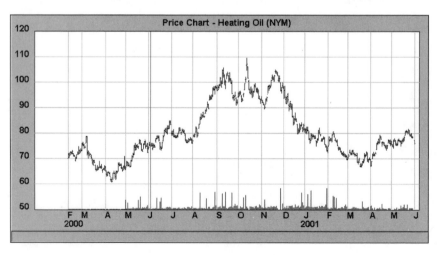

Price Chart - Heating Oil (NYM)

218

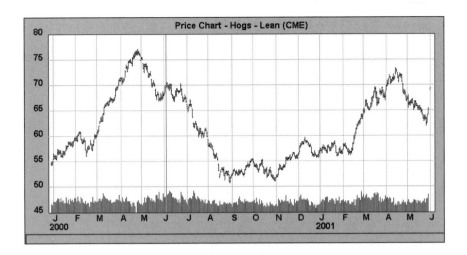

Price Chart - Hogs - Lean (CME)

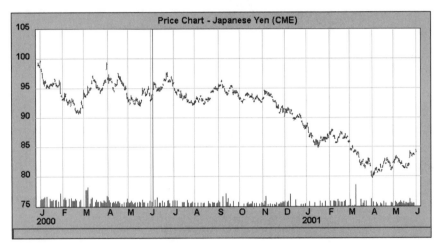

Price Chart - Japanese Yen (CME)

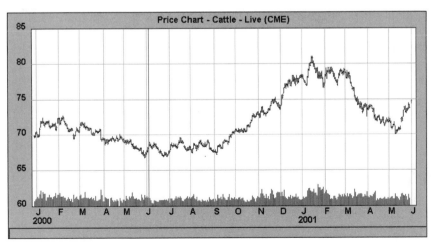

Price Chart - Cattle - Live (CME)

219

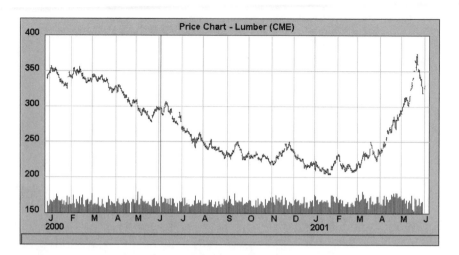

Price Chart - Lumber (CME)

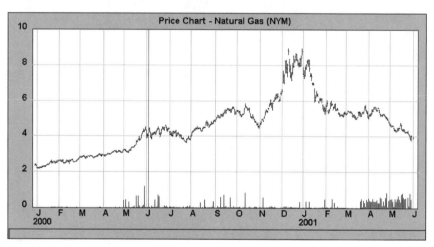

Price Chart - Natural Gas (NYM)

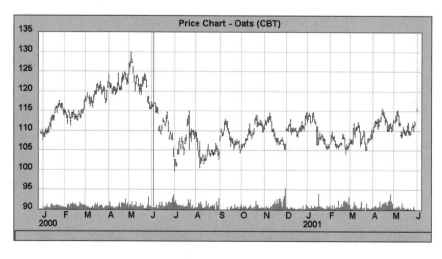

Price Chart - Oats (CBT)

220

Price Chart - Orange Juice (CTN)

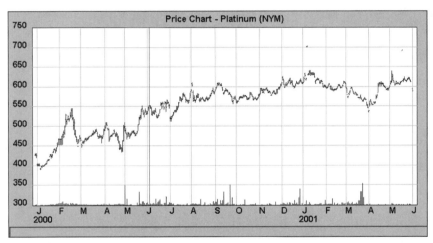

Price Chart - Platinum (NYM)

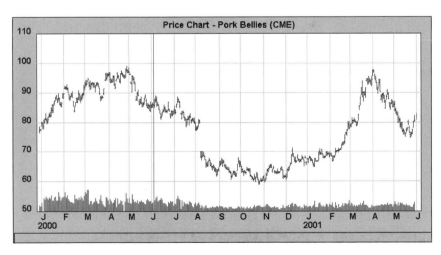

Price Chart - Pork Bellies (CME)

221

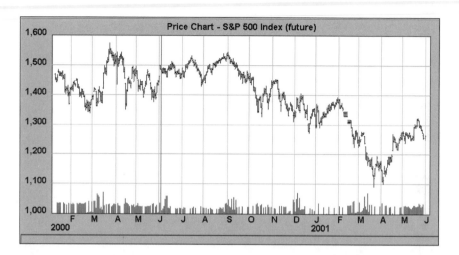

Price Chart - S&P 500 Index (future)

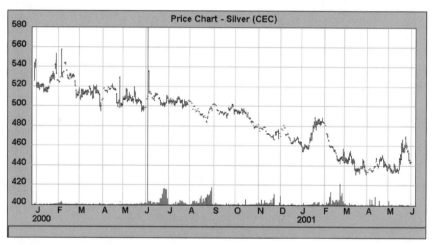

Price Chart - Silver (CEC)

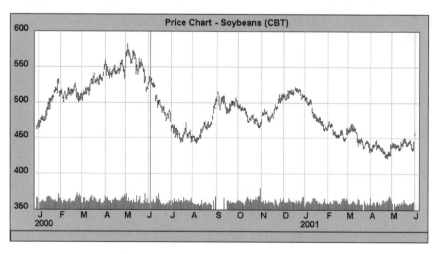

Price Chart - Soybeans (CBT)

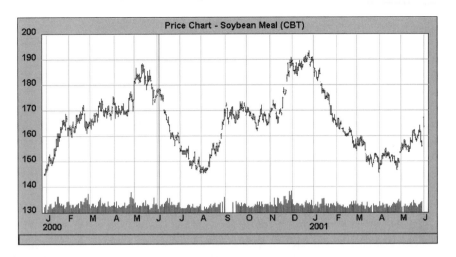

Price Chart - Soybean Meal (CBT)

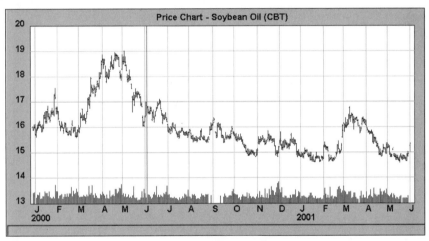

Price Chart - Soybean Oil (CBT)

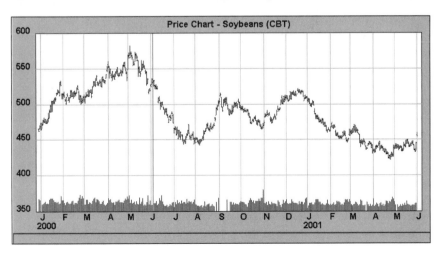

Price Chart - Soybeans (CBT)

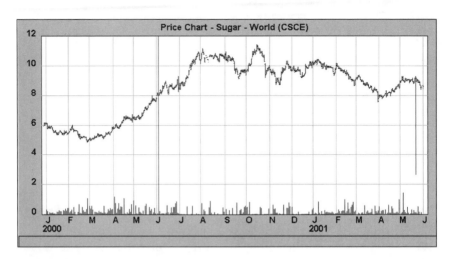

Price Chart - Sugar - World (CSCE)

Price Chart - Swiss Franc (CME)

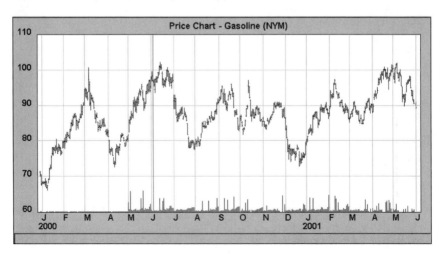

Price Chart - Gasoline (NYM)

224

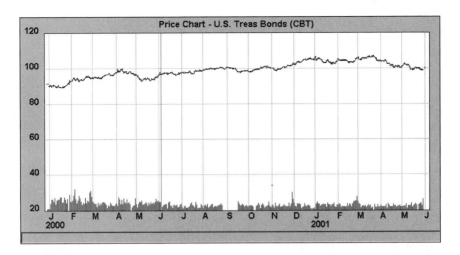

Price Chart - U.S. Treas Bonds (CBT)

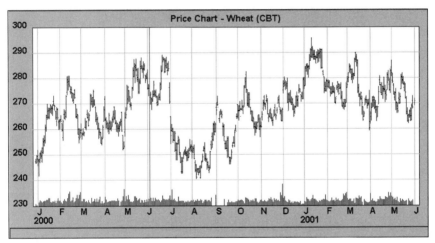

Price Chart - Wheat (CBT)

225

Appendix C

HISTORICAL COMMODITY PRICE RANGES (QUARTERLY)*

---

*All quarterly range charts created using EViews 3.1.

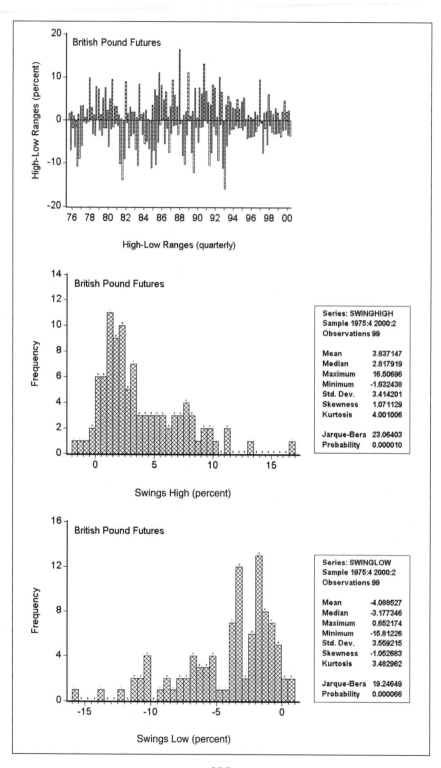

British Pound Futures

High-Low Ranges (percent)

High-Low Ranges (quarterly)

British Pound Futures

Frequency

Swings High (percent)

Series: SWINGHIGH
Sample 1975:4 2000:2
Observations 99

Mean	3.837147
Median	2.817919
Maximum	16.50696
Minimum	-1.632438
Std. Dev.	3.414201
Skewness	1.071129
Kurtosis	4.001006
Jarque-Bera	23.06403
Probability	0.000010

British Pound Futures

Frequency

Swings Low (percent)

Series: SWINGLOW
Sample 1975:4 2000:2
Observations 99

Mean	-4.088527
Median	-3.177346
Maximum	0.652174
Minimum	-15.81226
Std. Dev.	3.559215
Skewness	-1.052683
Kurtosis	3.482962
Jarque-Bera	19.24649
Probability	0.000066

228

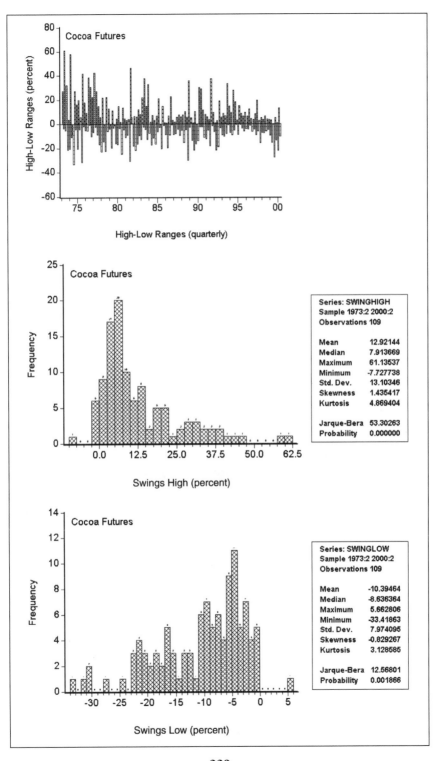

Cocoa Futures

High-Low Ranges (quarterly)

Cocoa Futures

Series: SWINGHIGH
Sample 1973:2 2000:2
Observations 109

Mean	12.92144
Median	7.913669
Maximum	61.13537
Minimum	-7.727738
Std. Dev.	13.10346
Skewness	1.435417
Kurtosis	4.869404
Jarque-Bera	53.30263
Probability	0.000000

Swings High (percent)

Cocoa Futures

Series: SWINGLOW
Sample 1973:2 2000:2
Observations 109

Mean	-10.39464
Median	-8.636364
Maximum	5.662806
Minimum	-33.41863
Std. Dev.	7.974095
Skewness	-0.829267
Kurtosis	3.128585
Jarque-Bera	12.56801
Probability	0.001866

Swings Low (percent)

229

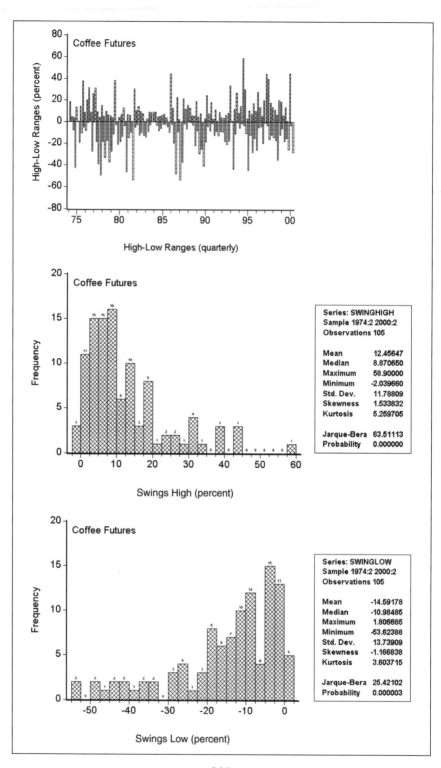

Coffee Futures

High-Low Ranges (quarterly)

Coffee Futures

Series: SWINGHIGH
Sample 1974:2 2000:2
Observations 105

Mean   12.45647
Median   8.870650
Maximum   58.90000
Minimum   -2.039660
Std. Dev.   11.78809
Skewness   1.533832
Kurtosis   5.259705

Jarque-Bera 63.51113
Probability   0.000000

Swings High (percent)

Coffee Futures

Series: SWINGLOW
Sample 1974:2 2000:2
Observations 105

Mean   -14.59178
Median   -10.98485
Maximum   1.806685
Minimum   -53.62388
Std. Dev.   13.73909
Skewness   -1.166838
Kurtosis   3.603715

Jarque-Bera 25.42102
Probability   0.000003

Swings Low (percent)

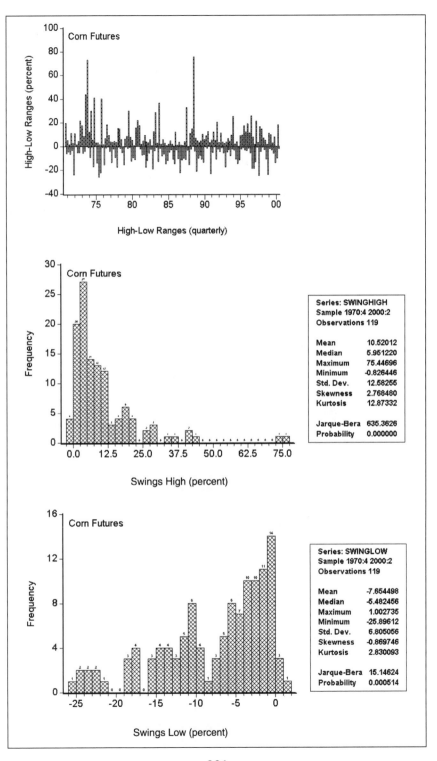

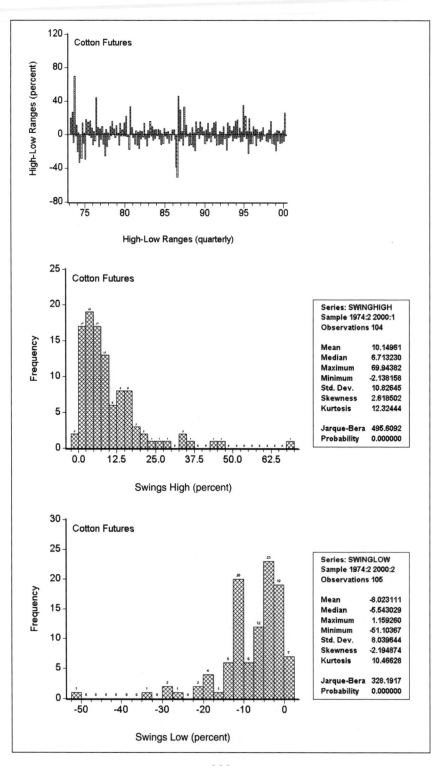

Cotton Futures — High-Low Ranges (percent) vs. High-Low Ranges (quarterly)

Cotton Futures — Frequency vs. Swings High (percent)

Series: SWINGHIGH
Sample 1974:2 2000:1
Observations 104

Mean	10.14961
Median	6.713230
Maximum	69.94382
Minimum	-2.138158
Std. Dev.	10.82645
Skewness	2.618502
Kurtosis	12.32444
Jarque-Bera	495.6092
Probability	0.000000

Cotton Futures — Frequency vs. Swings Low (percent)

Series: SWINGLOW
Sample 1974:2 2000:2
Observations 105

Mean	-8.023111
Median	-5.543029
Maximum	1.159260
Minimum	-51.10367
Std. Dev.	8.039644
Skewness	-2.194874
Kurtosis	10.46628
Jarque-Bera	328.1917
Probability	0.000000

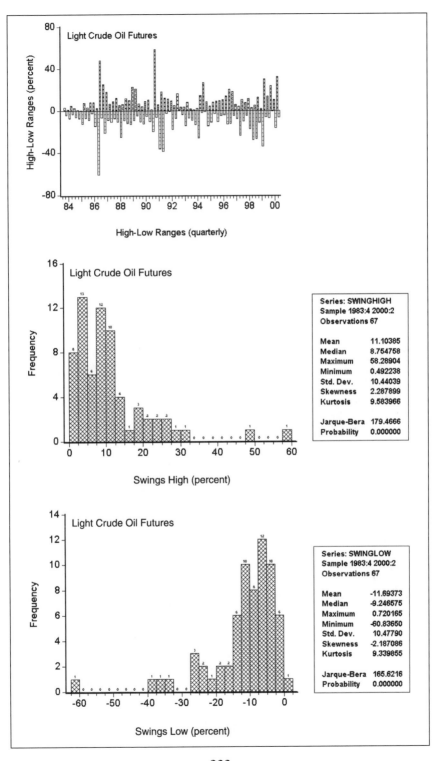

Light Crude Oil Futures

High-Low Ranges (quarterly)

Light Crude Oil Futures

Series: SWINGHIGH
Sample 1983:4 2000:2
Observations 67

Mean	11.10385
Median	8.754758
Maximum	58.28904
Minimum	0.492238
Std. Dev.	10.44039
Skewness	2.287899
Kurtosis	9.583966
Jarque-Bera	179.4666
Probability	0.000000

Swings High (percent)

Light Crude Oil Futures

Series: SWINGLOW
Sample 1983:4 2000:2
Observations 67

Mean	-11.69373
Median	-9.246575
Maximum	0.720165
Minimum	-60.83650
Std. Dev.	10.47790
Skewness	-2.187086
Kurtosis	9.339855
Jarque-Bera	165.6216
Probability	0.000000

Swings Low (percent)

233

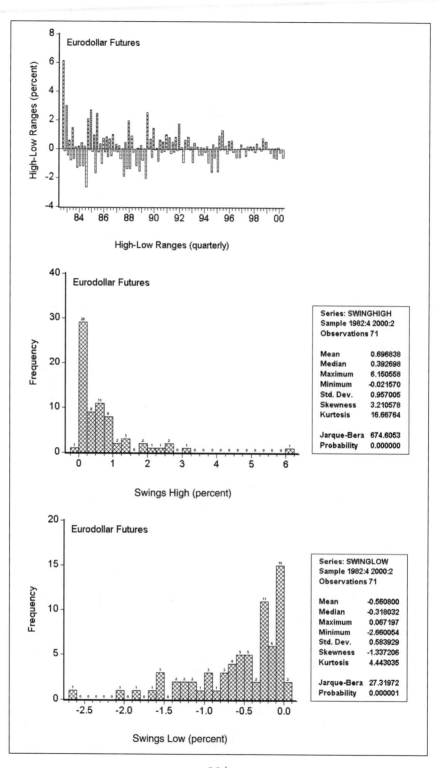

Eurodollar Futures (High-Low Ranges, percent, quarterly)

High-Low Ranges (quarterly)

Eurodollar Futures (Swings High, percent)

Series: SWINGHIGH
Sample 1982:4 2000:2
Observations 71

Mean	0.696838
Median	0.392698
Maximum	6.150558
Minimum	-0.021570
Std. Dev.	0.957005
Skewness	3.210578
Kurtosis	16.66764
Jarque-Bera	674.6053
Probability	0.000000

Swings High (percent)

Eurodollar Futures (Swings Low, percent)

Series: SWINGLOW
Sample 1982:4 2000:2
Observations 71

Mean	-0.560800
Median	-0.318032
Maximum	0.067197
Minimum	-2.660054
Std. Dev.	0.583929
Skewness	-1.337206
Kurtosis	4.443035
Jarque-Bera	27.31972
Probability	0.000001

Swings Low (percent)

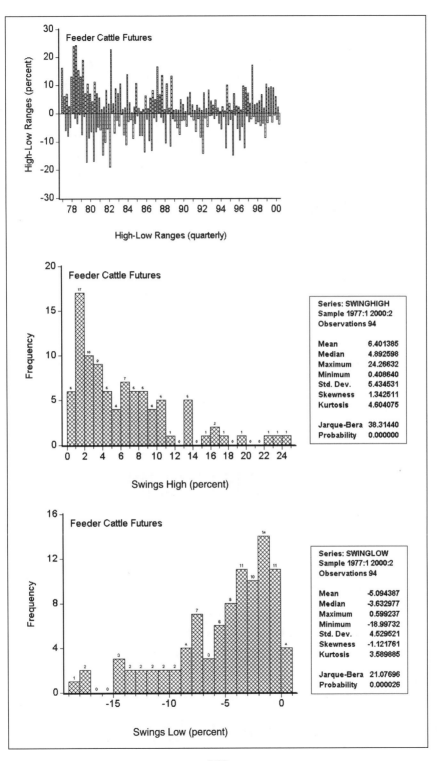

Feeder Cattle Futures

High-Low Ranges (quarterly)

Feeder Cattle Futures

Series: SWINGHIGH
Sample 1977:1 2000:2
Observations 94

Mean	6.401385
Median	4.892598
Maximum	24.26632
Minimum	0.408640
Std. Dev.	5.434531
Skewness	1.342511
Kurtosis	4.604075
Jarque-Bera	38.31440
Probability	0.000000

Swings High (percent)

Feeder Cattle Futures

Series: SWINGLOW
Sample 1977:1 2000:2
Observations 94

Mean	-5.094387
Median	-3.632977
Maximum	0.599237
Minimum	-18.99732
Std. Dev.	4.529521
Skewness	-1.121761
Kurtosis	3.589885
Jarque-Bera	21.07696
Probability	0.000026

Swings Low (percent)

235

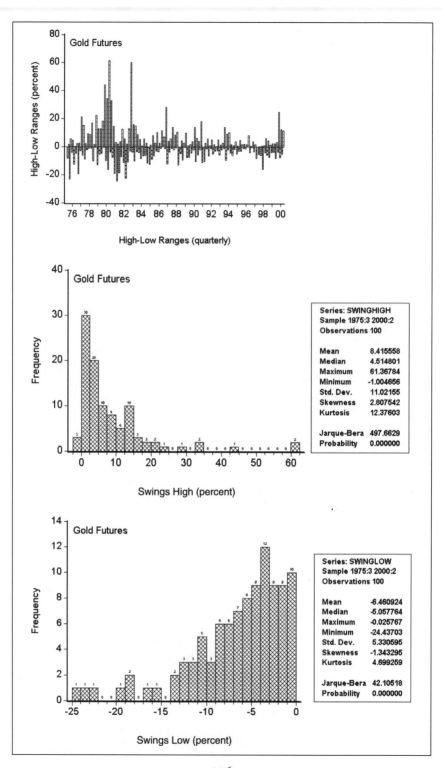

Gold Futures — High-Low Ranges (percent), High-Low Ranges (quarterly)

Gold Futures — Frequency vs Swings High (percent)

Series: SWINGHIGH
Sample 1975:3 2000:2
Observations 100

Mean	8.415558
Median	4.514801
Maximum	61.36784
Minimum	-1.004656
Std. Dev.	11.02155
Skewness	2.807542
Kurtosis	12.37603
Jarque-Bera	497.6629
Probability	0.000000

Gold Futures — Frequency vs Swings Low (percent)

Series: SWINGLOW
Sample 1975:3 2000:2
Observations 100

Mean	-6.460924
Median	-5.057764
Maximum	-0.025767
Minimum	-24.43703
Std. Dev.	5.330595
Skewness	-1.343295
Kurtosis	4.699259
Jarque-Bera	42.10518
Probability	0.000000

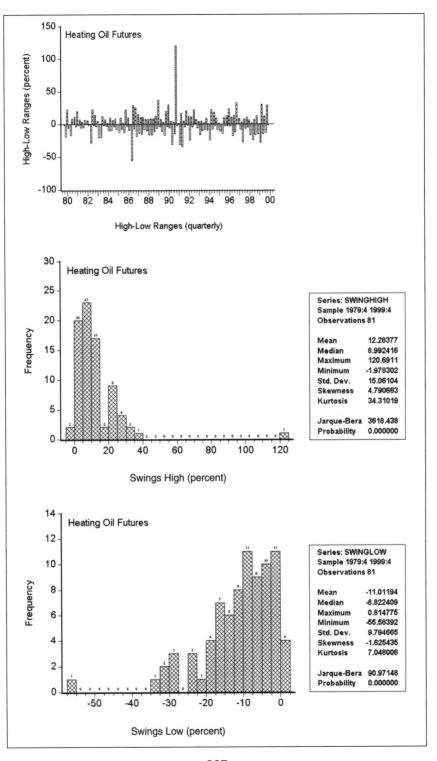

Heating Oil Futures

High-Low Ranges (quarterly)

Heating Oil Futures

Series: SWINGHIGH	
Sample 1979:4 1999:4	
Observations 81	
Mean	12.28377
Median	8.992416
Maximum	120.6911
Minimum	-1.978302
Std. Dev.	15.06104
Skewness	4.790663
Kurtosis	34.31019
Jarque-Bera	3618.438
Probability	0.000000

Swings High (percent)

Heating Oil Futures

Series: SWINGLOW	
Sample 1979:4 1999:4	
Observations 81	
Mean	-11.01194
Median	-8.822409
Maximum	0.814775
Minimum	-55.58392
Std. Dev.	9.794665
Skewness	-1.625435
Kurtosis	7.048006
Jarque-Bera	90.97148
Probability	0.000000

Swings Low (percent)

237

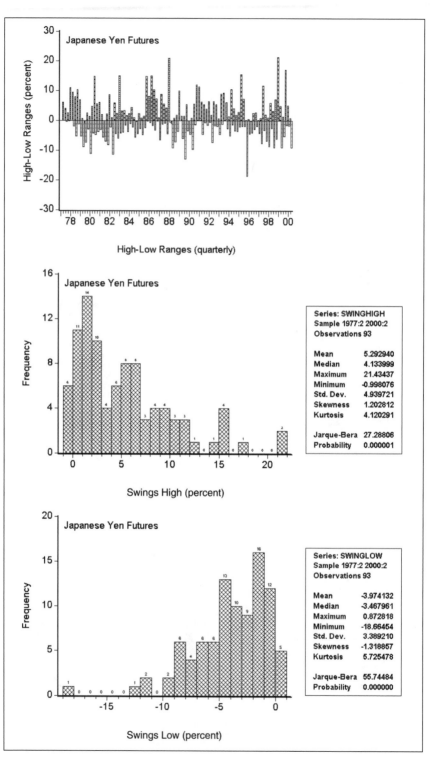

Japanese Yen Futures

High-Low Ranges (quarterly)

Japanese Yen Futures

Swings High (percent)

Series: SWINGHIGH	
Sample 1977:2 2000:2	
Observations 93	
Mean	5.292940
Median	4.133999
Maximum	21.43437
Minimum	-0.998076
Std. Dev.	4.939721
Skewness	1.202812
Kurtosis	4.120291
Jarque-Bera	27.28806
Probability	0.000001

Japanese Yen Futures

Swings Low (percent)

Series: SWINGLOW	
Sample 1977:2 2000:2	
Observations 93	
Mean	-3.974132
Median	-3.467961
Maximum	0.872818
Minimum	-18.66454
Std. Dev.	3.389210
Skewness	-1.318857
Kurtosis	5.725478
Jarque-Bera	55.74484
Probability	0.000000

238

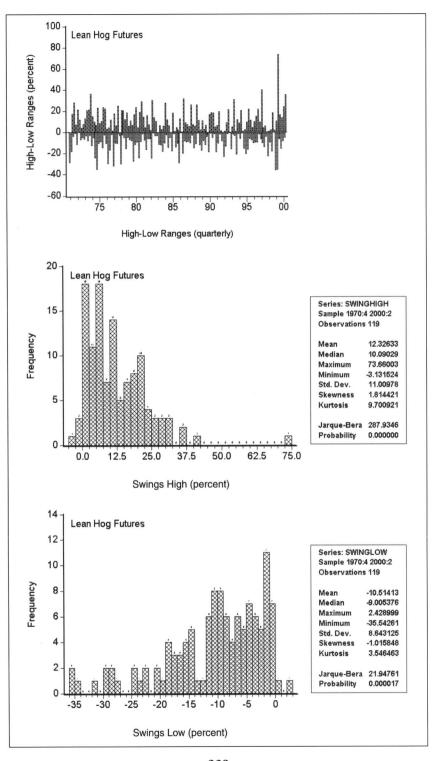

High-Low Ranges (quarterly)

Swings High (percent)

Series: SWINGHIGH
Sample 1970:4 2000:2
Observations 119

Mean	12.32633
Median	10.09029
Maximum	73.66003
Minimum	-3.131524
Std. Dev.	11.00978
Skewness	1.814421
Kurtosis	9.700921
Jarque-Bera	287.9346
Probability	0.000000

Swings Low (percent)

Series: SWINGLOW
Sample 1970:4 2000:2
Observations 119

Mean	-10.51413
Median	-9.005376
Maximum	2.428999
Minimum	-35.54261
Std. Dev.	8.643125
Skewness	-1.015848
Kurtosis	3.546463
Jarque-Bera	21.94761
Probability	0.000017

239

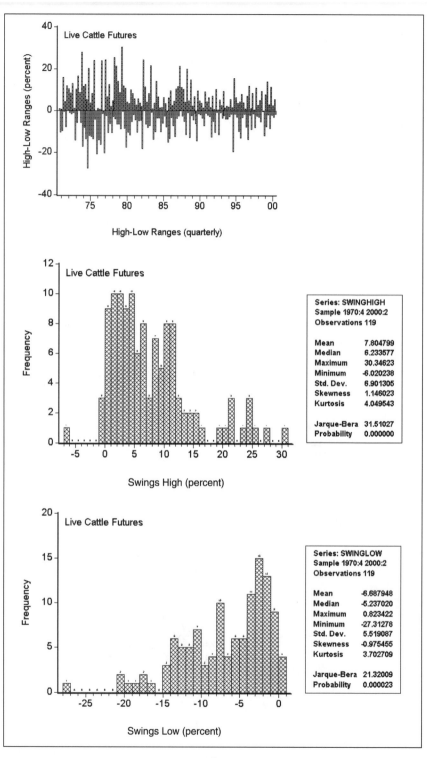

Live Cattle Futures

High-Low Ranges (quarterly)

Live Cattle Futures

Swings High (percent)

Series: SWINGHIGH
Sample 1970:4 2000:2
Observations 119

Mean	7.804799
Median	6.233577
Maximum	30.34623
Minimum	-6.020238
Std. Dev.	6.901305
Skewness	1.146023
Kurtosis	4.049543
Jarque-Bera	31.51027
Probability	0.000000

Live Cattle Futures

Swings Low (percent)

Series: SWINGLOW
Sample 1970:4 2000:2
Observations 119

Mean	-6.687948
Median	-5.237020
Maximum	0.823422
Minimum	-27.31278
Std. Dev.	5.519087
Skewness	-0.975455
Kurtosis	3.702709
Jarque-Bera	21.32009
Probability	0.000023

240

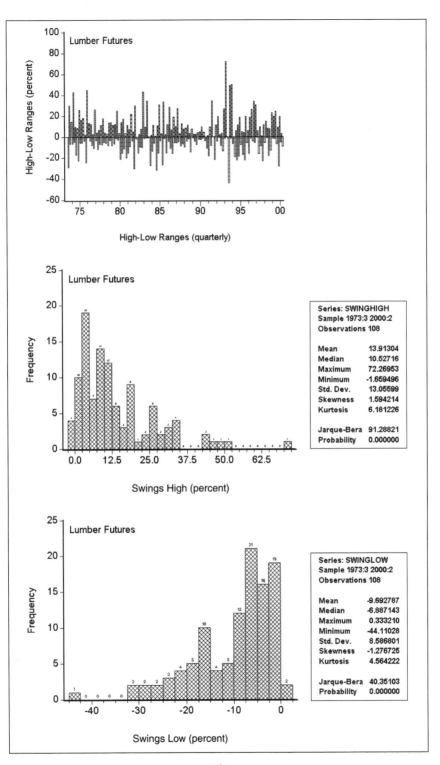

241

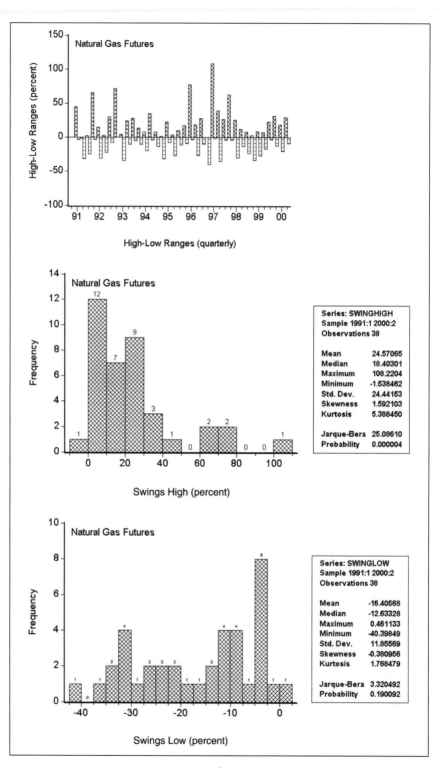

Natural Gas Futures — High-Low Ranges (percent), plotted quarterly from 91 to 00.

High-Low Ranges (quarterly)

Natural Gas Futures — Frequency vs Swings High (percent)

Series: SWINGHIGH
Sample 1991:1 2000:2
Observations 38

Mean   24.57065
Median   18.40301
Maximum   108.2204
Minimum   -1.538462
Std. Dev.   24.44153
Skewness   1.592103
Kurtosis   5.388450

Jarque-Bera 25.08610
Probability 0.000004

Swings High (percent)

Natural Gas Futures — Frequency vs Swings Low (percent)

Series: SWINGLOW
Sample 1991:1 2000:2
Observations 38

Mean   -16.40568
Median   -12.63328
Maximum   0.461133
Minimum   -40.39849
Std. Dev.   11.85569
Skewness   -0.380956
Kurtosis   1.768479

Jarque-Bera 3.320492
Probability 0.190092

Swings Low (percent)

242

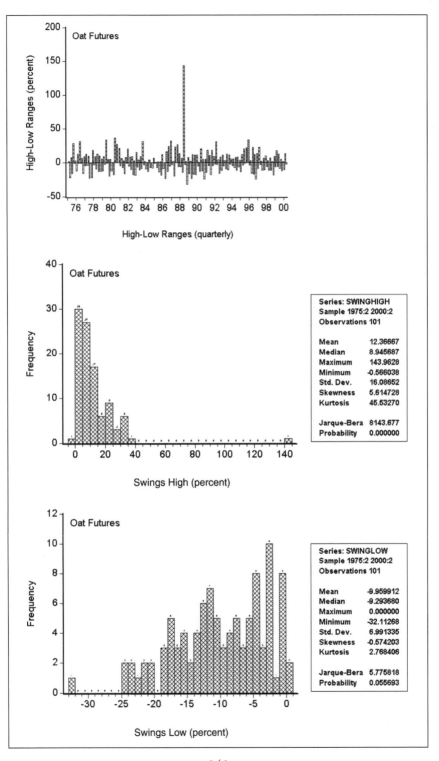

Oat Futures — High-Low Ranges (percent), High-Low Ranges (quarterly)

Oat Futures — Swings High (percent)

Series: SWINGHIGH
Sample 1975:2 2000:2
Observations 101

Mean	12.36667
Median	8.945687
Maximum	143.9628
Minimum	-0.566038
Std. Dev.	16.08652
Skewness	5.614728
Kurtosis	45.53270
Jarque-Bera	8143.677
Probability	0.000000

Oat Futures — Swings Low (percent)

Series: SWINGLOW
Sample 1975:2 2000:2
Observations 101

Mean	-9.959912
Median	-9.293680
Maximum	0.000000
Minimum	-32.11268
Std. Dev.	6.991335
Skewness	-0.574203
Kurtosis	2.768406
Jarque-Bera	5.775818
Probability	0.055693

243

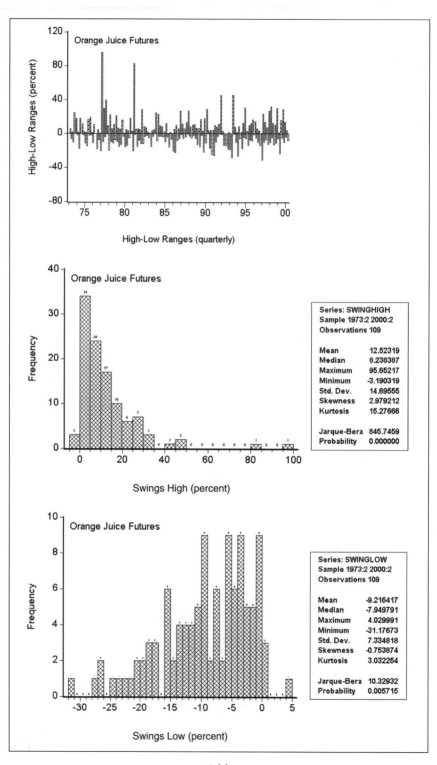

High-Low Ranges (quarterly)

Swings High (percent)

Series: SWINGHIGH
Sample 1973:2 2000:2
Observations 109

Mean	12.52319
Median	8.238387
Maximum	95.65217
Minimum	-3.190319
Std. Dev.	14.69555
Skewness	2.979212
Kurtosis	15.27666
Jarque-Bera	845.7459
Probability	0.000000

Swings Low (percent)

Series: SWINGLOW
Sample 1973:2 2000:2
Observations 109

Mean	-9.216417
Median	-7.949791
Maximum	4.029991
Minimum	-31.17673
Std. Dev.	7.334818
Skewness	-0.753874
Kurtosis	3.032254
Jarque-Bera	10.32932
Probability	0.005715

244

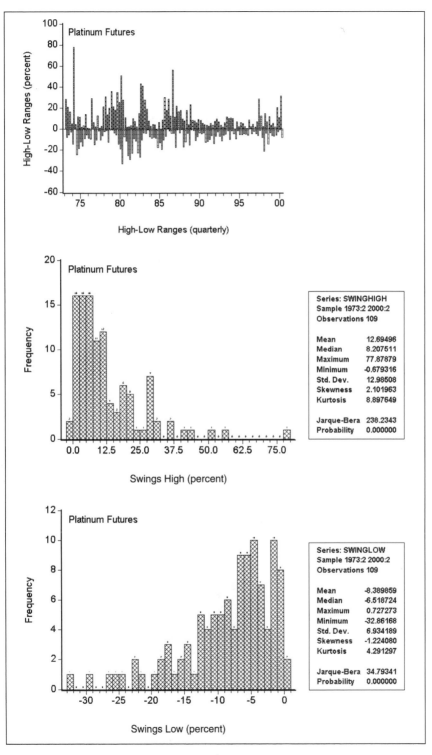

Platinum Futures — High-Low Ranges (quarterly)

Platinum Futures — Swings High (percent)

Series: SWINGHIGH
Sample 1973:2 2000:2
Observations 109

Mean	12.69496
Median	8.207511
Maximum	77.87879
Minimum	-0.679316
Std. Dev.	12.98508
Skewness	2.101963
Kurtosis	8.897649
Jarque-Bera	238.2343
Probability	0.000000

Platinum Futures — Swings Low (percent)

Series: SWINGLOW
Sample 1973:2 2000:2
Observations 109

Mean	-8.389859
Median	-6.518724
Maximum	0.727273
Minimum	-32.86168
Std. Dev.	6.934189
Skewness	-1.224080
Kurtosis	4.291297
Jarque-Bera	34.79341
Probability	0.000000

245

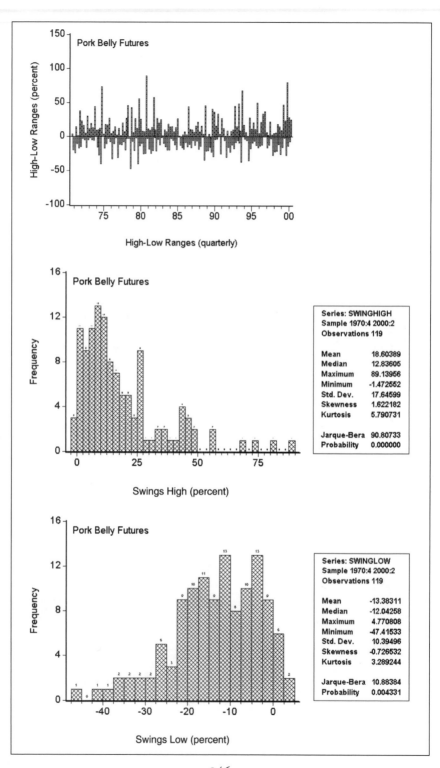

Pork Belly Futures — High-Low Ranges (percent) vs High-Low Ranges (quarterly)

Pork Belly Futures — Frequency vs Swings High (percent)

Series: SWINGHIGH
Sample 1970:4 2000:2
Observations 119

Mean	18.60389
Median	12.83605
Maximum	89.13956
Minimum	-1.472552
Std. Dev.	17.64599
Skewness	1.622182
Kurtosis	5.790731
Jarque-Bera	90.80733
Probability	0.000000

Pork Belly Futures — Frequency vs Swings Low (percent)

Series: SWINGLOW
Sample 1970:4 2000:2
Observations 119

Mean	-13.38311
Median	-12.04258
Maximum	4.770808
Minimum	-47.41533
Std. Dev.	10.39496
Skewness	-0.726532
Kurtosis	3.289244
Jarque-Bera	10.88384
Probability	0.004331

246

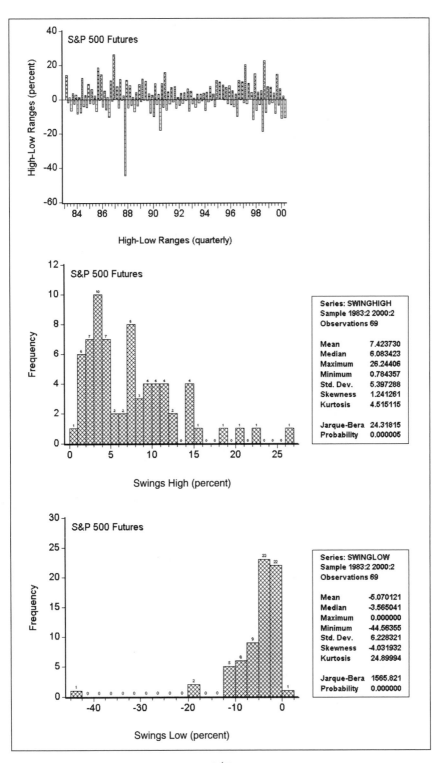

S&P 500 Futures

High-Low Ranges (quarterly)

S&P 500 Futures

Swings High (percent)

Series: SWINGHIGH
Sample 1983:2 2000:2
Observations 69

Mean	7.423730
Median	6.083423
Maximum	26.24406
Minimum	0.784357
Std. Dev.	5.397288
Skewness	1.241261
Kurtosis	4.515115
Jarque-Bera	24.31815
Probability	0.000005

S&P 500 Futures

Swings Low (percent)

Series: SWINGLOW
Sample 1983:2 2000:2
Observations 69

Mean	-5.070121
Median	-3.565041
Maximum	0.000000
Minimum	-44.56355
Std. Dev.	6.228321
Skewness	-4.031932
Kurtosis	24.89994
Jarque-Bera	1565.821
Probability	0.000000

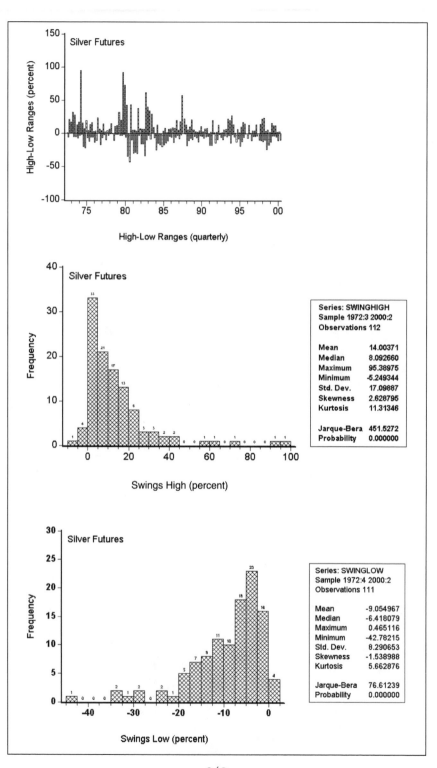

Silver Futures

High-Low Ranges (quarterly)

Silver Futures

Swings High (percent)

Series: SWINGHIGH
Sample 1972:3 2000:2
Observations 112

Mean	14.00371
Median	8.092660
Maximum	95.38975
Minimum	-5.249344
Std. Dev.	17.09887
Skewness	2.628795
Kurtosis	11.31346
Jarque-Bera	451.5272
Probability	0.000000

Silver Futures

Swings Low (percent)

Series: SWINGLOW
Sample 1972:4 2000:2
Observations 111

Mean	-9.054967
Median	-6.418079
Maximum	0.465116
Minimum	-42.78215
Std. Dev.	8.290653
Skewness	-1.538988
Kurtosis	5.662876
Jarque-Bera	76.61239
Probability	0.000000

248

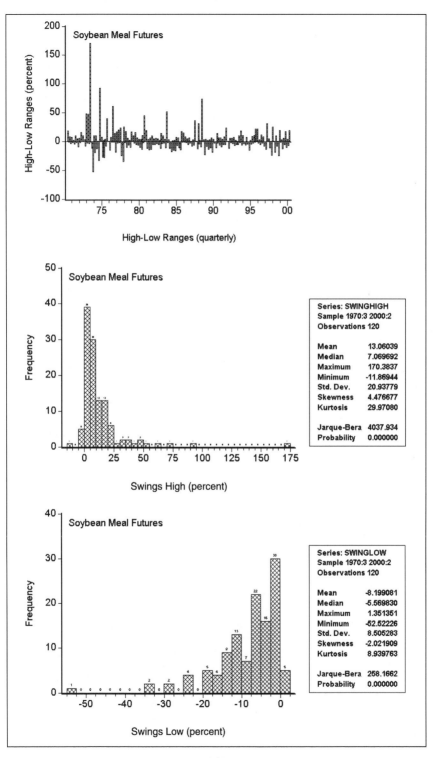

Soybean Meal Futures

High-Low Ranges (percent)

High-Low Ranges (quarterly)

Soybean Meal Futures

Frequency

Swings High (percent)

Series: SWINGHIGH	
Sample 1970:3 2000:2	
Observations 120	
Mean	13.06039
Median	7.069692
Maximum	170.3837
Minimum	-11.86944
Std. Dev.	20.93779
Skewness	4.476677
Kurtosis	29.97080
Jarque-Bera	4037.934
Probability	0.000000

Soybean Meal Futures

Frequency

Swings Low (percent)

Series: SWINGLOW	
Sample 1970:3 2000:2	
Observations 120	
Mean	-8.199081
Median	-5.569830
Maximum	1.351351
Minimum	-52.52226
Std. Dev.	8.505283
Skewness	-2.021909
Kurtosis	8.939763
Jarque-Bera	258.1662
Probability	0.000000

249

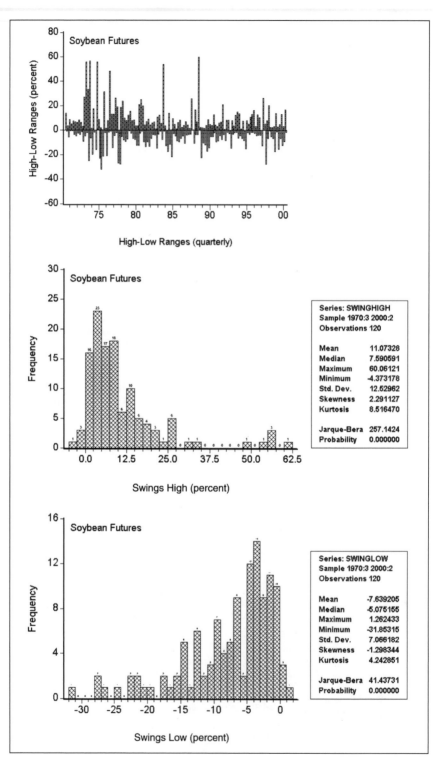

Soybean Futures

High-Low Ranges (percent)

High-Low Ranges (quarterly)

Soybean Futures

Frequency

Swings High (percent)

Series: SWINGHIGH	
Sample 1970:3 2000:2	
Observations 120	
Mean	11.07328
Median	7.590591
Maximum	60.06121
Minimum	-4.373178
Std. Dev.	12.52962
Skewness	2.291127
Kurtosis	8.516470
Jarque-Bera	257.1424
Probability	0.000000

Soybean Futures

Frequency

Swings Low (percent)

Series: SWINGLOW	
Sample 1970:3 2000:2	
Observations 120	
Mean	-7.639205
Median	-5.075155
Maximum	1.262433
Minimum	-31.85315
Std. Dev.	7.066182
Skewness	-1.298344
Kurtosis	4.242851
Jarque-Bera	41.43731
Probability	0.000000

250

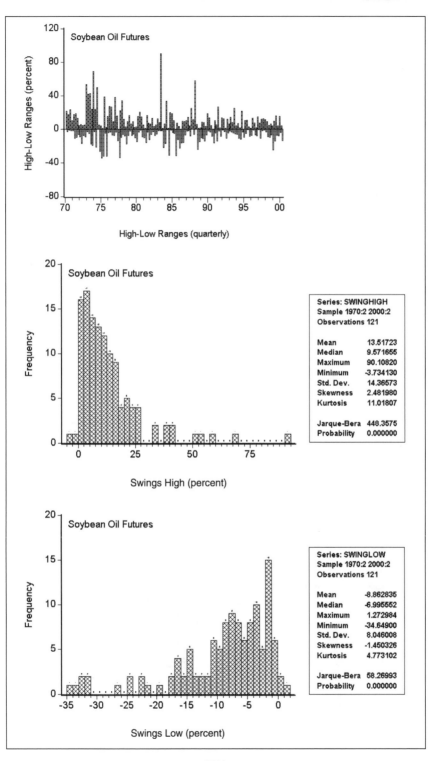

Soybean Oil Futures

High-Low Ranges (quarterly)

Soybean Oil Futures

Swings High (percent)

Series: SWINGHIGH	
Sample 1970:2 2000:2	
Observations 121	
Mean	13.51723
Median	9.571655
Maximum	90.10820
Minimum	-3.734130
Std. Dev.	14.36573
Skewness	2.481980
Kurtosis	11.01807
Jarque-Bera	448.3575
Probability	0.000000

Soybean Oil Futures

Swings Low (percent)

Series: SWINGLOW	
Sample 1970:2 2000:2	
Observations 121	
Mean	-8.862835
Median	-6.995552
Maximum	1.272984
Minimum	-34.64900
Std. Dev.	8.046008
Skewness	-1.450326
Kurtosis	4.773102
Jarque-Bera	58.26993
Probability	0.000000

251

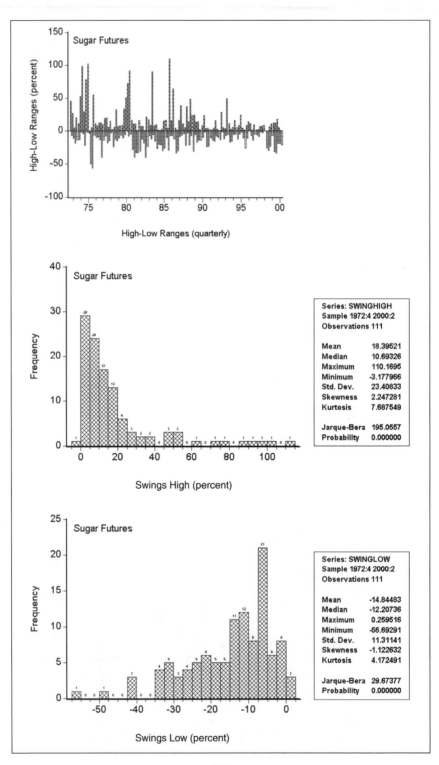

Sugar Futures

High-Low Ranges (quarterly)

Sugar Futures

Series: SWINGHIGH
Sample 1972:4 2000:2
Observations 111

Mean	18.39521
Median	10.69326
Maximum	110.1695
Minimum	-3.177966
Std. Dev.	23.40833
Skewness	2.247281
Kurtosis	7.687549
Jarque-Bera	195.0557
Probability	0.000000

Swings High (percent)

Sugar Futures

Series: SWINGLOW
Sample 1972:4 2000:2
Observations 111

Mean	-14.84483
Median	-12.20736
Maximum	0.259516
Minimum	-56.69291
Std. Dev.	11.31141
Skewness	-1.122632
Kurtosis	4.172491
Jarque-Bera	29.67377
Probability	0.000000

Swings Low (percent)

252

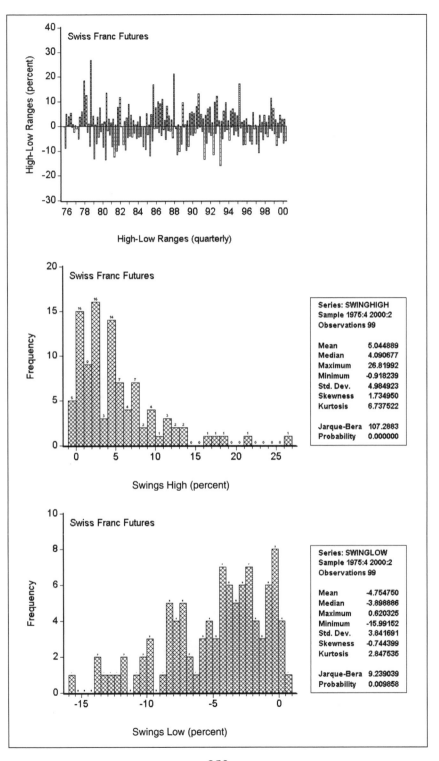

Swiss Franc Futures

High-Low Ranges (quarterly)

Swiss Franc Futures

Swings High (percent)

Series: SWINGHIGH
Sample 1975:4 2000:2
Observations 99

Mean	5.044889
Median	4.090677
Maximum	26.81992
Minimum	-0.918239
Std. Dev.	4.984923
Skewness	1.734950
Kurtosis	6.737522
Jarque-Bera	107.2883
Probability	0.000000

Swiss Franc Futures

Swings Low (percent)

Series: SWINGLOW
Sample 1975:4 2000:2
Observations 99

Mean	-4.754750
Median	-3.898886
Maximum	0.620325
Minimum	-15.99152
Std. Dev.	3.841691
Skewness	-0.744399
Kurtosis	2.847535
Jarque-Bera	9.239039
Probability	0.009858

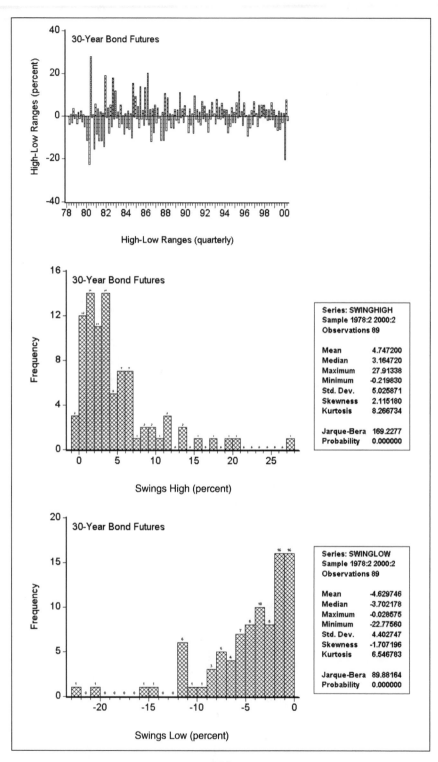

High-Low Ranges (quarterly)

Swings High (percent)

Swings Low (percent)

254

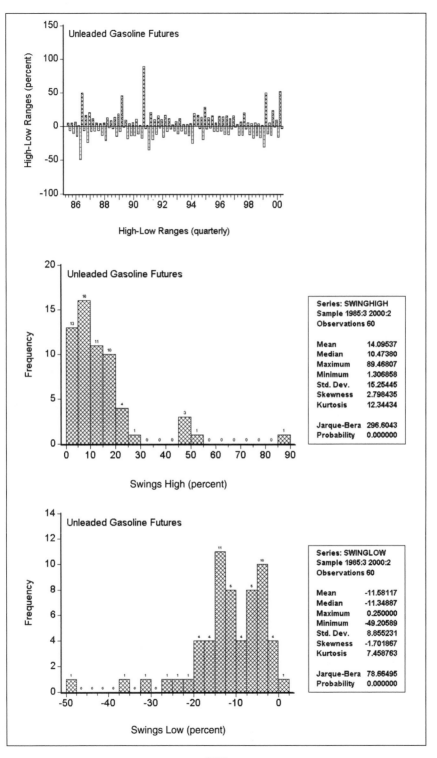

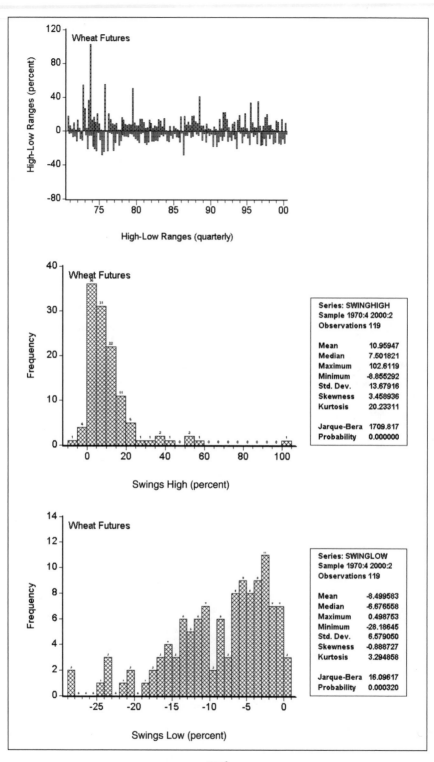

Wheat Futures

High-Low Ranges (percent)

High-Low Ranges (quarterly)

Wheat Futures

Series: SWINGHIGH
Sample 1970:4 2000:2
Observations 119

Mean	10.95947
Median	7.501821
Maximum	102.6119
Minimum	-8.855292
Std. Dev.	13.67916
Skewness	3.458936
Kurtosis	20.23311
Jarque-Bera	1709.817
Probability	0.000000

Swings High (percent)

Wheat Futures

Series: SWINGLOW
Sample 1970:4 2000:2
Observations 119

Mean	-8.499583
Median	-6.676558
Maximum	0.498753
Minimum	-28.18645
Std. Dev.	6.579050
Skewness	-0.888727
Kurtosis	3.294858
Jarque-Bera	16.09617
Probability	0.000320

Swings Low (percent)

256

Appendix D

SELECT FUTURES AND OPTION CONTRACT SPECIFICATIONS

Contract specifications are current as of March 10, 2001, and are subject to change. Verify any information herein with your broker before trading. Additional information can be obtained at the major exchanges. Please note that the daily price limits for futures are combined with those for options in the entry with the heading "Daily Price Limits."

Futures Contract—Soybeans

TRADING UNIT.   5,000 bushels.

TICK SIZE.   ¼ cent/bushel ($12.50/contract).

CONTRACT MONTHS.   September, November, January, March, May, July, August.

LAST TRADING DAY.   The business day prior to the 15th calendar day of the contract month.

TICKER SYMBOLS.   Open outcry: S; electronic: ES.

Option Contract—Soybeans

TRADING UNIT.   One CBOT soybean futures contract (of a specified contract month) of 5,000 bushels.

TICK SIZE. ⅛ cent/bushel ($6.25/contract).

CONTRACT MONTHS. September, November, January, March, May, July, August; and a monthly (serial) option contract is listed when the front month is not a standard option contract. The monthly option contract exercises into the nearby futures contract. For instance, an October option would exercise into a November futures position.

LAST TRADING DAY. The Friday preceding by at least two business days the last business day of the month preceding the option contract month.

TICKER SYMBOLS. Open outcry: CZ for calls, PZ for puts; electronic: OZS.

DAILY PRICE LIMIT. 50 cents/bushel ($2,500/contract) above or below the previous days settlement premium. Limits are lifted on the last trading day.

Source: Chicago Board of Trade.

Futures Contract—Live Cattle

TRADING UNIT. 40,000 pounds of 55 percent choice, 45 percent select-grade live steers.

TICK SIZE. 0.00025 = $10.00.

CONTRACT MONTHS. February, April, June, August, October, December, and seven months in the February bimonthly cycle.

LAST TRADING DAY. The last business day of the contract month.

TICKER SYMBOL. LC.

Option Contract—Live Cattle

TRADING UNIT. One live cattle futures contract.

TICK SIZE. 0.00025 = $10.00.

CONTRACT MONTHS. February, April, June, August, October, December, and serial months. There are six months in February bimonthly cycle and one serial month.

LAST TRADING DAY. Options trading shall terminate on the first Friday of the contract month. If that Friday is not a business day, then trading shall terminate on the immediately preceding business day.

TICKER SYMBOLS. Calls = CK, puts = PK.

DAILY PRICE LIMIT. N/A.

    Source: Chicago Mercantile Exchange.

Futures Contract—30-Year U.S. Treasury Bonds

TRADING UNIT. One U.S. Treasury bond with a face value at maturity of $100,000 or a multiple thereof.

TICK SIZE. $\frac{1}{32}$ of a point ($31.25/contract); par is on the basis of 100 points.

CONTRACT MONTHS. March, June, September, December.

LAST TRADING DAY. Seventh business day preceding the last business day of the delivery month.

TICKER SYMBOLS. Open outcry: US; electronic: ZB.

Option Contract—30-Year U.S. Treasury Bonds

TRADING UNIT. One U.S. Treasury bond futures contract (of a specified delivery month) having a face value at maturity of $100,000 or a multiple thereof.

TICK SIZE. $\frac{1}{64}$ of a point ($15.625/contract) rounded up to the nearest cent/contract.

CONTRACT MONTHS. The first three consecutive contract months (two serial expirations and one quarterly expiration) plus the next two months in the quarterly cycle (March, June,

September, December). There will always be five months available for trading. Monthlies will exercise into the first nearby quarterly futures contract. Quarterlies will exercise into futures contracts of the same delivery period.

LAST TRADING DAY. Options cease trading in the month prior to the delivery month of the underlying futures contract. Options cease trading at the same time as the underlying futures contract on the last Friday preceding by at least two business days the last business day of the month preceding the option contract month.

TICKER SYMBOLS. Open outcry: CG for calls, PG for puts; electronic: OZB.

DAILY PRICE LIMIT. None.

Source: Chicago Board of Trade.

Futures Contract—Dow Jones Industrial Average^{SM} Futures

TRADING UNIT. $10 times the Dow Jones Industrial Average^{SM} Index. The DJIA is a price-weighted index of 30 of the largest, most liquid U.S. stocks.

TICK SIZE. 1 point ($10).

CONTRACT MONTHS. March, June, September, December.

LAST TRADING DAY. The trading day preceding the final settlement day.

TICKER SYMBOLS. Open outcry: DJ; electronic: ZD.

Option Contract—Dow Jones Industrial Average^{SM}

TRADING UNIT. One Dow Jones Industrial Average^{SM} futures contract.

TICK SIZE. 0.5 ($5).

CONTRACT MONTHS. The front month of the current quarter plus the next three contracts of the quarterly cycle (March,

June, September, December). Additionally, serial-month options will be added such that four consecutive contract months will be listed.

LAST TRADING DAY. For quarterly expirations, the trading day preceding the final settlement day for the underlying futures contract. For serial expirations, the third Friday of the option contract month.

TICKER SYMBOLS. Open outcry: DJC for calls, DJP for puts; electronic: OZD.

DAILY PRICE LIMIT. Successive 10, 20, and 30 percent price limits based on the average daily close of the cash index in the last month of the preceding quarter. Price limits are effective only for limit moves below the previous day's close. If trading in CBOT DJIA^{SM} futures halts, options will also cease trading. Daytime price limits are coordinated with NYSE circuit breakers. All price limits are recomputed at the beginning of every quarter.

  Source: Chicago Board of Trade.

Futures Contract—S&P 500 Futures

TRADING UNIT. $250 times S&P 500 stock index.

TICK SIZE. 0.10 (10 pts) ($2.50/pt) (0.10 = $25.00).

CONTRACT MONTHS. March, June, September, December.

LAST TRADING DAY. N/A.

TICKER SYMBOL. SP/SP.

Option Contract—S&P 500 Futures

TRADING UNIT. One S&P 500 stock price index futures contract.

TICK SIZE. 0.1 = $25.00.

CONTRACT MONTHS. Four months in the March quarterly cycle and two months not in the March cycle (serial months). March, June, September, December.

LAST TRADING DAY. *Quarterly:* the business day immediately preceding the day of determination of the final settlement price (normally, the Thursday prior to the third Friday of the contract month). *Serial:* the third Friday of the contract month.

TICKER SYMBOLS. Clearing = SP; Ticker = OS.

DAILY PRICE LIMIT. Option trading is halted when the lead S&P futures lock limit.

    Source: Chicago Mercantile Exchange.

Futures Contract—Wheat

TRADING UNIT. 5,000 bushels.

TICK SIZE. ¼ cent/bushel ($12.50/contract).

CONTRACT MONTHS. July, September, December, March, May.

LAST TRADING DAY. The business day prior to the 15th calendar day of the contract month.

TICKER SYMBOLS. Open outcry: W; electronic: ZW.

Option Contract—Wheat

TRADING UNIT. One wheat futures contract (of a specified contract month) of 5,000 bushels.

TICK SIZE. ⅛ cent/bushel ($6.25/contract).

CONTRACT MONTHS. July, September, December, March, May; a monthly (serial) option contract is listed when the front month is not a standard option contract. The monthly option contract exercises into the nearby futures contract. For example, an August option exercises into a September futures position.

LAST TRADING DAY. The Friday preceding by at least two business days the last business day of the month preceding the option contract month.

TICKER SYMBOLS. Open outcry: WY for calls/WZ for puts; electronic: OZW.

DAILY PRICE LIMIT. 30 cents/bushel ($1,500/contract) above or below the previous day's settlement premium. Limits are lifted on the last trading day.

Source: Chicago Board of Trade.

Futures Contract—Corn Futures

TRADING UNIT. 5,000 bushels.

TICK SIZE. ¼ cent/bushel ($12.50/contract).

CONTRACT MONTHS. November, December, January, March, May, July, September.

LAST TRADING DAY. The business day prior to the 15th calendar day of the contract month.

TICKER SYMBOLS. Open outcry: C; electronic: ZC.

Option Contract—Corn

TRADING UNIT. One corn futures contract (of a specified contract month) of 5,000 bushels.

TICK SIZE. ⅛ cent/bu ($6.25/contract).

CONTRACT MONTHS. November, December, January, March, May, July, September; a monthly (serial) option contract is listed when the front month is not a standard option contract. The monthly option contract exercises into the nearby futures contract. For example, an August option exercises into a September futures position.

LAST TRADING DAY. The Friday preceding by at least two business days the last business day of the month preceding the option contract month.

TICKER SYMBOLS. Open outcry: CY for calls, PY for puts; electronic: OZC.

DAILY PRICE LIMIT. 20 cents/bushel ($1,000/contract) above or below the previous day's settlement premium. Limits are lifted on the last trading day.

Source: Chicago Board of Trade.

Futures Contract—Silver

TRADING UNIT. 5,000 troy ounces.

TICK SIZE. Price changes for outright transactions are in multiples of one-half cent (0.5¢ or $0.005) per troy ounce, equivalent to $25 per contract. For straddle or spread transactions, as well as the determination of settlement prices, the price changes are registered in multiples of one-tenth of a cent (0.10¢ or $0.001) per troy ounce, equivalent to $5 per contract. A fluctuation of one cent (1¢ or $0.01) is equivalent to $50 per contract.

CONTRACT MONTHS. Trading is conducted for delivery during the current calendar month, the next two calendar months, any January, March, May, and September thereafter falling within a 23-month period, and any July and December falling within a 60-month period beginning with the current month.

LAST TRADING DAY. Terminates at the close of business on the third last business day of the maturing delivery month.

TICKER SYMBOL. SI.

Option Contract—Silver

TRADING UNIT. One COMEX Division silver futures contract.

TICK SIZE. Price changes for outright transactions, including EFPs, are in multiples of one-half cent (0.5¢ or $0.005) per troy ounce, equivalent to $25 per contract. For straddle or spread transactions, as well as the determination of settlement prices, the price changes are registered in multiples of one-tenth of a cent (0.10¢ or $0.001) per troy ounce, equivalent to $5 per contract. A fluctuation of one cent (1¢ or $0.01) is equivalent to $50 per contract.

CONTRACT MONTHS. The nearest five of the following contract months: March, May, July, September, and December. Additional contract months—January, February, April, June, August, October, and November—will be listed for trading for a period of two months. A 24-month option is added on a July-December cycle.

LAST TRADING DAY. Expires on the second Friday of the month prior to the delivery month of the underlying futures contract.

DAILY PRICE LIMITS. *Futures:* Initial price limit, based upon the preceding day's settlement price, is $1.50. Two minutes after either of the two most active months trades at the limit, trades in all months of futures and options will cease for a 15-minute period. Trading will also cease if either of the two active months is bid at the upper limit or offered at the lower limit for two minutes without trading. Trading will not cease if the limit is reached during the final 20 minutes of a day's trading. If the limit is reached during the final half hour of trading, trading will resume no later than 10 minutes before the normal closing time. When trading resumes after a cessation of trading, the price limits will be expanded by increments of 100 percent. *Options:* No price limits for options.

TICKER SYMBOL. SO.

Source: New York Mercantile Exchange.

Futures Contract—Oats

TRADING UNIT. 5,000 bushels.

TICK SIZE. ¼ cent/bushel ($12.50/contract).

CONTRACT MONTHS. July, September, November, December, January, March, May.

LAST TRADING DAY. The business day prior to the 15th calendar day of the contract.

TICKER SYMBOLS. Open outcry: O; electronic: ZO.

Option Contract—Oats

TRADING UNIT. One oat futures contract (of a specified contract month) of 5,000 bushels.

TICK SIZE. ⅛ cent/bu ($6.25/contract).

CONTRACT MONTHS. July, September, November, December, January, March, May; a monthly (serial) option contract is listed when the front month is not a standard option contract. This monthly option contract exercises into the nearby futures contract. For example, an August option exercises into a September futures position.

LAST TRADING DAY. The Friday preceding by at least two business days the last business day of the month preceding the option contract month.

TICKER SYMBOLS. Open outcry: OO for calls, OV for puts; electronic: OZO.

DAILY PRICE LIMIT. 20 cents/bushel ($1,000/contract) above or below the previous day's settlement premium. Limits are lifted on the last trading day.

       Source: Chicago Board of Trade.

Futures Contract—Soybean Meal

TRADING UNIT. 100 tons (2,000 lbs/ton).

TICK SIZE. 10 cents/ton ($10/contract).

CONTRACT MONTHS. October, December, January, March, May, July, August, September.

LAST TRADING DAY. The business day prior to the 15th calendar day of the contract month.

TICKER SYMBOLS. Open outcry: SM; electronic: ZM.

Option Contract—Soybean Meal

TRADING UNIT. One soybean meal futures contract (of a specified contract month) of 100 tons.

TICK SIZE. 5 cents/ton ($5/contract).

CONTRACT MONTHS. October, December, January, March, May, July, August, September; a monthly (serial) option contract is listed when the front month is not a standard option contract. The monthly option contract exercises into the nearby futures contract. For example, a February option exercises into a March futures position.

LAST TRADING DAY. The Friday preceding by at least two business days the last business day of the month preceding the option contract month.

TICKER SYMBOLS. Open outcry: MY for calls, MZ for puts; electronic: OZM.

DAILY PRICE LIMIT. $20/ton ($2,000/contract) above or below the previous day's settlement premium. Limits are lifted on the last trading day.

Source: Chicago Board of Trade.

Futures Contract—Soybean Oil

TRADING UNIT. 60,000 lbs.

TICK SIZE. $1/100$ cent ($0.0001)/lb ($6/contract).

CONTRACT MONTHS. October, December, January, March, May, July, August, September.

LAST TRADING DAY.   The business day prior to the 15th calendar day of the contract month.

TICKER SYMBOLS.   Open outcry: BO; electronic: ZL.

Option Contract—Soybean Oil

TRADING UNIT.   One soybean oil futures contract (of a specified contract month) of 60,000 lbs.

TICK SIZE. $5/1000$ cent ($0.00005)/lb ($3/contract).

CONTRACT MONTHS.   October, December, January, March, May, July, August, September; and a monthly (serial) option contract is listed when the front-month contract is not a standard option contract. The monthly option contract exercises into the nearby futures contract. For instance, a November option would exercise into a December futures position.

LAST TRADING DAY.   The Friday preceding by at least two business days the last business day of the month preceding the option contract month.

TICKER SYMBOLS.   Open outcry: OY for calls, OZ for puts; electronic: OZL.

DAILY PRICE LIMIT.   2 cent/lb ($1,200/contract) above or below the previous day's settlement premium. Limits are lifted on the last trading day.

> **Source:**   Chicago Board of Trade.

Futures Contract—Cocoa

TRADING UNIT.   10 metric tons (22,046 lb).

TICK SIZE. $1.00/metric ton, equivalent to $10.00 per contract and approximately $5/100$ cent/lb.

CONTRACT MONTHS.   March, May, July, September, December.

LAST TRADING DAY. One business day prior to last notice day, which is 10 business days prior to last business day of delivery month.

TICKER SYMBOL. CC.

Option Contract—Cocoa

TRADING UNIT. One cocoa futures contract.

TICK SIZE. $1.00/metric ton, equivalent to $10.00 per contract.

CONTRACT MONTHS. "Regular options": March, May, July, September, December; "serial options": January, February, April, June, August, October, November.

LAST TRADING DAY. First Friday of the month preceding the contract month.

TICKER SYMBOLS. CC.

DAILY PRICE LIMIT. None.

Source: New York Board of Trade.

Futures Contract—Coffee

TRADING UNIT. 37,500 lbs. (approximately 250 bags).

TICK SIZE. $5/100$ cent/lb., equivalent to $18.75 per contract.

CONTRACT MONTHS. March, May, July, September, December.

LAST TRADING DAY. One business day prior to last notice day.

TICKER SYMBOL. KC.

Option Contract—Coffee

TRADING UNIT. One coffee "C" futures contract.

TICK SIZE. $1/100$ cent/lb., equivalent to $3.75 per contract.

CONTRACT MONTHS. "Regular options": March, May, July, September, December; "serial options": January, February, April, June, August, October, November.

LAST TRADING DAY. Second Friday of the calendar month preceding each regular or serial option month; provided, however, that for each option, there will be a minimum of four trading days between the last trading day of the expiring option and the first notice day of the expiring future.

TICKER SYMBOLS. KC.

DAILY PRICE LIMIT. None.

    Source: New York Board of Trade.

Futures Contract—Cotton No. 2

TRADING UNIT. 50,000 lb. net weight (approximately 100 bales).

TICK SIZE. $\frac{1}{100}$ of a cent (one point) per pound below 95 cents per pound. Five one-hundredths of a cent (or five points) per pound at prices of 95 cents per pound or higher. Spreads may always trade and be quoted in one-point increments, regardless of price levels.

CONTRACT MONTHS. Current month plus one or more of the next 23 succeeding months. Active trading months: March, May, July, October, December.

LAST TRADING DAY. Seventeen business days from end of spot month.

TICKER SYMBOL. CT.

Option Contract—Cotton

TRADING UNIT. One New York Cotton Exchange Cotton No. 2 futures contract.

TICK SIZE. $\frac{1}{100}$ of a cent.

CONTRACT MONTHS. March, May, July, October and December. The nearest 10 delivery months will be available for trading. Example: In August 1999, the October 1999, December 1999, March 2000, May 2000, July 2000, October 2000, December 2000, March 2001, May 2001, and July 2001 contracts will be available for trading.

LAST TRADING DAY. The last Friday preceding first notice day for the underlying future by at least five business days.

TICKER SYMBOLS. CT.

DAILY PRICE LIMIT. None.

Source: New York Board of Trade.

Futures Contract—Sugar No. 11

TRADING UNIT. 112,000 lb. (50 Long tons).

TICK SIZE. $1/100$ cent/lb., equivalent to $11.20 per contract.

CONTRACT MONTHS. March, May, July, October. January (commencing with January 2003).

LAST TRADING DAY. Last business day of the month preceding delivery month.

TICKER SYMBOL. SB.

Option Contract—Sugar

TRADING UNIT. One sugar No. 11 futures contract.

TICK SIZE. $1/100$ cent/lb., equivalent to $11.20 per contract.

CONTRACT MONTHS. "Regular options": March, May, July and October plus a January option on March futures; "serial options": February, April, June, August, September, November and December.

LAST TRADING DAY. Second Friday of the month preceding the contract month.

TICKER SYMBOLS. SB.

DAILY PRICE LIMIT. None.

Source: New York Board of Trade.

Futures Contract—Feeder Cattle

TRADING UNIT. 50,000 pounds of 700- to 849-pound medium-frame No. 1 and medium- and large-frame No. 1 feeder steers.

TICK SIZE. 0.00025 = $12.50.

CONTRACT MONTHS. January, March, April, May, August, September, October, and November; eight months listed at a time.

LAST TRADING DAY. Trading shall terminate on the last Thursday of the contract month, except that trading in the November contract shall terminate on the Thursday prior to Thanksgiving Day, unless a holiday falls on that Thursday or on any of the four weekdays prior to that Thursday, in which case trading shall terminate on the prior Thursday that is not a holiday and is not so preceded by a holiday.

TICKER SYMBOL. FC.

Option Contract—Feeder Cattle

TRADING UNIT. One feeder cattle futures contract.

TICK SIZE. 0.000125 = $6.25.

CONTRACT MONTHS. January, March, April, May, August, September, October, November, December, and flex options. Eight option months listed.

LAST TRADING DAY. Trading shall terminate on the last Thursday of the contract month, except that trading in the November contract shall terminate on the Thursday prior to Thanksgiving Day, unless a holiday falls on that Thursday or on any of the four weekdays prior to that Thursday, in which case trading shall terminate on the prior Thursday that is not a holiday and is not so preceded by a holiday.

TICKER SYMBOLS. Calls = KF; puts = JF.

DAILY PRICE LIMITS. N/A.

Source: Chicago Mercantile Exchange.

Futures Contract—French Franc

TRADING UNIT. 500,000 French francs.

TICK SIZE. 0.00002 = $10.00 (regular); 0.00001 = $5.00 (calendar spread).

CONTRACT MONTHS. Three months in the March quarterly cycle, March, June, September, December.

LAST TRADING DAY. The second business day before third Wednesday.

TICKER SYMBOL. FR.

Option Contract—French Franc

TRADING UNIT. One French franc futures contract.

TICK SIZE. 0.00002 = $10.00 (regular).

CONTRACT MONTHS. Three months in the March cycle and two months not in the March cycle (serial months), plus four weekly expirations.

LAST TRADING DAY. *Quarterly:* Trading in monthly options in the March quarterly cycle (i.e., March, June, September, and December) shall terminate at the close of trading on the second Friday immediately preceding the third Wednesday of the contract month. If the foregoing date for termination is an Exchange holiday, trading in monthly options shall terminate on the immediately preceding business day. *Weekly:* Trading in weekly options shall terminate at the close of trading on those Fridays that are not also the termination of trading of a monthly option. If the foregoing date for termination is an Exchange holiday, trading in weekly options shall terminate on the immediately preceding business day.

TICKER SYMBOLS. SF calls/puts = FR; ticker calls = FOC; ticker puts = FOP.

DAILY PRICE LIMITS. Option ceases trading when corresponding future locks limit.

Source: Chicago Mercantile Exchange.

Futures Contract—Orange Juice

TRADING UNIT. 15,000 pounds of orange solids (3 percent more or less).

TICK SIZE. Five one-hundredths of a cent per pound ($7.50 per contract).

CONTRACT MONTHS. January, March, May, July, September, November, with at least two January months listed at all times.

LAST TRADING DAY. Fourteenth business day prior to the last business day of the month.

TICKER SYMBOL. OJ.

Option Contract—Orange Juice

TRADING UNIT. One FCOJ futures contract.

TICK SIZE. Five one-hundredths of a cent per pound ($7.50 per contract).

CONTRACT MONTHS. In addition to a February option contract, each listed futures month will have its option month listed for trading (two Januaries, March, May, July, September, November). In addition, the nearest calendar month that is not a futures month will be listed (April, June, August, October, December).

LAST TRADING DAY. The third Friday of the month preceding named option month.

TICKER SYMBOLS. OJ.

DAILY TRADING LIMIT. (1) Ten cents per pound above or below settlement price of nearby month, 15-minute suspension. (2) Ten cents per pound above or below last traded price, 15-minute suspension. (3) After five 10-cent moves, the limit becomes 20 cents.

Source: New York Board of Trade.

Futures Contract—Platinum

TRADING UNIT. 50 troy ounces.

TICK SIZE. Price changes are in multiples of $0.10 (10¢) per troy ounce, $5 per contract.

CONTRACT MONTHS. Trading is conducted over 15 months beginning with the current month and the next two consecutive months before moving into the quarterly cycle of January, April, July, and October.

LAST TRADING DAY. Trading terminates at the close of business on the fourth business day prior to the end of the delivery month.

FUTURES DAILY PRICE LIMITS. *Futures:* There is no maximum daily limit during the current delivery month, the closest cycle month, and any months preceding it. In other months, the daily limit is $50 per sounce ($2,500 per contract). If the price in any of the back months settles at the limit for two consecutive days, limits will be expanded to $75 per ounce ($3,750 per contract) and, if the market settles at that limit for two consecutive days, prices will be expanded to the maximum daily limit of $100 per ounce ($5,000 per contract) on the following day.

TICKER SYMBOL. PL.

Options Contract—Platinum

TRADING UNIT. One NYMEX Division platinum futures contract.

TICK SIZE. Price changes are in multiples of $0.10 (10¢) per troy ounce, $5 per contract.

CONTRACT MONTHS. Trading is conducted in the nearest three contiguous calendar contract months, plus the next two months of the quarterly cycle of January, April, July, and October.

LAST TRADING DAY. Expiration occurs on the third Wednesday of each month.

OPTION DAILY PRICE LIMITS. *Options:* No price limits.

TICKER SYMBOL. PO.

    Source: New York Mercantile Exchange.

Futures Contract—Pork Bellies

TRADING UNIT. 40,000 pounds of frozen pork bellies, cut and trimmed.

TICK SIZE. 0.00025 = $10.00.

CONTRACT MONTHS. Five months of February, March, May, July, and August.

LAST TRADING DAY. The business day prior to the last three business days of the contract month.

TICKER SYMBOL. PB.

Option Contract—Pork Bellies

TRADING UNIT. One frozen porkbelly futures contract.

TICK SIZE. 0.00025 = $10.00.

CONTRACT MONTHS. Five months of February, March, May, July, August, and flex.

LAST TRADING DAY. The business day prior to the last three business days of the contract month.

TICKER SYMBOLS. Ticker calls = KP; ticker puts = JP.

DAILY PRICE LIMITS. Futures: $.03/lb, 300 points, $1,200; options: N/A.

    Source: Chicago Mercantile Exchange.

Futures Contract—British Pound

TRADING UNIT. 62,500 pounds sterling (British pounds).

TICK SIZE. 0.0002 = $12.50; 0.0001 = $6.25 (calendar spread).

CONTRACT MONTHS. Six months in the March quarterly cycle, March, June, September, December.

LAST TRADING DAY. The second business day before third Wednesday.

TICKER SYMBOL. BP.

Options Contract—British Pound

TRADING UNIT. One British pound futures contract.

TICK SIZE. 0.0002 = $12.50; 0.0001 = $6.25 for premium less than 0.0005, spreads w/net premium less than 0.0005, non-generic combo trades with total premium less than 0.0010.

CONTRACT MONTHS. Four months in the March cycle and two months not in the March cycle (serial months), plus four weekly expiration options.

LAST TRADING DAY. *Quarterly:* Trading in monthly options in the March quarterly cycle (i.e., March, June, September, and December) shall terminate at the close of trading on the second Friday immediately preceding the third Wednesday of the contract month. If the foregoing date for termination is an Exchange holiday, trading in monthly options shall terminate on the immediately preceding business day. *Weekly:* Trading in weekly options shall terminate at the close of trading on those Fridays that are not also the termination of trading of a monthly option. If the foregoing date for termination is an Exchange holiday, trading in weekly options shall terminate on the immediately preceding business day.

TICKER SYMBOLS. Calls/puts = BP; ticker calls = CP; ticker puts = PP.

DAILY PRICE LIMITS. *Futures:* 0.0001 = $6.25 for premium less than 0.0005, spreads w/net premium less than 0.0005, non-generic combo trades with total premium less than 0.0010; 1600. *Options:* Options cease trading when corresponding futures lock limit.

Source: Chicago Mercantile Exchange.

Futures Contract—Japanese Yen

TRADING UNIT. 12,500,000 Japanese yen.

TICK SIZE. 0.000001 = $12.50; 0.0000005 = $6.25 (calendar spread).

CONTRACT MONTHS. Six months in the March quarterly cycle, March, June, September, December.

LAST TRADING DAY. The second business day before third Wednesday.

TICKER SYMBOL. JY.

Option Contract—Japanese Yen

TRADING UNIT. One Japanese yen futures contract.

TICK SIZE. 0.000001 = $12.50; 0.0000005 = $6.25 for premium less than 0.0005, spread w/net premium less than 0.0005, nongeneric combo trades less than 0.0010.

CONTRACT MONTHS. Four months in the March cycle and two months not in the March cycle (serial months), plus four weekly expirations.

LAST TRADING DAY. *Quarterly:* Trading in monthly options in the March quarterly cycle (i.e. March, June, September, and December) shall terminate at the close of trading on the second Friday immediately preceding the third Wednesday of the contract month. If the foregoing date for termination is an Exchange holiday, trading in monthly options shall terminate on the immediately preceding business day. *Weekly:* Trading in weekly options shall terminate at the close of trading on those Fridays that are not also the termination of trading of a monthly option. If the foregoing date for termination is an Exchange holiday, trading in weekly options shall terminate on the immediately preceding business day.

TICKER SYMBOLS. Ticker calls = CJ; ticker puts = PJ.

DAILY PRICE LIMITS.   Futures: no limit between 7:20 A.M. and 7:35 A.M. Expanding limits; 800 points. Options: option ceases trading when corresponding future locks limit.

Source: Chicago Mercantile Exchange.

Futures Contract—Nikkei 225

TRADING UNIT. $5 times the Nikkei Stock Average.

TICK SIZE.   0.05 = $25.00.

CONTRACT MONTHS.   Four months in the March quarterly cycle. March, June, September, December.

LAST TRADING DAY.   The business day immediately preceding the day of determination of the final settlement price. The final settlement price is determined on the second Friday of the contract month by the Osaka Securities Exchange.

TICKER SYMBOL.   NK.

Option Contract—Nikkei 225

TRADING UNIT.   One Nikkei Stock Average Futures contract.

TICK SIZE.   0.05 = $25.00.

CONTRACT MONTHS.   Four months in the March quarterly cycle. Non-March quarterly cycle months may be listed based on demand.

LAST TRADING DAY.   The business day immediately preceding the day of determination of the final settlement price. The final settlement price is determined on the second Friday of the contract month by the Osaka Securities Exchange. Serial: The 3rd Friday of the contract month.

TICKER SYMBOLS.   Ticker calls = KN; ticker puts = JN.

DAILY PRICE LIMITS.   *Futures:* N/A; *options:* no limit.

Source: Chicago Mercantile Exchange.

Futures Contract—Eurodollars

TRADING UNIT. Eurodollar Time Deposit having a principal value of $1,000,000 with a three-month maturity.

TICK SIZE. 0.01 = $25.00.

CONTRACT MONTHS. March, June, September, December, Forty months in the March quarterly cycle, and the four nearest serial contract months.

LAST TRADING DAY. Futures trading shall terminate at 11:00 A.M. (London Time), 5:00 A.M. (Chicago Time) on the second London bank business day before the third Wednesday of the contract month. (Due to the 5:00 A.M. terminate time, the last day of trading for contracts listed on RTH will be the third business day immediately preceding the third Wednesday of the contract month).

TICKER SYMBOL. ED.

Option Contract—Eurodollars

TRADING UNIT. One Eurodollar Time Deposit Futures Contract.

TICK SIZE. 0.01 = $25.00 (regular).

CONTRACT MONTHS. March, June, September, December, six months in the March quarterly cycle and two serial months not in the March cycle.

LAST TRADING DAY. Quarterly: Options trading shall terminate at 11:00 A.M. (London Time) 5:00 A.M. (Chicago Time) on the second London bank business day before the third Wednesday of the contract month. Serial options and midcurve options trading shall terminate on the Friday immediately preceding the third Wednesday of the contract month. If the foregoing date for termination is an Exchange holiday, option trading shall terminate on the immediately preceding business day.

TICKER SYMBOLS. Ticker calls = CE; ticker puts = PE.

DAILY PRICE LIMITS. *Futures:* No limit on floor; 200 point limit on Globex2. *Options:* No limit; trading halts when primary futures contract is locked at limit.

Source: Chicago Mercantile Exchange.

Futures Contract—Gold

TRADING UNIT. 100 troy ounces.

TICK SIZE. Price changes are registered in multiples of 10¢ ($0.10) per troy ounce, equivalent to $10 per contract. A fluctuation of $1 is, therefore, equivalent to $100 per contract.

CONTRACT MONTHS. Trading is conducted for delivery during the current calendar month, the next two calendar months, any February, April, August, and October thereafter falling within a 23-month period, and any June and December falling within a 60-month period beginning with the current month.

LAST TRADING DAY. Trading terminates at the close of business on the third to last business day of the maturing delivery month.

DAILY PRICE LIMITS. *Futures:* Initial price limit, based upon the preceding day's settlement price, is $75 per ounce. Two minutes after either of the two most active months trades at the limit, trades in all months of futures and options will cease for a 15-minute period. Trading will also cease if either of the two active months is bid at the upper limit or offered at the lower limit for two minutes without trading. Trading will not cease if the limit is reached during the final 20 minutes of a day's trading. If the limit is reached during the final half hour of trading, trading will resume no later than 10 minutes before the normal closing time. When trading resumes after a cessation of trading, the price limits will be expanded by increments of 100 percent.

TICKER SYMBOL. GC.

Option Contract—Gold

TRADING UNIT. One COMEX Division gold futures contract.

TICK SIZE. Price changes are registered in multiples of 10¢ ($0.10) per troy ounce, equivalent to $10 per contract. A fluctuation of $1 is, therefore, equivalent to $100 per contract.

CONTRACT MONTHS. The nearest six of the following contract months: February, April, June, August, October, and December. Additional contract months—January, March, May, July, September, and November—will be listed for trading for a period of two months. A 24-month option is added on a June-December cycle. The options are American style and can be exercised at any time up to expiration. On the first day of trading for any options contract month, there will be 13 strike prices each for puts and calls.

LAST TRADING DAY. Expiration occurs on the second Friday of the month prior to the delivery month of the underlying futures contract. Beginning with the expiration of the December 2002 contract, options will expire on the fourth business day prior to the end of the month preceding the option contract month. If the expiration day falls on a Friday or immediately prior to an Exchange holiday, expiration will occur on the previous business day.

DAILY PRICE LIMITS. *Options:* No price limits.

TICKER SYMBOL. OG.

     Source: New York Mercantile Exchange.

Futures Contract—Light, Sweet Crude Oil

TRADING UNIT. 1,000 U.S. barrels (42,000 gallons).

TICK SIZE. $0.01 (1¢) per barrel ($10 per contract).

CONTRACT MONTHS. Thirty consecutive months plus long-dated futures initially listed 36, 48, 60, 72, and 84 months prior to delivery. Additionally, trading can be executed at an average differential to the previous day's settlement prices for periods of 2 to 30 consecutive months in a single transaction. These calendar strips are executed during open outcry trading hours.

LAST TRADING DAY. Trading terminates at the close of business on the third business day prior to the 25th calendar day of the month preceding the delivery month. If the 25th calendar day of the month is a nonbusiness day, trading shall cease on the third business day prior to the last business day preceding the 25th calendar day.

DAILY PRICE LIMITS. *Futures:* Initial limits of $3.00 per barrel are in place in all but the first two months and rise to $6.00 per barrel if the previous day's settlement price in any back month is at the $3.00 limit. In the event of a $7.50-per-barrel move in either of the first two contract months, limits on all months become $7.50 per barrel from the limit in place in the direction of the move following a one-hour trading halt.

TICKER SYMBOL. CL.

Option Contract—Light, Sweet Crude Oil

TRADING UNIT. One NYMEX Division light, sweet crude oil futures contract.

TICK SIZE. $0.01 (1¢) per barrel ($10 per contract).

CONTRACT MONTHS. Twelve consecutive months, plus three long-dated options at 18, 24, and 36 months out on a June-December cycle.

LAST TRADING DAY. Trading ends three business days before the underlying futures contract.

DAILY PRICE LIMITS. *Options:* No price limits.

TICKER SYMBOL. LO.
  Source: New York Mercantile Exchange.

Futures Contract—Unleaded Gasoline

TRADING UNIT. 42,000 U.S. gallons (1,000 barrels).

TICK SIZE. $0.0001 (0.01¢) per gallon ($4.20 per contract).

CONTRACT MONTHS. Trading in New York Harbor unleaded gasoline is specified for 12 months on a rolling basis commencing with the next calendar month.

LAST TRADING DAY. Trading terminates at the close of business on the last business day of the month preceding the delivery month.

DAILY PRICE LIMITS. *Futures:* Initial limits of $0.06 (6¢) per gallon are in place in all but the first two months and rise to $0.09 (9¢) per gallon if the previous day's settlement price in any back month is at the $0.06 per gallon limit. In the event of a $0.20 (20¢) per gallon move in either of the first two contract months, limits on all months become $0.20 per gallon from the limit in place in the direction of the move following a one-hour trading halt.

TICKER SYMBOL. HU.

Option Contract—Unleaded Gasoline

TRADING UNIT. One NYMEX Division New York Harbor unleaded gasoline futures contract.

TICK SIZE. $0.0001 (0.01¢) per gallon ($4.20 per contract).

CONTRACT MONTHS. Twelve consecutive months.

LAST TRADING DAY. Expiration occurs three business days before the underlying futures contract.

DAILY PRICE LIMITS. *Options:* No price limits.

TICKER SYMBOL. GO.

     Source: New York Mercantile Exchange.

Futures Contract—Heating Oil

TRADING UNIT. 42,000 U.S. gallons (1,000 barrels).

TICK SIZE. $0.0001 (0.01¢) per gallon ($4.20 per contract).

CONTRACT MONTHS. Trading is conducted in 18 consecutive months commencing with the next calendar month (for example, on October 1, 2001, trading occurs in all months from November 2001 through April 2003).

LAST TRADING DAY. Trading terminates at the close of business on the last business day of the month preceding the delivery month.

DAILY PRICE LIMITS. *Futures:* Initial limits of $0.06 (6¢) per gallon are in place in all but the first two months and rise to $0.09 (9¢) per gallon if the previous day's settlement price in any back month is at the $0.06-per-gallon limit. In the event of a $0.20- (20¢) per-gallon move in either of the first two contract months, limits on all months become $0.20 per gallon from the limit in place in the direction of the move following a one-hour trading halt.

TICKER SYMBOL. HO.

Option Contract—Heating Oil

TRADING UNIT. One NYMEX Division heating oil futures contract.

TICK SIZE. $0.0001 (0.01¢) per gallon ($4.20 per contract).

CONTRACT MONTHS. 18 consecutive months.

LAST TRADING DAY. Trading ends three business days before the underlying futures contract.

DAILY PRICE LIMITS. *Options:* No price limits.

TICKER SYMBOLS. OH.
Source: New York Mercantile Exchange.

Futures Contract—Natural Gas

TRADING UNIT. 10,000 million British thermal units (mmBtu).

TICK SIZE. $0.001 (0.1¢) per mmBtu ($10 per contract).

CONTRACT MONTHS. Thirty-six consecutive months commencing with the next calendar month (for example, on January 2, 2001, trading occurs in all months from February 2001 through January 2004), plus a long-dated contract, initially listed 36 months out.

LAST TRADING DAY. Trading terminates three business days prior to the first calendar day of the delivery month.

DAILY PRICE LIMITS. *Futures:* $1.00 per mmBtu ($10,000 per contract) for all months. If any contract is traded, bid, or offered at the limit for 5 minutes, trading is halted for 15 minutes. When trading resumes, expanded limits are in place that allow the price to fluctuate by $2.00 in either direction of the previous day's setlement price. There are no price limits on any month during the last three days of trading in the spot month.

TICKER SYMBOL. NG.

Option Contract—Natural Gas

TRADING UNIT. One NYMEX Division natural gas futures contract.

TICK SIZE. $0.001 (0.1¢) per mmBtu ($10 per contract).

CONTRACT MONTHS. Twelve consecutive months, plus 15, 18, 21, 24, 27, 30, 33, and 36 months on a June-December cycle.

LAST TRADING DAY. Trading terminates at the close of business on the business day immediately preceding the expiration of the underlying futures contract.

DAILY PRICE LIMITS. *Options:* No price limits.

TICKER SYMBOL. ON.

Source: New York Mercantile Exchange.

Futures Contract—Nasdaq 100

TRADING UNIT. $100 times the Nasdaq-100 Index.

TICK SIZE. 0.5 = $50.00.

CONTRACT MONTHS. Three months in the March quarterly cycle.

LAST TRADING DAY. The business day immediately preceding the day of determination of the final settlement price (normally, the Thursday prior to the third Friday of the contract month).

TICKER SYMBOL. ND.

Option Contract—Nasdaq 100

TRADING UNIT. One Nasdaq-100 Index® futures contract.

TICK SIZE. 0.05 = $5.00.

CONTRACT MONTHS. Three months in the March quarterly cycle and two months not in the March cycle (serial months) & Flex® options. March, June, September, December.

LAST TRADING DAY. *Quarterly:* The business day immediately preceding the day of determination of the final settlement price (normally, the Thursday prior to the third Friday of the contract month). *Serial:* The third Friday of the contract month.

TICKER SYMBOLS. ND.

DAILY PRICE LIMITS. *Futures:* Price limits corresponding to a 2.5, 5.0, 10.0, and 20.0 percent decline below the settlement price of the preceding pit session. *Options:* Options trading halted when lead Nasdaq 100 future locks limit.

Source: Chicago Mercantile Exchange.

Appendix E

FUTURES AND OPTION CONTRACT POINT VALUES

Silver (COMEX): $.01 = $50
Gold (COMEX): $1.00 = $100
Platinum (NYMEX): $1.00 = $50
Palladium (NYMEX): $1.00 = $100
Heating oil (NYMEX): $.01 = $420
Light crude (NYMEX): $1.00 = $1,000
Natural gas (NYMEX): $.01 = $100
Unleaded gas (NYMEX): $.01 = $420
Corn (CBOT): $.01 = $50
Wheat (CBOT): $.01 = $50
Soybeans (CBOT): $.01 = $50
Soybean meal (CBOT): $1.00 = $100
Soybean oil (CBOT): $.01 = $600
Oats (CBOT): $.01 = $50
Feeder cattle (CME): $.01 = $500
Live cattle (CME): $.01 = $400
Lean hogs (CME): $.01 = $400
Lumber (CME): $1.00 = $110
Japanese yen (CME): 1.00 = $1,250

British pound (CME): 1.00 = $625
Swiss franc (CME): 1.00 = $1,250
Coffee (NYBOT): $1.00 = $375
Cocoa (NYBOT): $1.00 = $10
Cotton (NYBOT): $.01 = $500
Orange juice (NYBOT): $.01 = $150
Sugar (NYBOT): $.01 = $1,120
S&P 500 (CME): 1.00 = $250
Dow Jones (CBOT): 1.00 = $10
Eurodollars (CME): 1.00 = $2,500
Treasury bonds (30-year): 1.00 = $1,000
Treasury notes (10-year): 1.00 = $1,000

Appendix F

FUTURES AND OPTION RESOURCES ON THE INTERNET

Industry Regulation

Commodity Futures Trading Commission (CFTC)
www.cftc.gov

National Futures Association (NFA)
www.nfa.futures.org

Futures Industry Association (FIA)
www.fiafii.org

Market Newswires and News Media

Dow Jones
www.dowjones.com

Bloomberg Business News
www.bloomberg.com

Market News Service
www.economeister.com

CNN
www.cnn.com

CBS Market Watch
www.cbs.marketwatch.com

MSNBC
www.msnbc.com

Financial Publications

Futures Magazine
www.futuresmag.com

Technical Analysis of Stocks and Commodities
www.traders.com

Feedstuffs
www.futuresmag.com

The Financial Times
www.ft.com

Barron's
www.barrons.com

Commodity Exchanges

Finding information about futures and futures markets is much easier than making money with that information. Perhaps the best places to go for information that is accurate and free are the exchanges themselves. Fortunately, the online revolution has made the journey a lot quicker. Most of the exchanges provide free access to delayed (and real time with certain contracts) quotes for major commodity markets, data on open interest and volume, contract specifications, intraday and daily price charts, market analysis, and educational resources. Following are the major U.S. commodity exchanges.

Chicago Mercantile Exchange (CME)
www.cme.com

The CME offers program-easy access to futures and options on futures information, with a couple of special features worth highlighting. For instance, you can register at the site for free futures quotes that automatically update on your computer screen. As part of a pilot program, there are several third-party data vendors from which you can choose to access the free quotes. The link to go directly to the free quotes information page is www.cme .com/web/live/. Only certain products, however, are accessible for viewing live.

Additionally, the CME offers a products calendar, which offers a snapshot of expiration dates, delivery dates, first notice dates, and so forth. There is also an excellent set of pages covering all you need to know about SPAN performance bond requirements (margin), including price limits and a volatility reference guide. Windows-based, user-friendly SPAN calculation software is also now available for purchase. For questions about SPAN requirements and purchasing the software, you can call 312-648-3646.

Chicago Board of Trade (CBOT)
www.cbot.com

The CBOT recently reorganized its web pages and the new structure makes access to futures and options on futures data and information, such as expiration calendars and historical and quotes data—a snap. The quotes and data pop-up menu on the arrival page is probably the most impressive feature. From here, you can go directly to tables containing historical data, agricultural, financial, equity index and metals settlement prices, latest quotes, and volume and open-interest statistics. There are also links in this menu to option and futures spread time and sales. The site also has an excellent "news room," including free audio market-wrap broadcasts covering equity, financial, and agricultural markets.

Other Futures Exchanges

New York Mercantile Exchange
   www.nymex.com
Coffee Sugar & Cocoa Exchange, Inc.
   www.nybot.com

Mid-America Commodity Exchange
www.midam.com
New York Board of Trade
www.nybot.com

U.S. Government Agencies

U.S. Department of Agriculture
www.usda.gov
U.S. Department of Labor Statistics
www.bls.gov
U.S. Department of Commerce
www.doc.gov

Data Vendors

Quote.com
www.quote.com
Futures Source
www.futuresource.com
CSI
www.csi.com
Genesis Financial Data Services
www.gfds.com

Options and Futures Analysis Software

OptionsVue
www.optionsvue.com
MetaStock
www.equis.com
Omega
www.omegaresearch.com

Appendix G

EQUITY-ONLY PUT-CALL RATIO DATA

Date	Oscillator	10DEMA	S&P 500
19990429	−55.20	38.20	1412.90
19990430	−77.55	36.40	1401.90
19990503	−48.20	36.60	1424.60
19990504	−49.27	36.70	1408.40
19990505	−77.17	37.00	1417.40
19990506	−105.39	37.00	1407.70
19990507	−60.30	37.60	1416.60
19990510	−66.24	38.10	1412.40
19990511	−177.67	37.90	1423.60
19990512	−86.08	38.10	1434.50
19990513	−76.20	38.00	1440.40
19990514	44.77	38.90	1404.70
19990517	−38.74	39.00	1406.40
19990518	−101.29	38.70	1406.60
19990519	−63.94	38.80	1414.60
19990520	−74.54	39.20	1407.90
19990521	275.04	40.90	1400.20
19990524	−59.62	41.00	1377.90
19990525	45.88	42.50	1349.90
19990526	−45.69	42.80	1369.90
19990527	59.90	43.80	1351.40
19990528	−48.45	43.00	1362.60
19990601	52.79	43.80	1361.00
19990602	12.80	44.60	1361.60
19990603	−11.45	44.90	1370.40
19990604	−77.98	44.70	1395.10

Date	Oscillator	10DEMA	S&P 500
19990607	−104.32	42.70	1397.60
19990608	12.77	43.20	1386.70
19990609	11.74	43.00	1384.20
19990610	12.73	43.40	1372.90
19990611	74.12	43.50	1361.70
19990614	103.50	44.70	1361.90
19990615	44.11	44.50	1370.90
19990616	−131.29	43.70	1395.30
19990617	−34.19	43.60	1407.90
19990618	−176.72	43.40	1409.20
19990621	−181.39	43.10	1412.40
19990622	0.00	43.00	1401.70
19990623	64.03	43.40	1394.70
19990624	74.10	43.90	1385.20
19990625	−31.40	43.00	1381.40
19990628	−72.07	41.60	1396.40
19990629	−38.83	41.00	1409.10
19990630	−184.00	40.60	1434.10
19990701	−181.88	39.50	1444.50
19990702	−139.99	39.20	1458.30
19990706	−206.07	39.20	1455.90
19990707	−71.81	38.60	1456.90
19990708	−16.89	38.00	1457.40
19990709	−106.44	36.70	1466.10
19990712	−48.93	36.70	1461.50
19990713	−35.60	37.20	1456.10
19990714	−117.52	36.90	1461.60
19990715	−122.57	37.40	1471.80
19990716	−274.49	37.70	1479.90
19990719	−18.07	38.60	1470.40
19990720	80.66	40.20	1439.90
19990721	54.64	41.20	1437.90
19990722	124.73	42.20	1420.20
19990723	66.02	43.50	1415.20
19990726	79.93	44.50	1407.20
19990727	−12.18	44.60	1416.10
19990728	72.85	45.80	1420.10
19990729	95.07	47.20	1402.20
19990730	114.79	49.20	1384.20
19990802	105.33	50.30	1388.60
19990803	163.33	50.90	1381.20
19990804	58.03	51.00	1361.40
19990805	214.93	51.20	1373.60

Date	Oscillator	10DEMA	S&P 500
19990806	255.06	52.30	1359.40
19990809	162.68	52.80	1355.40
19990810	308.58	54.70	1342.90
19990811	57.64	54.50	1356.40
19990812	26.20	53.90	1357.10
19990813	28.43	53.10	1385.30
19990816	72.53	52.80	1391.80
19990817	47.73	52.00	1399.40
19990818	31.78	51.70	1387.00
19990819	174.76	51.80	1379.40
19990820	176.32	51.00	1392.60
19990823	−112.89	48.70	1418.60
19990824	−124.38	46.20	1422.90
19990825	−50.12	45.50	1435.40
19990826	−29.74	45.10	1420.20
19990827	89.54	45.70	1404.10
19990830	88.57	45.90	1378.40
19990831	108.67	46.40	1372.20
19990901	477.58	49.30	1386.40
19990902	175.65	49.30	1372.60
19990903	−66.93	48.00	1414.90
19990907	−14.42	49.00	1404.80
19990908	95.29	50.30	1398.30
19990909	0.00	50.60	1397.40
19990910	−104.79	50.20	1406.70
19990913	75.58	49.90	1399.40
19990914	172.20	50.10	1389.90
19990915	179.34	50.30	1369.10
19990916	341.86	49.10	1370.70
19990917	230.25	48.80	1388.60
19990920	0.00	49.20	1385.90
19990921	236.88	50.60	1359.00
19990922	349.10	52.00	1358.90
19990923	204.90	53.10	1328.10
19990924	260.73	55.10	1325.60
19990927	88.49	55.20	1333.30
19990928	257.01	55.70	1331.40
19990929	91.14	55.20	1317.00
19990930	137.04	54.30	1335.30
19991001	186.03	54.60	1330.60
19991004	111.98	55.30	1355.80
19991005	−42.45	53.80	1352.80
19991006	−81.22	51.40	1371.80

Date	Oscillator	10DEMA	S&P 500
19991007	0.00	50.30	1366.10
19991008	123.71	49.50	1383.60
19991011	213.47	50.10	1384.10
19991012	113.57	49.30	1363.10
19991013	584.12	51.50	1326.60
19991014	387.51	52.20	1327.10
19991015	1380.22	55.20	1294.40
19991018	145.38	55.20	1302.80
19991019	−6.71	55.30	1311.60
19991020	0.00	55.70	1329.60
19991021	111.31	56.20	1333.10
19991022	185.03	56.50	1344.30
19991025	127.55	56.20	1338.00
19991026	114.11	56.20	1322.70
19991027	181.81	54.70	1342.60
19991028	20.98	53.10	1387.30
19991029	−73.84	48.60	1413.30
19991101	48.06	48.20	1399.60
19991102	233.57	49.60	1389.60
19991103	37.61	49.80	1397.60
19991104	−43.11	49.10	1405.60
19991105	−48.88	48.00	1421.70
19991108	−43.02	46.90	1420.30
19991109	62.92	46.50	1409.10
19991110	−20.77	45.20	1417.10
19991111	44.12	45.30	1425.00
19991112	0.00	45.60	1438.70
19991115	−123.97	44.70	1440.10
19991116	−95.07	43.00	1468.10
19991117	−79.46	42.50	1455.10
19991118	−255.78	41.70	1465.70
19991119	−256.88	41.10	1464.60
19991122	−69.52	41.00	1464.30
19991123	−37.28	40.50	1449.10
19991124	−103.23	40.00	1458.60
19991126	−50.06	39.30	1451.70
19991129	−40.16	39.10	1447.50
19991130	60.50	40.00	1428.60
19991201	−18.22	40.30	1439.60
19991202	−98.28	40.10	1449.30
19991203	−138.33	40.50	1475.60
19991206	−119.43	40.70	1462.60
19991207	−21.64	40.90	1452.90
19991208	−89.99	40.70	1442.50

Date	Oscillator	10DEMA	S&P 500
19991209	−152.51	40.70	1447.50
19991210	−172.49	40.50	1453.30
19991213	−139.08	40.10	1454.80
19991214	−52.29	39.60	1443.60
19991215	−83.44	39.40	1447.00
19991216	−76.88	39.60	1455.50
19991217	−231.78	39.50	1462.80
19991220	62.56	40.40	1453.30
19991221	−42.19	40.30	1472.80
19991222	−99.21	40.20	1475.80
19991223	−143.24	40.00	1498.70
19991227	−85.82	40.20	1496.10
19991228	63.11	41.20	1497.00
19991229	−59.83	41.00	1500.50
19991230	−27.59	41.10	1499.10
19991231	−21.88	41.20	1502.50
20000103	−196.93	41.00	1485.10
20000104	81.24	41.10	1430.10
20000105	0.00	41.30	1431.80
20000106	−21.99	41.70	1422.30
20000107	26.76	42.60	1478.80
20000110	−327.87	41.90	1493.30
20000111	−159.08	40.90	1472.60
20000112	−177.08	40.60	1460.30
20000113	−128.38	40.30	1476.80
20000114	−284.77	39.60	1496.30
20000118	−235.18	39.70	1487.80
20000119	−119.47	38.90	1490.80
20000120	−72.10	38.70	1475.30
20000121	−119.58	38.50	1472.00
20000124	−80.12	38.10	1430.10
20000125	44.83	39.50	1436.90
20000126	47.70	40.30	1433.70
20000127	0.00	41.00	1428.10
20000128	185.25	42.40	1384.80
20000131	19.93	43.40	1419.30
20000201	19.18	44.30	1435.10
20000202	23.48	44.80	1433.80
20000203	−142.05	44.30	1454.70
20000204	−23.86	44.50	1449.80
20000207	−105.22	44.20	1445.60
20000208	50.70	44.20	1464.50
20000209	47.48	44.20	1436.60
20000210	0.00	44.20	1437.50

Date	Oscillator	10DEMA	S&P 500
20000211	0.00	43.30	1415.10
20000214	42.77	43.40	1417.00
20000215	74.05	43.60	1428.30
20000216	24.91	43.60	1411.10
20000217	58.47	44.50	1403.80
20000218	408.96	45.80	1371.60
20000222	−23.59	46.30	1367.30
20000223	−137.50	45.50	1383.50
20000224	−72.70	45.00	1373.60
20000225	−121.15	44.50	1356.40
20000228	22.34	44.60	1366.00
20000229	−99.13	44.00	1390.30
20000301	−116.22	43.30	1403.30
20000302	−188.18	42.50	1403.20
20000303	−287.91	41.30	1429.00
20000306	−105.92	39.70	1413.30
20000307	−87.25	39.50	1370.10
20000308	−26.61	40.00	1384.50
20000309	−184.49	39.60	1422.50
20000310	−315.85	39.10	1417.80
20000313	−151.67	38.40	1401.50
20000314	−31.15	38.70	1380.00
20000315	95.56	39.40	1413.20
20000316	−150.85	39.70	1478.00
20000317	−224.49	40.10	1489.00
20000320	−77.59	40.20	1478.10
20000321	−169.43	39.80	1507.50
20000322	−133.41	39.40	1517.50
20000323	−160.19	39.50	1544.00
20000324	−126.77	40.00	1555.40
20000327	−105.33	40.10	1538.50
20000328	−41.87	40.00	1530.20
20000329	0.00	39.70	1530.50
20000330	−85.10	39.80	1504.30
20000331	−120.61	39.90	1515.30
20000403	−181.73	39.50	1528.20
20000404	68.88	40.40	1519.50
20000405	−24.18	40.80	1505.50
20000406	−98.15	41.00	1516.50
20000407	−200.77	40.60	1529.00
20000410	−106.29	40.60	1521.50
20000411	98.32	41.20	1519.00
20000412	186.47	41.90	1476.70
20000413	265.29	43.40	1456.00

INDEX